CULTURE AND SCHOOLING: BUILDING BRIDGES BETWEEN RESEARCH, PRAXIS AND PROFESSIONALISM

Dr Elwyn Thomas

Institute of Education, University of London

JOHN WILEY & SONS, LTD

Chichester · New York · Weinheim · Brisbane · Singapore · Toronto

Other Wiley Editorial Offices

John Wiley & Sons, Inc., 605 Third Avenue,
New York, NY 10158-0012, USA

WILEY-VCH Verlag GmbH, Pappelallee 3,
D-69469 Weinheim, Germany

Jacaranda Wiley Ltd, 33 Park Road, Milton,
Queensland 4064, Australia

John Wiley & Sons (Asia) Pte Ltd, 2 Clementi Loop #02-01,
Jin Xing Distripark, Singapore 129809

John Wiley & Sons (Canada) Ltd, 22 Worcester Road,
Rexdale, Ontario M9W 1L1, Canada

British Library Cataloguing in Publication Data

A catalogue record for this book is available from the British Library

ISBN 0-471-89788-4

DEDICATION

This book is dedicated to my son Christopher and his wife
Deborah

ACKNOWLEDGEMENTS

I wish to acknowledge the advice and assistance I received from the following persons during the writing of this book. First of all, I wish to thank Mr Cheah Syn Kay who helped with the drawing of figures and diagrams, Dr Christopher Williams for supplying me with a postcard of the wire toy from Botswana, and computer support from John Ekpoffiong. Discussions with Professor Angela Little relating to assessment and Dr Sheila Aikman about indigenous teaching and learning, were particularly useful. I would like to thank Christine Scotchmer, of the Child to Child Trust, for supplying me with the photographs of children for the front book cover. I also wish to acknowledge all the help and support I received from friends and family especially, my son Christopher and his wife Deborah.

ABBREVIATIONS

ADB	Asian Development Bank
APEID	Asia Pacific Programme of Educational Innovation for Development
BEP	Bilingual Education Project
CAPS	Continuous Assessment and Progression System
CEP	Community Education Project
CCC	Chinese Culture Connection
CHCs	Confucian Heritage Cultures
Cwd	Confucian work dimension
DES	Department of Education and Science
DFE	Department for Education
FD	Field Dependent
FI	Field Independent
I–C	Individualism–collectivism
IPBS	Institutionalised Public Basic Schooling
IT	Information Technology
KEEP	Kamehameha Elementary Education Project
LJ	*Lok Jumbish*
LLTE	Life Long Teacher Education
M–F	Masculinity–Femininity
M–H	Materialism–Humanism
MOW	Meaning of Work
MSD	Management self-development
PCM	Performance–Confucian–maintenance
P/D	Power/distance
PM	Performance–maintenance
SAL	Student Approaches to Learning
SIDA	Swedish International Development Aid
U/A	Uncertainty/Avoidance

UNDP	United Nations Development Programmes
UNESCO	United Nations Educational, Scientific and Cultural Organisation
WW2	World War 2

1

THE ROLE OF CULTURE IN EDUCATION AND SCHOOLING: AN INTRODUCTION

The main purpose of this book is to help educators improve educational practice in the ever-changing cultural contexts of school and society. It is hoped that the book will provide professionals not only with an awareness of the nature and implications of cultural change in schools and in teacher education, but enable practitioners to have access to knowledge as well as practical sources that will assist them to solve culture-specific problems related to teaching and learning. While schoolteachers and teacher educators are the main target that would hopefully benefit from this book, educational policy makers, administrators and researchers, as well as those who work in overseas educational development projects, should also find the book useful.

As societies become increasingly diverse as far as their cultural contexts are concerned, the role of education and schooling is having to change both in the goals that are set, and especially the ways those goals can be achieved in practice. There are several dilemmas facing societies where minority groups live alongside the majority population. The first of these dilemmas relates to how far the traditional customs, language and culture of the minority can adapt to those of the majority culture. A second dilemma exists, within and between countries that have highly developed educational systems, in which the challenges posed by trends for greater regional integration, for example (as posed by the advent of the European Union), affect the role of schools in developing a sense of national identity. A third dilemma involves modernisation and the wider process of globalisation, and how those responsible for policy and planning in education can meet the considerable challenges unleashed by the forces of social change which accompany these processes.

A fourth dilemma faced by educators since the end of WW2 has been the movement across countries and continents of people of different cultures. This has meant that where immigrant populations have arrived in significant numbers, educational systems have had to adapt to meet the challenge by making schooling more multicultural. In the light of these dilemmas, much of the discussion and examples cited in subsequent chapters will be drawn from cross-cultural and multicultural research, together with experiences of successful practice from different regions of the world.

Cross-cultural research has attempted to address issues such as cultural diversity and cultural uniformity, the nature of cultural identity and the existence of cultural universals with its implications for cross-country comparisons, and more recently the individualism–collectivism dimension. Most of these issues will emerge in the course of the book, but building bridges between current research into the dynamics of cultural diversity on one hand, and the application of research findings to problems of educational practice on the other, will be the main task of the present volume. Six areas will be emphasised in this bridge-building task, these are as follows:

- The cultural dynamics of learning and teaching
- Cultural context of educational assessment
- School and classroom management cultures

- The dynamics of changing classroom cultures
- Parental and community influences on the multicultural school
- Training and development of teachers for change and cultural diversity

By way of introduction, let us examine a variety of practical problems taken from each of the six areas, which exemplify the nature and extent of the bridge-building task ahead of us.

TEACHING AND LEARNING

Learning about Cultural Context from Children's Drawing: a Challenge for the Kenyan Primary-school Teacher

Most Samburu Kenyan primary-school children when asked to draw themselves as individuals, usually include other human figures in their drawings. Elsbeth Court (1994) has studied in depth the way different ethnic Kenyan children draw pictures of themselves standing or sitting, or when they eat or what their homes look like. In almost all cases, the drawing will include not one person standing or sitting, or one person eating, or just the picture of a house; the drawings will reflect a social depiction rather than an individual representation (see Figures 1.1(a) and (b)).

This means many more people will be drawn for the eating activity as shown in Figure 1.1(a), or just one other person will appear in the drawing as shown in Figure 1.1(b). In the case of drawing "my home" not only will significant other persons like family members and close friends be included, but animals and plants which are associated with the child's perception of his or her home will also appear.

The problem for a teacher is to be able to strike a balance between allowing children to interpret the world around them

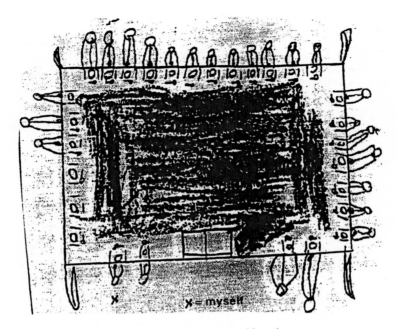

Figure 1.1a: Myself eating

Figure 1.1b: Myself eating

and encourage their particular brand of aestheticism, while meeting the need to develop the prescribed skills, knowledge and other attitudes to drawing (i.e. developing individualism) embodied by the school's art and drawing syllabus.

Enriching School Mathematics: Learning from Some Unexpected Sources

Let us now turn to the teaching of mathematics in situations in the poorer parts of a large city like Rio de Janeiro in Brazil. Terezhina Nunes (1994) has shown that street children in Rio, who are of primary-school age but do not attend school, when asked to perform mathematical operations like multiplication, division and ratio problems, do better than many of their peers who actually attend school. Again we see a serious disparity between learning and teaching strategies used by those who teach mathematics on one hand, and the teaching and learning strategies commonly practised in "out of school" environments as on the streets and market places on the other.

If the research carried out by Nunes and others like Schliemann & Carraher (1992) proves that the "everyday cognition" used on the streets of cities (and in rural villages) is more effective than formal teaching strategies practised in primary schools, then teachers need to be made aware of the use of these alternative ideas and strategies, and be able to meld them, where appropriate, into existing approaches used to teach mathematics. Teachers also need to reflect these alternative approaches in the way they will assess pupil performance in mathematics, this will be discussed further in Chapter 4 when we will examine the cultural dynamics of educational assessment.

CULTURAL PERSPECTIVES TO ASSESSING PUPIL LEARNING

Why Is It Sometimes Important to Include Rote Memorisation as Part of Pupil Assessment?

To what extent should formal modes of school assessment, outside developing countries, reflect locally based content and the application of preferred specific cultural learning sets and cognitive styles? For instance, research by Santerre (1975) has shown that there is a case for school assessment to reflect the needs for pupils to develop good memorising skills. Santerre has shown the importance of recitation in the early schooling and education of children from Islamic cultures, and so school assessment should, and in many cases does, recognise this situation.

The importance of memorising is not only confined to Islamic school settings; children from Confucian, and to a lesser extent Christian, traditions also put considerable store on the ability to recall information. Developing good mnemonic skills enables children to be more secure and comfortable about existing learning, as well as providing an essential base for the acquisition of higher-order linguistic and cognitive skills, leading to complex problem solving and even the development of creativity.

Why Is It Necessary to Balance the Role of Cultural Familiarity with the Necessity of Including More Global Content, When Assessing Pupils from Different Cultural Backgrounds?

In former colonial countries like Kenya, Zimbabwe and Malaysia, the curriculum in the main reflected that followed in the UK. Therefore, teaching and assessment of subjects such as history, geography and biology at the secondary-school level rarely referred to local examples and events. For instance, the history of the UK (or France in the case of Francophone territories) dominated the history syllabuses and geographical and biological content took working examples almost exclusively from those of the metropolitan country.

Much has been written on the effect of stimulus familiarity on cognitive outcomes especially in cross-cultural situations. If one equates the use of exemplars from local knowledge and skills with the concept of stimulus familiarity, then the inclusion of local materials would have implications for improving relevancy in school assessment. For instance, by including local examples of plants and animals in the study of biology, teaching about a local geographical feature and including areas of history which are related to the pupils' nation, would provide a basis for assessment that would be effective and relevant. This would not only enhance pupil interest, but hopefully pupil achievement as well.

By way of caution, however, the move to make curricula more interesting and relevant through overemphasising their local appeal may result in too much parochialism, shutting out important regional and global matters such as environmental and socio-political concerns; therefore some balance between the local context and outside influences has to be maintained. Nevertheless, the shift to localism is understandable as it represents a movement that aims to redress a formerly established ethnocentric situation. Methods of assessment should closely follow a culturally balanced curriculum and attempt to eliminate extra-cultural bias that has been all too evident in the past.

THE CHANGING NATURE OF CLASSROOM CULTURES

The exemplars discussed so far have mostly been taken from situations in developing countries; however, there are ample numbers of cases from the rich industrialised countries where schooling is facing stark challenges as far as the changing nature of classroom culture is concerned. In certain parts of the UK, teachers face a number of cultural challenges such as problems of anti-racism, the need for immigrant children to learn English while attempting to retain their mother tongue, and the broader problems of teachers trying to understand the social dynamics of multicultural classrooms. Let us examine firstly the issue of anti-racism in the classroom and secondly, broader issues concerned with classroom dynamics, such as cultural imbalance and bias.

Combating Anti-racism in Classrooms through More Enlightened Teaching Methods

Perhaps one of the most serious and difficult challenges faced by teachers is how to combat anti-racism in the classroom. Epstein (1997) has advocated the need to develop a particular type of pedagogy, which she calls an anti-racist pedagogy which fully involves teachers and children who come from diverse cultural backgrounds, so that they can share learning and teaching experiences with more equanimity.

The teaching packs used with multi-ethnic classes include among other elements, photographs which depict white and black children engaged in play and are used as part of the pedagogy. For example, children of between three and four years of age were asked what they liked about the images and what they did not. The teacher who uses stories in class which give a balanced view of the life and experiences of both black and white children, followed up with discussion of the stories, is another way Epstein advocates to combat racism among children. These are some of the approaches that teachers could use when faced with the demands of classroom multiculturalism. There is, it seems from the above, a clear need to develop a much wider view of pedagogy to help us address the changing dynamic of classroom cultures. This theme will be followed up in Chapter 3 on the dynamics of the teaching process.

Making Sense of the Perceptions of Classroom Dynamics

The challenge presented by anti-racism and cultural imbalances within classrooms is especially prevalent in schools situated in the poorer inner-city areas. This has prompted educational researchers and teacher educators to undertake research into the dynamics of multicultural classrooms, and where possible to engage teachers fully in this research. For instance, a typical problem would be the steps a teacher could take to provide learning environments which meet the needs of a growing number of children who come from different cultures and are in the same class. Research which addresses issues related to co-operative learning in cross-cultural contexts as in India (Singhal & Mohanty 1994), and in New Zealand and Singapore (Ward & Rzoska 1994) would form a valuable source of ideas for teachers, whether they are teaching in primary or secondary schools.

A pedagogical strand related to this issue would be the selection of teaching resources like books and audiotapes, and videos, to a provide a balanced view to the learners about the way a multicultural society should be developed, and the part which those children one day might play in that society. Another cluster of questions relating to changing classroom dynamics addresses problems that are associated with gender bias, children's rights, sexual orientation and where children find themselves in very difficult situations, as in refugee camps, war zones and famine areas, and who are still receiving some form of schooling (Thomas 1998).

Cross-cultural research which addresses cultural adjustment (Ward & Kennedy 1996), schooling as enculturation (Serpell 1993) and acculturation (Berry 1990; Berry & Sam 1997), would provide professionals with useful guidelines and background. Knowledge about this type of research would, in the first instance, act as a catalyst for improving educational practice and secondly, provide ideas for teachers to engage in research into cultural change in the classroom.

SCHOOL MANAGEMENT CULTURES

Much of school organisation and management is typified by a top-down approach in which the school principal or head teacher is usually the key decision maker. This pattern is well-nigh universal, whether we are discussing school management cultures in industrialised or less industrialised countries. Schools with a strong culture of top-down management are on the whole typified by a didactic and formal teaching mode. Where there are instances of a more relaxed interaction between teachers and learners, but where the management culture still remains top down, a greater chance of dissonance between school managers and teachers is likely to take place.

However, a school that has adopted an open and democratic management culture, which encourages more interactive learning and teaching and gives more opportunities for staff decision making, could result in teachers who have been used to more formal procedures becoming resistant to such changes. These instances are quite common in many developing countries, where school principals have been on management training schemes, and are keen to share the newly acquired skills with their staff colleagues. The task therefore is one of attempting to change teacher attitudes and behaviour in an ever-changing school management culture. If the instances described above are not resolved, it is more than likely that the effectiveness of the school will suffer. Borrowing new ideas and practices so that they can meld in with the old is not new in education; however, working towards a consensus would be to the benefit of all concerned, but it is not an easy option as we shall discover. Let us examine instances where cultural borrowing is taking place.

Borrowing from Particular Cultural Contexts to Improve School Management as well as Classroom Practice

Aikman (1994) found in her work with indigenous Peruvian groups that the consensual management styles practised by the elders of the Arakmut society also filter through to the way the primary schools are administered. Ideas about teaching and learning which may be introduced into the school curriculum are first discussed with teachers, pupils and parents, leading to more considered decision making that will affect the future of the indigenous culture. Similarly, the Teasdales (1994) in their work with the Aborigines in South Australia also found that many of the management practices used by the Aborigines in day-to-day decision making influenced school organisation and administration. By building into the indigenous management culture of the school ideas about school management which come from the wider Australian culture, means that a working consensus is more likely to be achieved.

A number of issues arise from cultural borrowing of any sort: firstly, how thoroughly have the cultures in question been researched for culture-specific practices, secondly, can all or some of the practices be effectively transferred, so that they can meld in with existing forms of school management, and thirdly, how can the melding process be effectively and sensitively achieved? Addressing these issues presents a particular challenge for multicultural school management practice. In Chapter 5 we will explore cultural aspects of management, focusing on the need for a measure of ownership and collaboration involving staff and head teachers.

PARENTS, COMMUNITY AND MULTICULTURAL SCHOOLING

The parents of pupils as well as the community in general have a major stake in the education and schooling of children. Firstly, because they pay the taxes which finance the school system, secondly, schooling provides their children with the means eventually to earn a living, and thirdly, they hope that the school will act as a conduit for enriching social and multicultural cohesion.

There are opposing views on the way parents and the wider community may play a part in the life and role of the school. One view is that schools do a better job if they are left alone to get on with the task of educating the pupil, and this view tends to be more typical of private schools or, less frequently, the better performing state schools. On the other hand, there are those who believe that schools would be the better for having more parental and community involvement. There are several levels of involvement as far as parents and the community are concerned. One level relates to the provision of extra finance; in this case monies are collected and donated to the school, and the head teacher or school governing body would use the money for books, playground facilities or anything else that may be required.

At another level, in many developing countries parents and community members would be requested to build a school classroom or indeed a whole school. At a third level, parents and religious leaders, representatives of local police forces, health care professionals and possibly non-governmental organisations such as Oxfam could provide assistance in the form of extra-curricular activities. Let us take a number of examples which illustrate some of these levels of involvement.

Tapping into Parental and Community Resources – the Case of a British Inner-city Primary School

It is not uncommon in many British inner-city schools to have over 50% of the pupil population representing at least six different ethnic groups. So there is a need for more teaching materials that can be specifically used with some or all of the different groups, e.g. Bangladeshi or Pakistani. These schools like other state schools have their budgets controlled by a school governing body, and their financial allocation usually just covers the needs of the National Curriculum. There is usually no money available for extra teaching and learning materials. Parents, therefore, could be asked to contribute the extra money and sometimes they do. However, parents and other community members who are from the Bangladeshi- or Urdu-speaking communities could themselves be the teaching source.

It would therefore be the task of the head teacher and some of the staff to mobilise, and where possible supervise, the parents in identifying and selecting suitable materials, so that they may be used in class. Building cultural bridges which involve parents and teachers as envisaged above promotes an interculturalism that would not only benefit an interested cultural group within the school, but would help enrich teachers and other pupils in a culture that they know little about. This enrichment process is discussed further in Chapter 6 as part of the bridge building that needs to take place between school and society. Let us now turn to another example of community involvement, this time from an African country.

Tapping into Parental and Community Resources – the Case of the Kenyan Harambee School

Village communities in Kenya often agree to build and continue to finance primary schools with some financial help from the government. These schools are called Harambee schools. Parents and community leaders are asked to provide the money, and where possible the skills to build most of the classrooms (Hill 1991). There are no demands on the community to be involved with the curriculum or to give support for teachers' salaries, this is usually the responsibility of the government. When a school is built and starts to function, the community does not usually withdraw from the enterprise but continues to support the school. This request is made by the authorities, firstly because the school needs to be maintained, and secondly it strengthens the concept of community ownership and the cultural identity of the school, of its teachers and its pupils.

The Harambee model has since the 1960s continued to be used, and has even been copied in a modified form in other developing countries. Politicians in countries like the UK have also seen positive aspects of this model as a means of supplementing school budgets. The essence, however, of this type of community–school partnership is that it can provide a sound basis for ensuring cultural values are part of the school's identity through the concept of community ownership (Hill 1991).

Tapping Parental and Community Resources – Other Experiences

The cross-cultural research on cultural identity and particularly the work done by Aikman in Peru and the Teasdales in Australia have shown how essential it is to examine the dynamics of the background of a cultural group. By focusing on the concept of ownership, it is seen how central it is to the success of schooling, especially among indigenous and other multicultural groups. Where institutions encourage a greater degree of ownership among its members and significant others (like parents in the case of schools), we can expect a greater degree of commitment from all concerned. Recent international research on school effectiveness and school improvement goes some way to underline this contention, which describes how the value of parental and community interest assists schools in achieving their academic and social objectives.

Apart from the two examples above, there are a growing number of instances from both developing and developed countries in which the multiculturalism of the school is being influenced by parents and the community. Since about the beginning of the 1970s, parents in countries like Hawaii, Turkey and Scotland have begun to take a more active role in classroom activities, often complementing the role of the teacher, especially as school helpers in early childhood education. Some of these activities will be discussed in more detail in Chapter 6.

Furthermore, where the children and parents are recent immigrants, activities may include help from parents on language skills. Another instance arises when parents may need to explain to teachers about specific cultural and religious attributes, which could influence the ways their children approach certain problem-solving tasks. Parents could also be called upon to clarify meanings and ways of approaching social and emotional problems which children experience at home, and which could be barriers to learning when they get to school. These cases are typical of the problems of inner-city children, some of whom have recently arrived in either London, Paris or Munich from Bangladesh, Morocco, Turkey and the former Yugoslavia respectively.

DEVELOPING IMAGINATIVE TEACHER EDUCATION PROGRAMMES FOR THE MULTICULTURAL CLASSROOM

In countries like the USA, the UK, Australia and more recently Germany, Italy and France, coping with the challenges of the multicultural classroom brought about by the effects of immigration since the 1970s and earlier has become the norm. In all these countries, attempts have been made to train teachers to cope with the increasing problems of teaching and managing classrooms that have as many as 20 different nationalities, and an equal number of spoken languages and dialects.

Therefore, there is a greater need than ever before to develop pre-service and in-service courses which include components that train teachers to cope with the increasing number of cross-cultural problems. These programmes would, it is hoped, provide teachers with a more substantive base from which to tackle not only cross-cultural learning and instructional issues, but would also enable teachers to identify culture-specific social and emotional dilemmas such as cultural adjustment and culture shock.

It is quite common that such dilemmas can often arise between pupils of differing cultural and linguistic backgrounds sharing the same classroom. Newly trained teachers, especially those who teach in inner-city areas, where the bulk of the problems associated with the effects of multiculturalism arise, will need to have an ongoing exposure to innovative repertoires of pedagogical skills and specialised knowledge, to meet the challenge of providing effective communication for use inside and outside the classroom. Pedagogical models which may include some of these repertoires are discussed in more depth in Chapter 3. These teachers will also need to develop attitudes which put an emphasis on adaptability, tolerance, even-handedness and a great deal of resourcefulness. Teachers may even find it valuable to learn a minority language such as Urdu or Hindi, in the British context.

Let us discuss examples of how teacher education programmes may be developed to meet two problem areas related to multicultural education. The first concerns bilingualism, and the second relates to training teachers to cope with cultural diversity within the classroom.

Teaching in English to Newly Immigrant Primary-school Children: the Implications of Transitional Bilingualism for Teacher Training

Newly arrived immigrant Bangladeshi children who have come to the UK will soon become aware that they will need to acquire English (L2), which is the dominant language of their adopted culture, and in which they will have to communicate sooner rather than later. While L2 is the principal language of instruction, in most cases Bangla (L1) will also be pursued as a parallel means of communication at home and among their Bangladeshi peers in school.

This means, in essence, that teachers will need to develop an integrative pedagogy in which most instruction will be in L2, but they will need to be aware of the pitfalls of second-language learning as well. As research by Mohanty & Perregaux (1997) shows, bilingualism does not just imply learning two languages, but two different cultures are being experienced as well. By providing opportunities through teacher education programmes which emphasise an awareness of recent practices in cross-cultural bilingual education, and the underpinning of these practices from research on the social psychology of language, this would contribute to a more culture-sensitive pedagogy.

Where teachers have a working knowledge of the mother tongue, e.g. Bangla language, they also learn about the acculturative processes which Bangladeshi children are experiencing in their new and bewildering society. The acculturation model developed by Berry (1980a, 1984, 1990) would be a valuable framework for teachers, as it would assist them to understand the dynamics of classroom acculturative processes, hopefully providing for a more sympathetic and sensitive style of teaching in transitional bilingual situations that we have discussed above.

A bilingual language policy which advocates a close and integrative relationship between the two languages in question, is likely to lead to stable bilingualism, language maintenance, and provide better opportunities for social integration. The teacher is a key player in this process of social integration, but all teachers need to receive continuous and substantive injections of support through imaginative and innovative in-service programmes. These are essential if teachers are to become more adaptive, creative and relevant to the changing dynamics of the multicultural classroom.

Let us now turn from a specific multicultural problem like bilingualism and its implications for teacher training, to a wider issue of how teachers may be prepared to become more culture-sensitive and hopefully more effective as cultural bridges. The idea of the teacher as a cultural bridge spanning the space between cultural context and community will be developed at length in Chapters 3, 4 and 7. In these chapters, issues concerning language of instruction, modes of assessment and forms of appropriate training for fulfilling this bridge-building role will be discussed.

Training Teachers for Cultural Diversity

There are a number of ways in which teacher education programmes might address the problem of training teachers to become effective at coping with the challenges of the multicultural classroom. One way would be to supplement an existing monocultural curriculum with bits of information about various cultural groups that make up a society, and this is often manifested in the form of a single course on *multicultural education*. This is currently done in countries like France, and to a lesser extent in the USA and UK, and is usually associated with the *melting pot* theory of society. According to some educational researchers, this approach smacks of condescension and even cultural imperialism (Tabachnick & Zeichner 1993).

Another way would be to take a purely *pluralistic* approach, which would recognise that teachers need to be trained cross-culturally with a great deal of emphasis on developing their cultural sensitivities. This means that a teacher education curriculum will need to be infused with issues related to cultural diversity, and that the trainees should be actively engaged in developing strategies and cultural resources that will be part of classroom instruction. Let us take a Malaysian classroom situation that shares some key features with classrooms all over South East Asia and typifies the type of pluralistic approach to teaching discussed above.

Preparing Teachers for the Malaysian Multicultural Classroom

In a typical Malaysian classroom one would find pupils from ethnic Malay, Chinese and Indian cultural backgrounds. These different cultural backgrounds reflect different religions, languages and traditions. Although national policy dictates that the language of instruction will be Bahasa Malaysia for the purposes mainly of national unity, all teachers are faced with reconciling all the cultural differences that emerge on a day-to-day basis. In other words, while upholding national identity as a necessity, there is also the need to recognise cultural diversity.

A first priority for a training programme would be to sensitise trainees to teaching a multi-ethnic class. A key step in the sensitisation process involves giving the trainees an awareness that they can themselves often be the cultural barrier if they are not trained in the skills of reconciling both issues. They should be prepared to take on the role of an acceptor as well as a donor of cultural attitudes through intercultural communication. Another feature of a multicultural training programme would be get teachers to reflect on their experience as agents of multicultural education, and to value the fact that pupils will bring many types of cultural resources with them to the classroom, which could be used in teaching and learning for the whole class.

Educating teachers to act as *cultural bridges* would span many of the above-mentioned features in a teacher education programme, so making teacher education more sensitive to the problems of cultural diversity. This would hopefully not only convert the situation into one that could benefit both the academic and social outcomes of schooling, but could lead to a teaching profession that would be better prepared, as well as being sympathetic to meeting the complexities of multicultural education and schooling. There is growing evidence that training is already being given to Malaysian teachers to meet the challenge of cultural diversity in the schools (Thomas 1996).

FOUR KEY PROCESSES AND THE NOTION OF CULTURE AS AN ALL-EMBRACING ENTITY

The discussion so far has introduced several key processes, and as they will surface from time to time throughout this book, it is necessary to establish at the outset what they mean. There are four key processes, as follows:

- Culture
- Education
- Schooling
- Teacher education

In many instances, all four processes are closely interlinked, and there are situations in which the links are strongly reciprocal as in the case of education and schooling. Figure 1.2 attempts to provide a perspective on how these four processes relate to one another.

We can perceive culture to be a binding wider concept which embraces two key education subcultures, namely formal and informal education. The culture of formal education is shaped by government policies which control teacher education, formal schooling, and ultimately what goes on in classrooms.

One might also include non-formal education within the formal educational process, insomuch that it is almost always linked to some form of institutionalisation; however, the

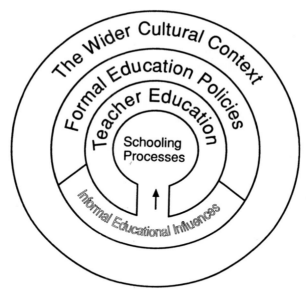

Figure 1.2: Cultural context, educational processes and schooling

definition of non-formal education remains a controversial issue within the subject of educational development. On the other hand, informal education derives its structure and influence from family, ethnic and community sources. Informal education is, in the main, non-institutionalised.

There are varying degrees of reciprocity between formal and informal education cultures. For instance, with groups such as the Australian Aborigines and the Peruvian indigenous peoples, there is often a close liaison between formal and informal education cultures. In countries such as Singapore and Thailand, there is very little interflow between the two education cultures. The increasing role of the school as an agent of cultural transmission in modern societies has meant that the influence of the culture of informal education has diminished significantly. However, it will be shown in several parts of the present book that it may be unwise for those who are responsible for formulating education policy to ignore completely the value and strengths offered by the informal education culture in any society.

The school, which is one of the main ways in which education is disseminated, would have a specific role to play in the relationship between culture and education; for instance, it can promote through the school curriculum certain values, norms and customs of a particular society. In other words, education in its broader sense and schooling as a more specific form of education are both important conduits in the transmission of culture. Turning to teacher education, and its relationship to this all-embracing notion of culture, teachers and the education they receive are at the heart of the process of cultural transmission. Their influence is therefore pivotal, and so there is a need to enhance this influence further by investing in sound teacher development which emphasises not only academic and professional expertise but aims to make teachers more culture sensitive and informed, in the part they play in cultural transmission.

It is not the purpose here to give a set of strict definitions of the four processes; however, it is necessary to provide a sketch of what these processes are likely to constitute in the context of the present book, in order to act as a working basis for what follows in subsequent chapters. Let us therefore elaborate further on each of the four processes.

Culture as an All-embracing Concept

Culture, the most elusive of the four processes, has been viewed as a interpretative process by Serpell & Hatano (1997) in which humans interpret their own nature. Humans are unique in the way they acquire behavioural traits and through socialisation pass on these traits to subsequent generations. To other workers, culture is more about meanings (Rohner 1984), while culture in the form of context and the general properties of settings plays a crucial part in understanding the nature of human behaviour (Bronfenbrenner 1979), and the inseparable nature of the person from the cultural context of activity (Schweder 1990). The cultural structuring of human development as envisaged by Super & Harkness (1997) views cultural processes in the form of niches which recognise the roles of customs and cultural variability, mental activities of the child, and the role of significant others such as parents who provide specific cultural contexts.

The above views about culture provide a mosaic of perceptions from which it is possible to draw several underlying and interlinking features. These features include generational and developmental processes, and the acquisition of behavioural characteristics by individuals and groups which determine the roles and nature of traditions and customs. A dominant feature which most analyses of culture uncover is the need to recognise the importance of context. Cultural context may be about many things, such as preferred language usage, unique ways of thinking and problem solving, the sanctity of certain cultural values and the holding of well-established attitudes. Above all, context is about how individuals and groups interact with one another, and how adaptable to change a particular group is. The more adaptable a cultural group is to innovation and change, the greater the possibility of cultural variation leading to the likelihood that new and enriched cultural systems will emerge in the longer term.

Education and Culture

The features which typify culture as a concept and a process have a certain commonality with education. The process of acquisition, be it applied to language, cultural values, social attitudes or learning and teaching, makes up a substantial part of most educational processes, be they formal (i.e. schooling) or informal (i.e. incidental and/or non-institutional). Again the development of children's abilities and interests, as well the search for personal identity and the realisation of a person's self-esteem, may be considered as cardinal functions of education. Education is also about contexts involving different age levels, different socio-economic groups, varied ethnic and linguistic minorities, indigenous cultures as well those cultural groups that have established effective educational systems, as in the richer industrialised nations of the world.

From the start it is important to make a distinction between education and schooling, as although the two processes are closely interrelated, the philosophical, sociological and political perspectives from which they are often analysed provide sufficient insight for professional educators to develop praxis that is aimed on one hand at the realisation of extrinsic societal goals (which is what schooling attempts to accomplish), and on the other the realisation of an individual's intrinsic goals, often called personal development or self-development. This focus on development is the essence of education as a continuous and total process. Education can therefore be perceived as a continuum which includes at one end a set of informal non-institutionalised learning experiences, to highly institutionalised venues such as schools and colleges at the other. In between, there often exist opportunities for a non-formal but institutional training with an emphasis on technical and commercial skills.

Therefore formal, non-formal and informal forms of education can be viewed as being part of the total educative process which can be experienced by all people at different times of their lives. This broad view of education makes it akin to the notion of culture as an all-embracing process. However, while schooling is part of the wider educative process, it has very specific features which distinguish it from education and these will be discussed below.

Schooling and Culture

As much of this book deals mainly with schools and schooling let us examine further the nature of both. The school is an institution in which a child learns, is taught, interacts and socialises with peers and other teachers. It is remarkably similar in physical appearance and general organisation throughout the world (Thomas 1992). Children are housed in units called classrooms usually equipped with desks or tables and chairs, supplied with teaching and learning aids, the amount and quality varying from one society to another. In many situations, especially in poor countries, the classroom may take the form of an open air venue like under a tree. But the main goal of the school is the same, that is to promote learning. The ratio of children to a teacher varies from country to country and between parts of a country. In richer countries there may be as few as 10 pupils per teacher, in very poor countries we may meet as many as 70 or 80 pupils to one teacher, and where many of the pupils are likely to be sitting on the floor.

Schooling is the process that goes on in the school and can be thought of as a distinctive form of enculturation which is formalised through the curriculum. Schooling has a prescribed length of time, e.g. 6–12 years (although this varies in different countries), during which pupils learn, are taught and interact with peers. The rationale for schooling throughout the world is surprisingly universal, schools attempt to engender self-realisation, provide society with citizens that are skilled, knowledgeable and able to participate in an effective and efficient division of labour, and to act as an agent of intergenerational cultural transmission.

The blueprint for the knowledge and skills to be taught in all schools is embodied in the curriculum, and it is the main function and responsibility of the teacher to ensure that curriculum objectives are achieved to the best of his/her ability. While schooling is distinctive as an institution and as a process, it is not the only form of enculturation as Serpell & Hatano (1997) point out; non-formal as well as informal educational processes often sit side by side with formal schooling, especially in non-industrialised countries.

Schooling should also be seen as a process which continues the *apprenticeship* of the child not only in exploring new fields of cognitive and psychomotor domains, but also developing social and emotional domains. While the concept of apprenticeship as described by Rogoff (1990) in her cross-cultural research is, in general, seen to be a universal process, cultural variability determines the kind of impact which apprenticeships may have on how children arrive and embark on their schooling career. This means that pre-school-age children who come from different cultures will bring with them particular and often unique ways of structuring and responding to the teaching–learning environment of the school. Those who are responsible for schooling have, by and large, not always recognised the crucial importance that a child's previous experience (or entering behaviour) is already varied, and often so rich that it can act as a sound basis from which new knowledge and different modes of thinking and problem solving can be initiated and developed.

While schooling is recognised as having a universal agenda which stakes out that all pupils should be introduced to the knowledge and skills necessary for functioning in a modern society, it should also be recognised that school has other agendas which it needs to address, and which impinge on the social and cultural goals of that society. Therefore, while schooling is seen as part of the wider process of education, a contextual approach to schooling and the understanding of how children think and develop will reflect the need for varied approaches to learning and teaching in school, especially those that reflect local circumstances and aspirations. Teachers, as well as the pupils they teach, also come from varied and rich cultural backgrounds and these aspects need to be developed and used as a basis from which culture-sensitive pedagogies could ultimately emerge, a subject that will be elaborated upon in Chapter 3.

Within the schooling process it is also necessary to be aware of a number of subcultural systems which not only include the obvious pupil/teacher culture, but other cultural contexts such as the pupil/pupil culture (or peer culture), teacher cultures (including the cultures of teaching), and the school culture which includes the school ethos and its relationship with school management. Differing classroom climates which arise from the effect of innovation and the application of new ideas, and which bring about cultural change, are also a growing feature of schooling as we enter the millennium. In other words, the school and the process of schooling represent a whole complex of cultural and subcultural systems, which need to be considered when we are advocating proposals for improved praxis to enhance educational quality.

There is also the increasing influence of significant others from outside the school. It is not only in the rich industrialised countries that we have parents, the community, religious organisations and the world of work taking an active interest in the schooling process. In many developing countries, we find this state of affairs to be a growing trend as well. For instance, in many countries of Latin America and Africa, a growing number of parents are involved in financing schools and wanting a say in what is taught and how it is taught. In Chapter 6 we will examine in more depth how cultural bridges may be developed between school and society, involving not only parents but significant others such as employers, religious and municipal authorities, and welfare groups.

Teacher Education and Culture

Turning finally to teacher education and its relationship with our view of culture, the training of teachers can best be thought of as a process of lifelong teacher education (LLTE), in which professionalisation is seen as an enabling feature that will assist teachers to continually develop their potential (Thomas 1993, 1997b). It is becoming more and more acceptable to think of teaching as a set of cultures, which teachers are able to experience as they unlock their potential through taking part in the process of LLTE and training. A model of LLTE which addresses the issue of making teachers more culture sensitive will be the essence of sound teacher development especially in the context of multicultural education.

How would teacher development benefit from the growing number of research findings about the cultural context of learning and teaching? Would a teacher's lifelong education and training be enhanced if recent ideas on teacher support mechanisms became part of in-service teacher education? The answer to these questions would hinge not only on where and how teachers have access to new ideas emanating from research about pedagogy, it would also depend on how they used the information to improve their praxis, once it is in their possession. One of the principal tasks facing teacher education and its relationship with culture and multiculturalism is how the teacher-training curriculum can accommodate the need to treat issues like cultural identity alongside cultural uniformity, actually engaging in meaningful and sensitive treatment of acculturative and enculturative processes in the classroom, and how different pedagogies can be developed which are both sensitive and effective for successful multicultural schooling.

THREE CONTEXTUAL SCENARIOS

Culture, education, schooling and teacher development will be examined in this book within at least three contextual scenarios (see Figure 1.3). The first contextual scenario relates to the *cultural demography* of schools and classrooms. It refers to classrooms that have pupils and teachers who come from a variety of linguistic, ethnic, religious and social backgrounds. Such contexts are described as *multicultural*, and the number and diversity of multicultural classrooms have increased significantly over the last few decades in almost all parts of the world. The increase in the number of multicultural classrooms has brought with it headaches for administrators and

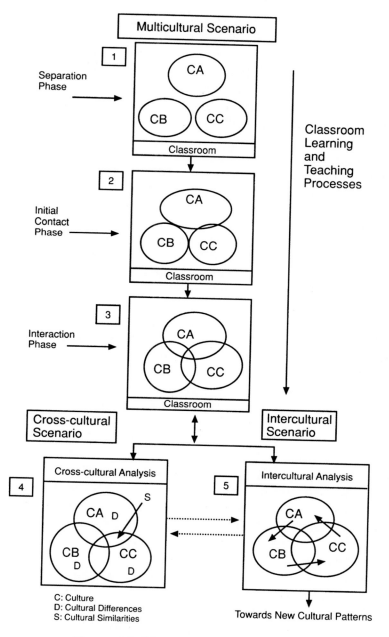

Figure 1.3: Three contextual scenarios

many challenges for teachers and pupils. One of the challenges is to provide optimum teaching and learning conditions that will satisfy the needs of most learners. Another challenge is to develop classroom climates which are conducive to meaningful and mutually beneficial social interrelationships between pupils and between teachers and their pupils, so that effective schooling can take place.

The multicultural contextual scenario can be envisaged as being made up of three sequential phases. The first is called a *separation phase* in which the pupils' cultural identities (i.e. A, B, C) are likely to be seen as separate during the early days or weeks of schooling. The second is a *contact phase* in which pupils are starting to get to know each other. The third is the *interaction phase*, in which the various cultural identities are interacting with one another in class group work, during play and school visits and other pursuits. This phase will continue until the class members move on to another class or leave the school for good. The multicultural scenario is one in which all members, irrespective of cultural origins, experience together the processes of teaching and learning.

A second contextual scenario to be examined in this book will be the *cross-cultural* scenario. Cross-cultural studies of individual and social behaviour aim to discover similarities as well as differences between cultures, leading, it is to be hoped, to a better understanding of how members of different cultures learn and think, how they are motivated, how they interact with one another and, of particular concern here, how cultural differences and similarities affect the education and schooling of children and young people.

A key challenge in many countries is the need for the school to be at the forefront of developing national identity and citizenship based on traditional values, while at the same time accommodating cultural pluralism. The cross-cultural scenario informs all three phases of the multicultural scenario, and through researching similarities and differences between the different cultural identities, educators will be provided with a wealth of information about the dynamics of multicultural classrooms. Armed with this information, it is to be hoped the teachers will receive sound training in addressing issues related to cultural diversity, and perhaps even carry out research themselves.

A third contextual scenario is called *intercultural*, and involves an analysis of the relationships between two or more different cultures that result from long-term contact. Like the cross-cultural scenario, the analysis may examine differences and similarities, but with the goal of detecting new cultural patterns of behaviour. This scenario provides educators and researchers with opportunities to observe the development of unique patterns of behaviour associated with teaching as well as learning. This could lead to better levels of schooling and social interaction in the multicultural classroom. Intercultural analyses could also provide more culture-sensitive pedagogies. What the foregoing describes is a study at the interface between two or more cultures which will hopefully provide us with an *intercultural* dimension to the impact of culture on the schooling process.

AIMS OF THE BOOK

It is the *general* aim of this book to apply selected cross-cultural and multicultural research, that has originated over the last 25 years in fields not always directly related to education, for the use of educators to assist them in improving their praxis, and which may even stimulate them to carry out cross-cultural research into multiculturalism and schooling.

A more *specific* aim of the present book, however, is to give the reader an insight into how the different views about culture and the different methods used by cross-cultural researchers can solve particular multicultural problems that arise in schools and classrooms from all over the world. It will become clear to the reader that as different facets of the schooling process (such as learning, teaching, managing) are examined in the chapters that follow, rarely does one find that there is only one solution to a particular problem.

Another *specific* aim of this book is to clarify the relationship between praxis, theory building and research. Sound praxis in most fields of study, and especially education, emanates from sound theories, and sound theories in general generate valuable bases for research. Throughout this book, the relationship between the above three activities will be explored in some depth, as we consider the six areas selected for the bridge-building task mentioned earlier in this chapter. However, application and praxis in the context of the multicultural classroom will remain at the heart of this book.

BOOK AND CHAPTER STRUCTURE

Chapters 2–4 will concentrate on the need to examine the changing nature and role of pedagogy as it is used in the dynamic environments of multicultural classrooms. The processes of learning and teaching, and the interplay between the two, will be examined from a number of perspectives. These will include the suitability of content, the efficacy of how content is presented to the learner, and how learners, whether they attend school or not, structure their learning experiences in particular cultural contexts, and what implication this may have for assessment, and the transfer of skills and knowledge to other tasks.

Chapters 5 and 6 will examine the influence of certain groups of significant players who share in, and are entrusted to different degrees with, the responsibility of fulfilling the goal of effective schooling. Among these players will be the school managers (or head teachers), and the management culture they adopt and which invariably influences both staff and pupils. This, it will be shown, has a profound effect on the effectiveness of pupil learning and the way teachers relate to their various roles in the classroom. The growing influence of out-of-school factors such as parents, religious leaders, community officials, the media, personal computers and the Internet is becoming more common. It is recognised, therefore, that the teacher will not be the only person who can transmit knowledge, skills and attitudes to his/her pupils in the future. While the need for effective and well-motivated teachers will always be a requirement, there are many in the community who have valuable life and work experiences to offer children, as well as what the children can contribute to each other. Therefore, the emphasis in Chapter 6 will highlight the cultural support which school pupils may draw, from not only their teachers but their parents, siblings, peers and other members of the community.

It is clear that teacher education and training should equip teachers for new roles and expectations, and a wider understanding of the many cultures that exist in our societies and beyond them. Therefore the final chapter will discuss the need for sound and imaginative teacher education, that will focus on cultural diversity providing an essential base for praxis as well as teachers' professional development.

Chapters 2–7 will be structured along the following lines. There will be an introduction which will give a brief background to the issues and problems the chapter aims to address. This will be followed by a number of key questions which, in essence, will provide the framework for the chapter. The key questions will broadly focus on issues relating to the subject of the chapter, e.g. learning, teaching, the relevant cross-cultural research that has been carried out into the subject and allied fields, and the possible applications of the research to education praxis. In each chapter, there will be a discussion of a number of case studies taken from different countries, which show actual or possible applications of the cross-cultural research that was discussed earlier in each chapter. Finally, there will be a summary of the main issues that were discussed in the body of the chapter, followed by suggestions for further reading.

SUMMARY

In this introductory chapter, we have covered a number of pivotal areas in the study of cultural influences on schooling. In the course of this book, all these areas will be expanded upon as we examine their relevance and importance to developing sound praxis and teacher professionalism. The following summary attempts to distil the gist of what has been discussed in this chapter:

1. The main thesis of this book is to build bridges between relevant current cross-cultural research into the dynamics of cultural diversity, and the achievement of better educational practice in the classroom.
2. Six areas are emphasised in this bridge-building task, which include the cultural dynamics of learning and teaching, the cultural context of educational assessment, the social dynamics of classroom and school management cultures, parental and community influences on schooling and preparing teachers for cultural diversity.
3. The four key processes of cultural development, education, schooling and teacher education are closely interlinked and constitute an all-embracing notion of culture, which will underpin the development of sound strategies for good praxis as well as qualitative teacher development.
4. The four key processes will be examined within three overlapping contextual scenarios: the first refers to the *multicultural* demography of classrooms, especially multicultural classrooms, the second is *cross-cultural* in nature providing a comparative perspective to cultural differences in schools and classrooms, and the third is referred to as *intercultural*, and concentrates on the cultural interactions that take place between different cultural groups and indi-

viduals within classrooms, and the possible generation of new cultural patterns.

SUGGESTIONS FOR FURTHER READING

Berry, J.W. (1990). The psychology of acculturation. In J. Berman (Ed.), *Cross Cultural Perspectives: Nebraska Symposium on Motivation*. Lincoln: University of Nebraska Press, pp. 201–234.

Keats, D.M. (1997). *Culture and the Child: A Guide for Professionals in Child Care and Development*. Wiley Series on Culture and Professional Practice. Chichester: Wiley.

Schliemann, A., Carraher, D. & Ceci, S.J. (1997). Everyday cognition. In J.W. Berry, P.R. Dasen & T.S. Saraswathi (Eds), *Handbook of Cross Cultural Psychology* (2nd edn), Volume 2. Boston: Allyn & Bacon, pp. 177–216.

Serpell, R. & Hatano, G. (1997). Education, schooling and literacy. In J.W. Berry, P.R. Dasen & T.S. Saraswathi (Eds), *Handbook of Cross Cultural Psychology* (2nd edn), Volume 2. Boston: Allyn & Bacon, pp. 339–376.

Thomas, E. (Ed.) (1994). *International Perspectives on Culture and Schooling: A Symposium Proceedings*. London: University of London, Institute of Education Publication.

THE CULTURAL DYNAMICS OF LEARNING PROCESSES

This chapter will focus on the learning process, and it will be discussed as part of the total cultural dynamic of schooling. The other part of the dynamic is the process of teaching. Both learning and teaching are salient in the overall transaction between the two principal players, namely the learner and the teacher. The term "transaction" denotes interactions, and in this chapter and the one that follows it (which will focus on teaching), the discussion will attempt to emphasise the close interrelationships that exist between these two activities.

However, in the interests of manageability and clarity, a single chapter has been devoted to each process. Another reason for doing this is that there is an increasing amount of cross-cultural research, which needs to be considered, and which will hopefully throw light on how the cultural contexts of both learning and teaching can be better understood and eventually practised.

This chapter will be structured around three key questions, as follows:

1. How does research into the cultural contexts of learning assist teachers to make schooling more relevant?

2. How does recent cross-cultural research into the learning of key curriculum subjects (i.e. literacy, mathematics) provide ideas and guidelines for better teaching and learning in multicultural classrooms?
3. To what extent have findings from cross-cultural research into some key psychological processes (i.e. cognition, memory) provided educators with a better understanding of the cultural dynamics of learning in the classroom?

Let us therefore proceed to address the first of the three questions posed above.

SCHOOLING, CULTURAL CONTEXT AND LEARNING

The research from cross-cultural and multicultural sources shows that there are widely differing contexts within which various researchers have carried out their work. This also points to the fact that the researchers themselves have particular interests and concerns, which affect their perceptions and basic assumptions behind the process of schooling. For instance, some researchers such as Rogoff and Serpell have concentrated on examining learning and teaching in countries such as Guatemala and Zambia respectively, where economic support for schooling is often meagre. Not only have these workers therefore been concerned with questions of how teachers and learners can use the limited resources they have at their disposal, but in doing so they have stressed that relevant schooling in a particular context is as important as trying to aim at an alien (i.e. Western) view of schooling.

So-called Western forms of schooling have been charged with de-emphasising key cultural learning and pedagogical processes, which are more meaningful and effective in the long run for the children of non-Western countries. In doing so, Serpell in particular has raised serious doubts about the whole notion of schooling with its strong association with

Westernisation, as being the most appropriate form of enculturation for young people from developing countries. Other authors such as Bruner, Olson and Goodnow have viewed cultural context which has implications for schooling not only in economically disadvantaged situations, but in an affluent country like the USA. In the USA and similar countries, learners and teachers appear to be reticent to accept, or are even unaware of, the value of what Bruner has labelled *folk psychology* and *folk pedagogy*, which according to these workers are attributes that we all possess. Olson & Bruner (1996) have summarised folk psychology and folk pedagogy as alternative models of mind and pedagogy, in which an insider's (i.e. each person's) view of thinking, learning, knowing and teaching is as important as the current dominance of externalist theories (as espoused in educational psychology).

The genuine possibility of constructing useful ways of explaining how children and adults may organise their learning and its transference to others will assist both to manage their lives more meaningfully and effectively. These contentions are the essence of what folk psychology and folk pedagogy are about. An awareness by teachers of these alternative ways of thinking, learning and teaching is also valuable, as teachers will be able to organise experience for children while applying it to themselves at the same time.

Formal schooling, consistently and persistently, is allowed to override the merits of the experience we gain from learning informally (or incidentally), and how it is passed on to other people. This is in part due to the historical setting of the school, and the importance attached to it over the years by society. Society has come to see school as the key agent in preparing children for the world of work, with its overemphasis on credentialism. There is, however, a clear need for benchmarks in the form of standardised qualifications and attainment criteria, otherwise access to work and higher education would be based on a free for all or maybe even a lottery.

Much of what is taught at school is in need of reappraisal, so that it meets the changing needs of society as we enter the next millennium. It is clear that a reappraisal will also need to address the ways schooling can tap into the out-of-school cultural experiences of children, be they from the rich industrialised countries of the world or from the poorer developing societies. To carry out this reappraisal more effectively, we need to understand more about the cultural dynamics of learning and some of the key factors that influence the process. Let us consider briefly these factors below.

Five Key Factors in the Cultural Dynamics of Learning

From the views of those psychologists (some of whom have been mentioned above) who are critical of the shortcomings of schooling, whether it be in the poorer or more affluent parts of the world, a number of key factors enter into the cultural dynamics of learning. The first factor is that of the nature of cultural *context*. The second is about the need to identify *meaningful* patterns of learning and teaching, so that schooling can be seen to contribute to the third factor, namely that of *relevance*. A fourth factor relates to *adaptation to change*, enabling schooling to meet the challenge of modernisation and globalisation. A fifth factor is the need to attain a *balance* in terms of what is taught, and how it is taught.

As we enter the next century, educators will need to select appropriate research in order to devise new teaching and learning strategies which encompass the above five factors. Finding the correct balance however, will be the hardest task in view of the rapidly changing demands which are being made on school systems everywhere. The problem of achieving balance, is intimately related to how content and process in learning and teaching can be addressed in different cultural contexts. All five factors will be referred to in the course of our discussions of recent research, which has been carried out into cross-cultural and multicultural contexts and has application to school praxis. We will also attempt to relate research findings to different school scenarios in different parts of the world, to see if there are some common problems which the findings address. However, as *context* plays such a fundamental role in the cultural dynamic of learning, it is necessary to discuss the nature of context in a little more depth before discussing specific subject areas that are taught in schools.

Context as a Special Factor in the Cultural Dynamics of Learning

There is a tendency to regard context as being reducible to either a study of just an individual or groups of individuals, or the environment in which people live and work. Context is far more complex than this, as Schliemann, Carraher & Ceci (1997) point out. Human cognition and indeed other aspects of behaviour are best understood as a set of interactions involving an interplay between the individual and the situations in which the individual participates. Context for the most part is not an explanatory concept; it mostly refers to a complex of behaviours which reflect the actions of an individual or individuals, and the characteristics of a particular setting in which these behaviours are taking place. It is therefore necessary to analyse the setting, the individual's, mental and physical features in a less discrete and polarised manner.

Context is better viewed in terms of relationships between persons and the cultural arenas in which they act (Little 1994). This enables us to focus more succinctly on situations from which meaning and relevance arise when we are examining the cultural context of learning. It is the dynamic interplay that exists between the individual and his or her setting, that informs us about the real nature of what characterises a particular learning set or situation. While it is important to be aware of this contextual dynamic interplay by those studying the learner, it is equally important that the teacher and those responsible for planning the school curriculum are also aware of it.

We will explore all five factors listed above in the course of our discussion about the cultural dynamic of learning as exemplified through a number of key school subjects, and with reference to certain key psychological processes that are closely related to the cultural context of learning. We will therefore continue in the section that follows to address the second question that was posed earlier.

CROSS-CULTURAL RESEARCH INTO LEARNING KEY CURRICULUM SUBJECTS

Literacy, mathematics, science, language acquisition and bilingualism have been chosen as the school subjects for analysis, in view of their fundamental importance in the schooling process. We will first examine the cross-cultural research on literacy.

Literacy Learning as an "Access Card" to Better Communication and Thinking Skills

There are various ways of interpreting literacy – some workers such as Gibson and Levin (1975) see it as the ability to interpret meaning from orthography, others such as Illich (1991) view literacy as a complex system of knowledge, skills and attitudes which transcend a varied set of human activities. Serpell & Hatano (1997) have put forward their views on literacy in the context of education and have distinguished between two broad phases in which literacy plays a salient role. The first phase is *foundational*, during which reading and writing are acquired, and the second is *functional*, in which literacy is used as a means of entering into a world of cultural knowledge which may lead to higher levels of cognitive functioning. The key issues affecting both learners and teachers are how literacy relates to communication, and what effect it has on the cognitive capacities of children. It will become clear that the task of schooling will eventually be one of providing the pupil with an "access card" in the form of sound literacy skills.

Teasing out the relationship between literacy and communication is easier than investigating its effect on cognition and, especially, on cognitive development. As far as literacy and cognition are concerned within the context of the school, there are several approaches to the relationship between these two processes that need to be discussed. The descriptions of the approaches that follow will illustrate some of the problems that have to be overcome, if literacy learning is to be both meaningful and relevant, and that the "access card" can be part of a generally accepted currency. There are three well-known approaches to why children and adults need to be literate and these are discussed below.

Learning to be Literate as a Means of Enlightenment

When children first attend school and therefore begin the formal processes of learning to read and write, to what extent does school learning actually enable children to release their intrinsic potentialities of interpreting written text for the organisation of ideas? Furthermore, does this release of potential empower children eventually so that they may acquire a higher-order cultural awareness of their society, enabling them to engage in the possibilities of using logic, science and religion for their own self-esteem and advancement? This is sometimes referred to as the *classical torch* view of literacy and has been criticised on the grounds that it divides literates from non-literates, and that if school does not achieve the goal of literacy for many of its pupils, they are doomed when they reach the adult world, making them unable to participate effectively in day-to-day cultural interaction and the high culture of their society. While schooling should be a means of enlightenment and learning, teaching pupils to be literate is an essential first step in the process whatever the arguments about likely social divisions that may occur.

There is, however, according to Street (1984), an underestimate of the general cognitive capacity of non-literates, who often have a rich oral capacity and in which attendance at school has not for various reasons been realised. The inability of the school to realise this capacity may also be a feature of the way literacy is taught. Much of school learning as far as literacy is concerned, is mainly focused on highlighting what Street calls the "technological" features of writing, and this means that the important social and cultural context of those pupils learning to read and write is ignored. A more moderate line taken by those who perceive the role of schooling in literacy as some form of enlightenment states that literacy acts as a torch to empower people in specific ways, assisting them in day-to-day tasks. In other words, the value of literacy in this context depends on what people do with it once they have mastered the basic skills. For instance, being able to read instructions for those working in jobs that require a need to follow set procedures as in operating machines allows these people to participate in this type of work.

At a more highly skilled and intellectual level, being literate enables individuals to take part in scientific, philosophical and literary activities. The recent work of Olson (1991) shows that written language in whatever context it is used enhances not only ways of communication but develops different forms of thinking as well.

Literacy as a Key to Social Learning and Political Awareness

The failure of schooling in many countries over the last few decades to deliver on the promises of social equality and equal opportunity among the population has been seen by social and political scientists as the reason behind the gulf that is developed when individuals are not taught to be literate.

Being literate is like having a key which opens a number of important doors into society. Those who have the key gain access to a whole new world of opportunities denied to those who are non-literate. The literacy gulf, often wide in many poor countries of the world, is a recipe for political and social disenfranchisement and with which comes a rejection of socio-cultural norms and values.

Literacy as Collaboration

This view of literacy embodies cognition as a process of social distribution and has been the focus of research by Gardner (1991), Hutchins (1991) and Serpell & Hatano (1997) who envisage literacy as a "cultural resource at the disposal of the participants in various socially organised activities" (p. 347). In this context, literacy has a powerful mediating influence in which it can be used by members of a community having different but complementary goals, and in which the engagement with literacy reflects a collaboration. The work of Reder (1987) with minority groups of Laotian, Hispanics and Eskimos in the USA, and Wagner (1993) with Moroccan adults, shows how different participants within a community can share various types of functional literacy, so that what we end up with is a collaborative act or set of acts. It appears from the research carried out by these authors that schooling plays little or no role in these processes. In fact literacy develops in spite of schooling or may indeed be parallel and separate from it.

Three Possible Strategies to Obtaining the Literacy "Access Card" as Part of Meaningful Learning in School

In the light of the above discussion, what can teachers learn from these perspectives to literacy, so that schooling can meet both foundational and functional requirements of all children from whichever country they come? It appears that there are at least three key strategies teachers might consider when they face the task of teaching their pupils to read and write.

The *first strategy* is to recognise that each child has the capacity to be literate, and that teachers have a duty to exploit this as far as possible. This exploitation on the part of teachers may involve a variety of ways in getting pupils to learn orthography, sentence construction and sequence as well as phonetics and eventually semantics. There is no one particular way of doing this. Different situations call for the use of different approaches; this is especially true of teaching literacy in the poorer countries of the world. Also teaching children to be literate in societies which are pluralistic presents teachers with particular challenges, especially if they are minority languages. In these situations teachers have to resort to a variety of methods some of which are bound to be branded as traditional. This situation has to be recognised, where most schools have no access or expertise to update their teaching methods and where paucity of essential teaching materials is the norm.

A *second strategy* is to recognise that each child's capacity to learn literacy is a function of his or her previous background reflected in home and socio-economic conditions. The nature of children's background factors varies in extent and in the richness of the experience which they bring to school. It is therefore the role of the teacher to find out as much as possible about the child's background factors, and to selectively meld certain features that are relevant to the teaching and learning of literacy for that context. This hopefully will not only mean that more non-literate children become literate, it will also avoid many children being marginalised both socially and politically.

A *third strategy* relates to making the learning of literacy more effective and relevant, and embraces the concept of sharing and collaboration. Where classroom teaching is planned by teachers to include peer interaction and peer instruction, this would provide valuable opportunities for children who come from different social and cultural backgrounds to use their particular language in different ways and for different purposes and situations. This means that by setting active classroom collaboration tasks which involve learning to read and write, exposure to the different uses to which the same language can be put will be experienced by all the learners. This makes for a greater degree of understanding and awareness on the part of teachers and learners, of the sheer variety and diversity that exist in other languages as well as their own.

Learning Mathematics and Science: Facing up to Some Cross-cultural Issues in Praxis

One, Two or More Types of Mathematics Learning?

Knowledge and skills which are developed in the school, the home and in the workplace have their own special learning dynamic. Since the 1980s, there has been a growing body of research into the teaching and learning of mathematics in "out of school" and "in school" cultures. Attempts have been made to explain the differences between these cultures. The research carried out by Lave (1977) and Reed & Lave (1979) investigated Liberian tailors' ability to solve arithmetical problems on the job and whether they had attended school. These researchers showed that everyday experience at work gave opportunities to emphasise competencies that manipulate quantities that receive much less attention in the classroom.

This resulted in far fewer errors being made by the tailors in their day-to-day tasks than had they been taught these operations at school. On the other hand, schooling provides the wherewithal to solve problems by using symbols, emphasising the need to learn, giving the possibility of transferring concepts across to other areas of knowledge, and providing general principles so that they can be applied to the solution of a wider range of complex problems.

This has the effect of increasing problem complexity, as well as enriching the variety of problems that can be tackled. Time and again research with children and adults shows that where mathematical operations are intimately practised in real life situations such as at home or in the workplace, it is crucial to understand the interface between the learning process and the setting. Therefore, understanding how setting and process bring the problem and possible solutions together is a necessary skill in which every teacher needs to be experienced. One of the key problems associated with the teaching of numeracy is to train pupils to develop the competency of being able to use symbolic representation. This enables children to master mathematical concepts which eventually leads them to engage in effective mathematical reasoning.

The work of Carraher, Carraher & Schliemann (1987) and Nunes (1994) has shown the quality and effectiveness of mathematical reasoning and its application, as employed by Brazilian street children in their everyday situations. Their research showed how street children performed in comparison to their school peers when it came to the speed of performing basic operations, and their application of these operations to tasks such as selling and bartering. The street children mainly used oral strategies to solve their number problems, but using the usual school-based stepwise sequence of operations to solve the problem was perceived to be slow and unnecessary for their immediate context. Introducing a set routine (a feature of school mathematics learning), often applied to non-real situations, removes the relevance of the particular mathematical operation, e.g. addition or division, from the street task.

In other words, mathematical operations are better understood at this level where solutions of problems are linked into real, relevant and therefore more meaningful contexts. While rule-bound procedures are necessary, they are not always understood by all pupils as they can often be counterproductive in generating solutions to "out of school" mathematical problems. Strategies that are employed to solve problems "out of school" are often more flexible and provide constant reference to the task at hand, reinforcing the meaningfulness of the situation.

At this point in the discussion we need to raise the question of whether there are two types of mathematics. Is there a school mathematics, and an "out of school" or everyday mathematics that is proving to be as effective? A perusal of recent research findings does indeed seem to indicate this perception. According to Nunes, Schliemann & Carraher (1993), school mathematics tends to be concerned with getting pupils to master numeracy and problem solving through rule following, which emphasises number manipulation and computation. However, out-of-school mathematics focuses on everyday tasks, where manipulation of quantities is directly linked to task immediacy, which therefore gives an instant meaning to the numeric computations associated with the task.

Both types of mathematics appear to be important to learning, for they are likely to contribute to a better understanding of numeracy and higher mathematical concepts, e.g. solving equations, in the long run. While many cross-cultural psychologists emphasise, quite correctly, the value of everyday cognition and the way schooling can benefit from incorporating many of its facets, teachers will still need to address the value of rule learning and subsequent rule application. This is directly linked to learning transfer and all the implications this process has for understanding the use of mathematics across school subjects such as science, technology and design.

The specific nature of "out of school" situations has limitations when it comes to transfer of knowledge and skills. As it is in science, so it is in mathematics, learning of rules and principles enables us to solve more complex problems through analysis, application and prediction. This will enable learners to be more analytical and creative, both qualities necessary for enhancing the quality of mathematics thinking.

The challenge for teachers and teacher educators will be to provide training regimens that will address both types of mathematics learning, by giving opportunities for teachers to devise teaching and learning situations that will "cash in" on the strengths of both. As we have seen from the selected research findings reported above, everyday mathematics is closely bound up with culture-specific patterns of informal learning and instruction. This has important implications for the nature of programmes which seek to give more relevant training for teachers. There is a growing desire, therefore, for training programmes to address the need to enable all teachers to develop culture-sensitive adaptive strategies, which will make their pedagogy not only more meaningful and effective but innovative as well. However, for understanding higher mathematical principles set routines are essential.

Enriching School Science through Learner Experiences

It has been shown since about the beginning of the 1980s, that children develop a substantial knowledge about science from their own life experiences in addition to that which they may get at school (Hatano 1990). One has only to examine the development of science education worldwide to recognise that there are several worlds for the child learning science. There is the world of school science with its emphasis on learning of facts, rules and principles and their application to often unreal and remote situations which children would rarely if ever meet in their whole lives. Then there is the world of out-of-school science, with its roots in informal observations of nature, involving such activities as insect and bird recognition, the identification of plants and minerals and their possible use at home and in the community for food and construction purposes.

There is also the world of learning science through play. Children in many parts of Africa have very well-developed abilities to construct, through imitation, toys that often closely resemble objects like cars and lorries. They use waste materials such as unwanted wire, cardboard, plastic and other junk items to construct toys (see Figure 2.1). In many cases these toys and other playthings are constructed in quite a complex

Figure 2.1: A wire toy made by a Botswana child

and sophisticated manner. The author has observed wire toy cars that resemble well-known makes such as Minis and Toyotas being constructed in Malawi, complete with gear changes and even brakes (Thomas 1999). To what extent do these different worlds of the child coincide, and is there any conscious link made between what is taught in school for instance about mechanics, or nutrition and health, technical drawing, woodwork and art, and this other everyday world of science? Alas! the answer to the question in most cases is no.

The school, in general, does not effectively attempt to link these out-of-school experiences and activities with the school science curriculum. It seems that teachers are, in the main, unaware of the potential everyday science has for their pupils. An equally pressing issue is that where there is an awareness of the potential, most teachers do not have the opportunities or the money to follow up these experiences as part of in-service teacher education programmes.

Some teachers, it must be said, may not be motivated any rate, for they may have been taught to devalue certain aspects of their culture, especially when it may be seen to substitute for so-called Western knowledge and skills. Not only are toy substitutes perceived to be third-rate alternatives to the real thing, but the skill and knowledge gained in their construction are seen to be of a poorer order than that which the school can deliver. It would be valuable, therefore, if a number of linking strategies could be developed in which teachers were able to incorporate relevant components from some of these out-of-school repertoires into the school science curriculum.

For instance, let us examine Figure 2.1 to observe the potential which constructions such as these have for teaching science in the late primary-school years, and in the early secondary-school period. The construction of parts like wheels, steering column, axles, etc., and the functional relationship between the parts, open up interesting insights into the development of children's psychomotor and spatial abilities. It also stimulates problem solving, such as getting the model to move smoothly, and in some toy constructions even gear changes can be accomplished. Some wire toys even have small electrical batteries attached to bulbs at the front, acting as headlights. Teachers of science could develop quite valuable lessons in mechanics, electricity and spatial relationships based on these naturally developed abilties.

Cross-cultural Agendas of Language Acquisition and Bilingualism in the Classroom

Research on language acquisition has gradually turned away from cross-cultural validation of linguistic models based on

Chomsky, towards perceiving the process as a mainly cultural phenomenon in which all languages are acquired in a socio-cultural matrix. The process of acquisition is intimately bound up with a socially embedded system of communication. The emphasis in cross-cultural research has changed from focusing on the relative merits and demerits of monolingualism and multilingualism, to one in which the need to speak more than one language is linked with the achievement of both social and societal objectives.

While there are undoubted political agendas related to policies followed by governments as to which language/s all the population must learn, e.g. Bahasa Malaysia in Malaysia, English in the UK and the USA, bilingualism or multilingualism should also be seen as acquiring a set of competencies which will serve the needs of an individual living in a multicultural society. This will lead ultimately to the benefit of that society.

Having to learn more than one language has important implications for schooling; for instance, it means the curriculum will be more crowded and the time devoted to other subjects will be shortened accordingly. Furthermore, a school which encourages its pupils to be bilingual has to ensure that there are sufficiently qualified teachers available to meet this need. This is a perennial problem in many countries where there is a bilingual education policy, such as in Malaysia, Canada and Wales.

But far more important than an overcrowded curriculum or having insufficient teacher expertise are the consequences that bilingualism or multilingualism has for three key elements in the pursuit of effective multicultural education and schooling, namely *cognitive outcomes, pedagogy and language acquisition, and intercultural socialisation*. Let us examine each of these three elements in the light of current cross-cultural research being carried out on bilingualism.

Bilingualism and Cognitive Outcomes

It was Lambert (1977) who pointed out the failure of researchers to control for tests administered in the second language of bilingual children. Socio-cultural and sometimes economic differences as well as test bias, account for the fact that there were so many negative findings about school performance in the early studies of bilingualism. Bilingualism was viewed as a mental burden, and immigrant children as well as more established linguistic minorities were made to feel ashamed to use their own language in preference to the official tongue. However, this trend in negative findings has thankfully now been reversed mainly due to better methodology, and fairer tests that are now being used in the field.

A key feature in the more recent research linking bilingualism to cognitive outcomes is that IQ tests have gradually been replaced by measures that have concentrated on information processing and assessments of metalinguistic abilities. Work in India by Mohanty and his co-workers with the Kond ethnic group has shown how bilingual children gave better performance on a range of cognitive tests than did monolingual children. The samples of both types of children who were drawn from the same culture were controlled for age, sex and socioeconomic status. It was also reported that the success of the bilingual children was not the result of school, as they grew up as simultaneous users of Kui, the group language and Oriya, the provincial language. Further work especially from the Indian subcontinent seems to support that fact. Rather than bilingualism being a disadvantage to better cognitive performance, bilingualism appears to have a cognitive "push" as a result of the child being effectively conversant in more than one language.

However, it is important for teachers to recognise that the nature of being bilingual needs to be explored thoroughly, with regard to the impact that bilingualism has on a child's rate of cognitive growth. It is important to question the extent to which the progressive acquisition of L2 tends to replace L1 or enrich it. In other words, does bilingualism have an *additive* or a *subtractive* function? According to research by Cummings (1987), the additive outcome of bilingualism is a function of the learner's proficiency as a bilingual. This means that the child is good in both languages. This led Cummings to propose that there are two thresholds, a lower one in which the child is sufficiently effective as to avoid any negative effects, and a higher one which leads to faster cognitive growth.

The role of the teacher, in the light of this, would be to assess how proficient the child is in the two languages concerned, and where possible develop teaching and learning strategies which enable the child to reach the higher threshold as soon as possible in the early school years. Catching the child early in his or her school career means that operating in two languages becomes a natural process, which increasingly facilitates the child's cognitive performance whichever language is used.

Before examining the intercultural context of bilingualism, it is necessary to mention the relationship between bilingualism and metalinguistic awareness, and the enhancement of metacognition. An interesting view concerning the relationship between being bilingual and being sensitive to the meaning of sentences, intonation and a better understanding of rules particularly when learning other languages takes us into the realm of metalinguistic awareness.

Having this awareness enables the child to reflect and resolve conflicts often thrown up by different rules of language use. According to Mohanty and Perregaux (1997), this has the effect of generalising to other metacognitive processes. The generalising effect means in cognitive terms that the bilingual child is likely to be more effective in performing a range of intellectual tasks.

Pedagogy, Language Acquisition and Bilingualism

It is clear from the above discussion that bilingualism is not an isolated condition; in fact in most societies, especially in the middle- to lower-income countries, bilingualism as well as multilingualism is often the norm. Another trend which emerges from current research is that being bilingual is more than likely to have considerable cognitive benefits, although the findings would need to be carefully examined, as there are contextual factors such as frequency of languages spoken at home, which come into play in some instances.

Pertinent to these trends as they affect schooling is how the learning of L1 relates to the learning of L2. In view of a dominant monolingual bias, the model for first-language acquisition has become the point of reference for analysing the learning process of L2. The appearance of various learning strategies, the occurrence of certain errors, the order and sequence of acquisition in L2, mirror those that occur for L1. This points to the fact that when two languages are being learnt, the activities of learning and teaching appear to have much in common as far as basic processes are concerned. The existence of this commonality has prompted some researchers such as Roulet (1980, 1995) to argue the case for developing an "integrated pedagogy".

However, the issue surrounding whether the type of pedagogy should be integrated or otherwise is not only related to the immediate context of schooling. The pre-school history of bilingual development is also an important factor. The acquisition of two or more languages during early childhood is usually a natural process, often spontaneous, adaptable and without a formal pedagogical mode of instruction. However, there are styles of pedagogy which are involved in the language acquisition process, which are often unique, often effective and which are practised at home, mostly by mothers or mother substitutes (including older siblings) and which must play a crucial role in the acquisition process. An effective school pedagogy would certainly benefit from research carried out at this level of language acquisition.

Another observation which needs to be made on the early development of bilingualism is that bilinguals develop a flexibility in the way they use languages in different situations. When they have reached the third stage of Saunders' (1988) model of becoming bilingual, that is the stage of maximal differentiation (the earlier two stages being varying degrees of non-differentiation), the bilingual person is adept at making the correct decisions about what language can be used, for what purpose, in what conditions and with whom.

According to Baker (1993) a single language system exists which underpins the bilingual's L1 and L2, which may be fused in such a way that it develops as an integrated linguistic cognitive system, which the bilingual can call upon when a particular situation presents itself. It would be in the interests of teachers who are faced with learning and instruction in bilingual contexts to know about this integrative system and how it works. A discussion of an integrated pedagogy in Chapter 3 takes up some of these points.

Bilingualism and Intercultural Socialisation

Socio-psychological as well as socio-cultural factors are as important as cognitive and pedagogical factors in the cross-cultural agenda of language acquisition. Enhanced language learning and the consequent effect on better cognitive performance take place in societies where there are positive forces which encourage learning of several languages as a means of survival. There is, in other words, a strong social motivating set of influences which are also at play. This brings us at this point to examine the element of bilingualism in intercultural socialisation and its effect on schooling.

It is now accepted that sharing languages goes a considerable way towards sharing cultures. This has clear implications for not only language policy at the national level, but also for its implementation at the level of the school. There are obviously also important implications for a multicultural society. The role played by languages in intercultural communication and therefore socialisation, needs an understanding of the social psychological processes which underpin some situations in which language contact leads to additive and stable interaction, whereas in others we get subtractive and often inflamed outcomes.

There are a number of social psychological models that educators should be aware of in the context of bilingualism and intercultural socialisation. One particular model would be that of the so-called *ethnolinguistic vitality* model of intergroup relations. This model has been developed by Giles, Bourhis & Taylor (1977) in which they identified a set of three group vitality factors which might predict the outcome in possible language contact situations. These factors are (a) sociopolitical and economic support of the ethnolinguistic group, (b) demographic size and distribution and (c) institutional support including education, media and influence of organised language movements, e.g. the Welsh Language Society.

Another model is that of Clement (1980) which associates itself with competence in a second language and competence linked to levels of social motivation. At the first or primary level of motivation, there is a fear on the part of an L1 speaker of not being sufficiently competent in L2, so that there is a strong desire to become integrated in order to become proficient; this, however, can conflict with the need to retain proficiency in L1 at the same time. There is, in other words, an antagonistic motivational interplay set in train which determines the net primary motivational tendency.

The second motivational tendency results in the L1 speaker developing competency in L2. While the outcome of this interplay may be acceptable for conditions which allow the L1 speaker a choice; however, where the L1 speaker is forced to learn an L2, the resolution of the motivational conflicts is likely to be difficult. It is in these situations that educational language policy needs to be made clear. Teachers facing the former situation of choice are likely to have difficulties at any rate with the usual problems of L2 teaching and learning, but where there is an ethos of compulsion and especially where the compulsion has political overtones such as the Soweto case in South Africa in the 1970s, and many of the former Soviet republics, the teacher's task is even more problematical.

Berry's work on acculturation is particularly relevant in the debate about how schooling can cope adequately with the challenge of implementing bilingual and multilingual policies. The acculturation strategies model proposed by Berry (1990; Berry & Sam 1997; see Figure 2.2) addresses the psychological processes in situations of contact between different groups. Attitudes towards acculturation involves choices along two dimensions, the first relating to one's own identity

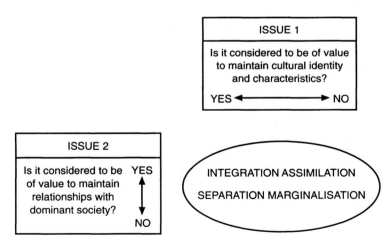

Figure 2.2: Berry's acculturation strategies

and the other by maintaining a relationship with the other group. The resolution of the particular attitude dimension taken is then expressed as one of four outcomes, these being *assimilation, integration, separation* and *marginalisation*.

Berry's model can be readily applied to intercultural bilingual socialisation. An integrative relationship which fosters language contact leads to stable bilingualism and language maintenance. Where bilingualism follows a transitional pathway, and where the policy is gradually to assimilate the minority group, one may be witnessing an eventual loss of the minority language either with or without the consent of the outgroup. Where separation is a policy from either the in-group or out-group, we get Berry's condition of acculturative separation leading to marginalisation, with all the potential dangers of inclusiveness and enclavicism which are distinct features of both dimensions.

Berry's acculturation model provides an awareness on the part of teachers of the socio-cultural complexities of classroom bilingual situations to be found in many countries around the world. Government-inspired language policies that encourage both marginalisation and assimilation present teachers with particular problems relating to classroom cohesion and discipline. The model is also valuable from the perspective of the policy maker, who may be confronted with making decisions about language policy in a multicultural society. For instance, in countries such as Malaysia, Singapore, Canada and Wales, integrative policies have been more or less adopted in these countries, allowing a successful *modus vivendi* to exist among the various linguistic groups. Berry's model sensitises educational policy makers and planners to the dangers of adopting policies that could foster explosive separation and marginalisation within a society, as the cases of Sri Lanka and South Africa have shown in recent years.

Having examined subject disciplines which are part of a school curriculum, let us address the third question posed at the beginning of this chapter, namely the recent cross-cultural research into some of the key psychological processes that underpin the cultural dynamic of learning activities in the classroom.

PSYCHOLOGICAL PROCESSES: IMPLICATIONS FOR PUPIL LEARNING

In this section, we will examine selected cross-cultural research that has been carried out into a number of key psychological processes and have pertinence to *context, meaningfulness, relevance, adaptation to change* and *achieving balance*, which are the five key factors identified earlier. The psychological processes examined below underpin the need to be numerate, be literate, to understand science and to be conversant in first or second language where appropriate. Four psychological processes have been selected, with cross-referencing to related fields such as perception, personality and values. The four main processes are as follows:

- Cognition
- Memory
- Motivation and learning
- Transfer of learning

Cognition

Research into a number of fields of cognition has pertinence to translating theory into praxis, these include *cognitive style, general abilities, cognitive development, reasoning and problem solving.* Let us first examine cognitive style.

Cognitive Style

Approaches using cognitive style look for interrelationships in cognitive performance, and it is assumed that different abilities develop in relationship to different eco-cultural settings depending on the demands placed on the individual. Field dependent (FD) and field independent (FI) cognitive styles have received the most attention in cross-cultural research. The recent work by Berry (1991) links cognitive style to acculturative processes, in which socialisation plays a key part. Socialisation involving family, school and society does appear to show that it has an effect on cognitive style across cultures, i.e. differentiation is affected by a greater degree of socialisation. However, the evidence is weak for within-cultural differences.

For teachers, the implications of the research on cognitive style seems to suggest that they should be aware of how children's performance in different subject domains may be a function of cognitive style. It is clear that in some instances, it would be useful for the teacher to promote conditions in the classroom that would actively encourage FD styles as in social studies, teamwork and language learning in groups, while FI styles might be better developed in subjects like aesthetics, mathematics and creative writing, and philosophical thinking.

In reality, cognitive style is more a function of context as there are instances during the school day in which both forms of styles may be evident and indeed necessary. For instance, in group work involving practical science or geography, sharing and tolerance of others which characterise FD styles would be among the most preferred social competencies (FD style). However, after group sessions in the field or laboratory pupils will be required individually to find time to reflect (FI style) on the practical work carried out, and tease out for themselves its significance to the particular topic.

General Abilities

The existence of *general ability* (*"g"*) is based on the idea of a unitary cognitive underpinning to intelligence, and this notion has arisen from extensive research carried out involving testing the performance of children on verbal, spatial, numerical and other tasks. According to workers such as Carroll (1983) and Sternberg (1985), the notion of "g" is central to any description of intelligence. The notion of "g" assumes that a central cognitive processor accounts for varying levels of intelligence across individuals in any population. Where there are large clusters of rich eco-cultural experiences for an individual to pursue, an "enriched" cognitive environment enhances the development of both potential "g" as well as actual "g". Where the clusters are small, this typifies a "deprived" environment, and means that both forms of "g" have less chance of development.

Cross-cultural studies of intelligence have shown the existence of more specialised factors besides "g" (Burg & Belmont 1990; Vernon 1969). The history of attempting to disentangle the distinctions between intelligence A (genetic), intelligence B (potentiality) and intelligence C (test performance) has been bedevilled with both conceptual and methodological problems, leading in many cases to classic cases of ethnocentric bias. These problems unfortunately clouded any rational debate on a subject which is important for praxis in the classroom.

Attempts by Eysenck (1988) and Vernon (1990) to determine more precisely what constitutes intelligence A, through measuring brain activity, have yet to yield more light on the debate. More recently, Rushton (1995) and others have also added to the discussions on the nature of intelligence, by claiming that within group differences, test scores can be applied to across-group differences on such tests. This strongly suggests that if "g" exists it is a universal concept.

The danger of this interpretation is that cultural differences may be ignored in playing a role in explaining the cross-group differences in test scores. However, these observations should not be thrown out of court entirely, for there may be evidence (either available or forthcoming) that could shed light on the presence or not of a central cognitive processor that accounts for varying levels of intelligence across different individuals.

The cultural view of intelligence does not subscribe to a deficit hypothesis as far as intellectual abilities are concerned, and this stance is reflected in the work of McShane & Berry (1988). They examined a number of *deficit* and *difference* models of explanation for individual and group differences using test scores. In *deficit* models genetic, psychological as well as sociological factors such as poverty and deprivation are called into play to produce usually negative value judgements about individuals. On the other hand, *difference* models view intellectual processes as essentially similar across cultures, but that levels of competence and performance are functions of particular cultural contexts.

Pertinent to the focus of the present book is the fact that schooling has been found to be a useful predictor of intelligence test scores by workers such as Ceci (1994), accounting for significant variation. It may be that schooling as well as socio-cultural factors including socio-economic status, parental education and religious education contribute to a common "*a*" factor, which is translated as an *acculturation factor*. If this is the case, then the effects of schooling and its relationship to society will need to be subjected to greater scrutiny by educators and parents, as well as researchers.

Cognitive Development

Piaget's cognitive developmental theory has been the focus of many cross-cultural research studies since the mid 1970s. Of particular interest to schooling have been those studies carried out on concrete and formal operational thinking. Tasks devised to explore conservation, simple logic and spatial thinking when applied to different cultures have shown that, in some instances, there may be a complete lack of concrete reasoning. This is because the context in which the members of a culture operate does not seem to need this type of thinking. However, Dasen (1982) has shown that with training, children can think in concrete terms if the opportunity arises. This means that cultural differences often show up as differentials in terms of performance rather than a lack of competence.

Cole & Scribner (1977) have argued that the application of Piagetian tasks to adults often assigns them to a type of child-like status, and that applying value judgements to whether they should or should not reach a certain status needs to be avoided, as there are strong eco-cultural reasons for the way adults and indeed children in some cultures perform. However, the role of training (which is closely related to schooling), appears important in changing a certain status in the level of concrete operational thinking, and so the implications for educators are significant for improving learning and teaching. That is, instruction strategies could include specific intervention schedules that would enhance a child's understanding of number, or substance conservation, or act as a preparation for children to solve problems using deductive and hypothetico-deductive reasoning.

From the evidence of cross-cultural studies examining the role of schooling in performance on formal operational tasks, instruction in many situations does make a difference (Dasen & Heron 1981; Shea 1985). Keats (1985), comparing formal operational thinking in Australian students with ethnic Malay, Indian and Chinese Malaysians, found that on a proportionality training session, what differences existed between and within the groups were due to performance factors rather than being related to competence.

Studies by Tape (1994) in the Ivory Coast, using tasks such as permutation, the pendulum and flexibility of rods with both schooled and unschooled children, found that unschooled children use a variety of thinking styles. For instance, the styles that would be more experiential are characterised by a greater use of symbolism and what Tape calls "a pragmatic action type logic", which is a feature of Bantu philosophy and essentially an informal type of thinking. The lessons to be drawn from the above, are that we should be careful about using situations that are not culturally suitable for non-schooled children, otherwise we draw the wrong conclusions about children's performance and their competency to carry out cognitive tasks (Mishra 1997).

However, this caution also extends to those children attending school and who come from different culural backgrounds. In determining the level of formal operational thinking (mainly dominated by pedagogies which emphasise analytical and experimental thinking styles), it is important that the teacher is aware of the emic dimension to thinking styles that reflect cross-cultural forms of analysis and interpretation, when solving formal operational problems. It is becoming clear that there are cultures that do not need to use scientific reasoning in everyday situations. Therefore, before we assign a final stage of development to a member of such a culture, we should try and understand the *cognitive value system* of that culture, and find out how far the person has developed.

Clearly the role of teachers is crucial here. For instance, the indigenous Peruvian or Australian Aborigine teachers should be encouraged during their training to select from their indigenous cognitive value system and incorporate some of these values into their teaching strategies (Aikman 1999; Teasdale & Teasdale 1994). However, it should not be seen that culture-specific cognitive values need to replace the analytical and experimental tradition so fundamental to good scientific reasoning. Here is a case where adaptation to change and providing some form of balance by the teacher are essential, as both approaches can be used alongside the other in order to make learning easier, relevant, more meaningful as well as enriching the dynamic of the learning process.

Reasoning and Problem Solving

One of the ultimate goals of schooling is to provide pupils with a set of mental skills which will enable them to solve a range of problems, many of which will be part of their everyday experience. However, schooling is also about developing mental abilities that facilitate pupils to develop general thinking strategies, which they can apply to a particular situation, thereby enabling learning transfer to take place. Since about the beginning of the 1980s, most cross-cultural research into reasoning and problem solving has centred on verbal or syllogistic reasoning, and in mathematics, deductive and conditional reasoning have also been investigated.

Workers such as Cara & Politzer (1993) working in Malaysia with ethnic Chinese, Indian and Malay native speakers, found that when they were given reasoning problems to solve in English, the outcomes were not that different than if they used their own languages. This suggests that reasoning may not be so constrained by linguistic–cultural features as might have been thought was the case. Contrary to the case of linguistic factors, however, socialisation may have a key role in determining how children perform on deductive reasoning tasks, as Hollos & Richards (1993) found with their studies of Nigerian secondary-school-age boys and girls. Their differential performance on a reasoning science task involving the conditions for healthy growth of plants showed that adolescent boys, who have more outdoor experiences, did better than their female counterparts, who have to stay at home to look after the younger children.

In these circumstances, teachers need to develop strategies to compensate for the lack of out-of-door experience of girls, and so arrange for appropriate and frequent field excursions as part of science lessons. It is unlikely in the short term that there would be much cultural change in the duties accorded to males and females on the part of Nigerian society, especially in rural areas. It is the school that will be left with the problem of compensation for girls, and in doing so would slowly change the culture, eventually ending up with both boys and girls having equal learning opportunities.

Syllogistic reasoning involves logical truths that are different from actual empirical events. The explanation of logical truths requires an understanding and an ability to infer relationships, and so actual truths are explained on the basis of actual experience. Scribner & Cole (1981) have shown that schooling contributes substantially to the ability to reason syllogistically. However, when comparing the performance of non-schooled children with schooled children, Bickersteth & Das (1987), working among Indian children, produced findings suggesting that, when the syllogisms use content familiar to both samples, the differences in task performance were not significant. The examples cited in Figure 2.3 were used in these workers' research.

This once again raises the issue of relevance and meaning when learners are faced with reasoning and problem-solving tasks that are encountered in school. It seems from the research studies quoted above, that teachers need to ensure that tests and learning materials include content which reflects a considerable degree of familiarity for the learner.

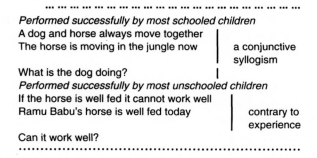

Figure 2.3: Examples of syllogisms used with Indian children by Bickersteth & Das (1987)

Previous research in this area of syllogistic reasoning carried out by Luria (1976) used unfamiliar content with children from different cultures, which gave biased results. This led to researchers and practitioners drawing incorrect implications about the ability of children from different cultural groups when faced with reasoning tasks that involved syllogisms. We will return to the issue of familiarity in Chapters 3 and 4 when discussing how teachers need to be able to build it into their methods of teaching and pupil assessment, so reflecting the use of familiar concepts in tests and other measures of cognitive performance.

Memory

There have been many cross-cultural studies on the role of culture on memory and learning. Much of the research work in this area has examined mnemonic performance through storytelling. When different cultures are tested for recall of stories, as in the case of Steffensen & Calker's (1982) work with American and Australian Aboriginal women, better recall was seen to be consistent with familiar cultural settings for the storytellers.

However, other workers such as Mandler *et al.* (1980) showed that storytelling was a culturally universal process, in which people often resort to using familiar mnemonic coding strategies in situations where they meet unfamiliar objects or events. In other words, there is a reinterpretation of the newer elements of an unknown situation into terms of the known. Therefore, if Scribner and her associates are correct, the differences in recall of stories consistent with one's own cultural knowledge, indicate that people from different cultures have similar capacities when using mnemonic principles.

Schooling and the culture of a particular school have also been shown to have an influence on learning and memory. Comparative studies by Wagner (1985, 1993) involving traditional

Koranic and Sanskrit, schoolchildren and children from Western schools, showed that rote memory was the dominant form of learning among the non-Western children. The use of organisational strategies by both types of children in memory tasks also differed, the Western children preferring to memorise the importance of events rather than the importance of objects, as was the case with the Sanskrit and Koranic sample. Teachers have to make decisions under these circumstances, about the need to get their pupils to develop memory skills that favour the importance of prioritisation in a particular task, and when it is necessary to emphasise memory skills focusing on concrete lists of words and symbols. A question of balance also arises here, where there is a need for both memory strategies.

The quality of schooling is also a key factor in cognitive test performance. Schools that are poorly equipped and have poorly trained teachers, as well as a lack in learning technology and library facilities, have been shown to have a negative influence on effective learning and recall. Other factors that influence learning and memory include the pupils themselves, parental interest in their children's progress and the nature of the examination system. Many examination systems in Asia emphasise rote learning (Murphy 1987), which has often been seen as the key reason for labelling these pupils as passive, and lacking in creativity and objectivity.

However, Lin (1988) has argued that we should see these strategies as being culturally valued, and in the case of Chinese students being directly related to the system of filial piety. Therefore, where rote learning is highly valued in a school system, it does not mean than other forms of learning and memory strategies are absent in children, or that they cannot acquire them. It has been shown that where learning situations are so planned that a number of equally valued strategies can be used, Chinese pupils perform as well as children from Western societies and in some cases significantly better (Biggs 1996).

Motivation and Learning

A number of research workers have observed that cultural groups that exist in different social environments like schools, colleges and the workplace seem to be motivated by a range of different factors, and this has resulted in the exploration of various models in order to assess these factors (Berry 1980a; Triandis 1980; McInerney 1994). However, motivation is a difficult notion to operationalise in multicultural settings, as we come up against the emic–etic dilemma. In other words, are the same agents at play for everyone when they are motivated irrespective of cultural differences (etic), or are the motivational agents culture specific (emic)? McInerney (1994) found in his work with Australian Aborigines and Navajo Indians that the same motivational systems exist as for the majority groups, e.g. sense of purpose, sense of competence, pursuing excellence.

But factors like group concern and affiliation which are more culture specific, may not contribute greatly to school success in the mainstream. If teachers were trained to unleash these special cultural features, such values could be valuable for enhancing school achievement as well, giving better opportunities for all cultures that make up the school population in a society. Teachers would not be the only agents in this process of adaptation, school administrators also have a key role in creating the working and organisational climate within their school, one which is conducive to a well-balanced and adaptive cross-cultural atmosphere.

When motivation is linked to productivity in the workplace and accompanied by the learning of skills and knowledge, cultural factors play a key role. For instance, where the culture is predominantly collectivist, as it is in most Confucian heritage cultures (CHCs), the rewards be they either monetary or socially driven are often shared among the group in the interests of group harmony. This is in contrast to individualistic societies, where the reward structure is based on an autonomous principle of self-actualisation in competition with other group members.

There are of course many instances where the two systems work side by side as in Singapore and Hong Kong, but this *collectivist motivation* is beginning to be eroded in many Asian tiger economies. One has only to observe the educational systems in these countries to realise that the power of the examination system and how it determines the individual's need to achieve are having a diluting effect on collectivism. Large class sizes, excessive homework and examination-driven teaching strategies mean that *individualist motivation* is in the ascendancy. Techniques for reward and punishment vary across cultures as far as pupil achievement is concerned. In Oriental societies particularly, praise is rarely given for good performance, while punishment usually takes the form of ridicule or even shaming (Ho 1981). Praise is only given in most Asian situations for exceptional achievements, and rarely given publicly (Salili, Hwang & Choi 1989). In Western societies such as the USA and UK the opposite is the case.

Biggs (1996) has been particularly influential in discussing the role of motivation as an important variable in the whole process of learning. The work of Biggs and others will be discussed further in Chapter 4, in which we will examine the motivational effects of assessment, feedback and "backwash" on learning. However, at this juncture it is important to point out that by manipulating motivation through school examinations, teachers have considerable power over not only what their pupils learn but how they learn. The work of Biggs on SAL (Student Approach to Learning) shows how a certain type of test item, included in an examination, is associated with how well they perform as a result of their preferred learning styles.

SAL was stimulated by the earlier research of Marton & Saljo (1976), on how students approached learning through the use of "surface" and "deep" strategies. "Surface" approaches to learning are characterised by using a preponderance of memory and factual information, while learners using "deeper" approaches tend to favour analysis and abstraction. Biggs (1979) showed that where examinations were constructed to test for factual recall, surface learners performed well, whereas in examinations which tested for analysis and abstraction, learners using deeper learning strategies did better.

In contrast to the Asian experiences described above, in Africa the work of Lave & Wenger (1991) among Liberian tailors on the role of apprenticeship as a learning and teaching strategy where productivity and skill learning are both involved, showed that praise is necessary in order to derive a balance between learning and production, thereby ensuring that intrinsic motivation is part of the participatory process within the group. Serpell & Hatano (1997) have pointed out that institutionalised public basic schooling (IPBS) has generated a new form of motivation, in which total pupil achievement in school is only ascertained through the use of test scores. Does this mean that learning geared to tests and examinations is the only worthwhile learning that seems to matter?

Cole & Griffin (1983) found that children's learning that is measured by test scores does not necessarily mean that they have understood all that has been achieved in the tests. In other words, achievement motivation can lead to results in which pupils *perform* well in a certain task or tasks, but may not show sufficient *competency*. For instance, learning successfully how to perform quadratic equations is one matter, but application of the principle underlying the use of quadratic equations in science requires competence in the application and a deeper understanding of the concepts involved. It may be that we need to examine more closely the different forms of pedagogy which reflect culture-sensitive and culture-valued modes of delivery, so providing culture-specific motivational features that can become melded into existing forms of instruction.

Transfer of Learning

Much of the research carried out on everyday cognition and how particular cognitive processes dovetail or not with schooling throws light increasingly on the process of learning transfer. In the earlier section of this chapter, we compared the strengths and weaknesses of everyday mathematics as developed on the streets of many Brazilian cities, with that taught in school. A general principle seems to emerge, as it has with similar research findings from elsewhere in the world on this topic, that whatever school mathematics does not do for pupils in primary schools, it *does* aim to lay down the basic principles from which pupils may be able to work out problems which are not part of their daily experience. On the other hand, everyday mathematics is very situational, which is a kind of "on the job" type of learning, which takes place in a very pragmatic environment, often linked to the immediate survival of the individual.

Brazilian children of different schooling levels were asked to work out a series of permutations on a money lottery task and it was found that those children who had substantial amounts of schooling in mathematics performed significantly better when it came to working out more complex series of combinations (Schliemann & Acioly 1989). It seemed that the failure by non-schooled children to transfer procedures is probably linked to their reliance on the memory of a limited number of operations. This makes them rely on so-called practical "on the street" *procedural knowledge*, which has limitations when it comes to learning transfer, involving higher levels of thinking, i.e. working out more complex permutations. For higher cognitive operations such as solving equations, predicting events and application of rules, schooling is necessary as it emphasises so-called *conceptual knowledge* which enables the child to engage in increasingly complex permutational thinking.

It appears, therefore, that a specific everyday learning situation such as street bartering, weaving or serving petrol at a garage emphasises in the main only skills and knowledge limited to those specific situations. These limitations tend to exclude the use of a general set of principles because of the high degree of task specificity. However, the research from South America suggests that even with a minimum amount of schooling, this may be sufficient to effect a transfer of learning that could lead to higher conceptual knowledge and skills being developed. Therefore a key influence of schooling is that the process takes children beyond their own experience, allowing them to tackle new problems in terms of previous knowledge and skills that have been learnt.

For transfer of learning to be effective, teachers should be aware of the procedural background knowledge and skills which many childen bring with them from their culture to the classroom. However, teachers must then be prepared to actively develop learning which can build upon this *procedural* background, so that *conceptual* knowledge can be introduced by the teachers, and allowed to be fully exploited by the learner. This will involve an understanding and application of rules and principles to new problem-solving tasks. Once the thirst for conceptual knowledge is initiated, it will act as a catalyst for sound intellectual development as children move from primary into secondary education.

SUMMARY

In concluding this chapter, we will summarise the main steps exploring the cultural dynamics of the learning process, and how they might relate to improved praxis in the classroom:

1. It must always be remembered that learning and teaching are intimately linked to each other, and that any discussion on the cultural dynamic of learning is reciprocal to a discussion about the dynamics of teaching.
2. In order to make sense of the growing amount of cross-cultural research that is available, and its impact on

schooling, five key factors have been identified to help link research to praxis; the factors are *context, meaning, relevance, adaptation* to change and *balance*.

3. To understand the cultural dynamics of learning, *context* is among the most important of the five key factors. This is because context is about constantly changing sets of interactions between people, and the arenas in which they live. School contexts differ profoundly from the poorest to the well resourced, so translating research for the improvement of praxis is in itself an exercise in studying the appropriate context.

4. Three key questions were posed in the chapter which were: (i) How does research into cultural contexts of learning assist teachers to make schooling more relevant? (ii) How does cross-cultural research into learning of curriculum subjects provide ideas and guidelines for better teaching and learning? (iii) To what extent have findings from cross-cultural research into key psychological processes provided educators with a better understanding of the cultural dynamics of learning in the classroom?

5. This chapter has examined the cultural dynamics of learning through research that has been carried out on two domains, namely basic school subjects and psychological processes.

6. The basic school subjects consist of literacy learning, mathematics, science and language acquisition and bilingualism, while the psychological processes include cognition and learning, memory, learning transfer and motivation.

7. Whether *learning to be literate* is viewed as means of enlightenment, a key to socio-political awareness or as social collaboration, there is a foundational and functional role that has to be addressed in any schooling process, and realisation of this role is essential for all children (and adults) as it is the "access card" to their future success.

8. Recent cross-cultural research on *mathematics* learning shows that there are at least two types, namely, *out* of

school and *in* school. The task for teachers is to take advantage of both, for the former provides a valuable pragmatism to solving everyday numerical problems, while the latter is essential for more complex application and learning transfer.

9. Teaching *science* in schools which draw children from diverse cultures requires teachers to be trained to explore, select and value the experience children bring with them from their home and community, for this would not only enrich classroom teaching, but assist in children's understanding of scientific concepts and principles.

10. Cross-cultural studies on *language acquisition* especially in the context of *bilingualism* show that there are implications for teaching and learning in terms of cognitive outcomes, pedagogy and intercultural socialisation. Teachers should be aware of the fact that bilingualism appears to provide a "cognitive push", and so stimulate better quality thinking; it is also likely to make pedagogy more culture sensitive and provide a greater degree of multicultural understanding, and hopefully successful acculturation.

11. Recent cross-cultural research into *cognition, learning, memory, motivation* and *learning transfer* has shown how much these processes provide an essential underpinning for the understanding and application of the principles of classroom learning. The challenge lies in training teachers to recognise the importance of this research and to put it into practice.

SUGGESTIONS FOR FURTHER READING

Olson, D.R & Bruner, J.S. (1996). Folk psychology and folk pedagogy. In D.R. Olson & N. Torrance (Eds), *Handbook of Education and Human Development: New Models of Learning, Teaching and Schooling*. Oxford: Blackwell, pp. 9–27.

Rogoff, B. (1990). *Apprenticeship in Thinking: Cognitive Development in Social Context*. New York: Oxford University Press.

Schliemann, A.D., Carraher, D. & Ceci, S.J. (1997). Everyday cognition. In J.W. Berry, P.R. Dasen & T.S. Sarawathi (Eds), *Handbook of Cross Cultural Psychology*, Volume 2, *Basic Processes and Human Development*. Boston: Allyn & Bacon, pp. 177–216.

Watkins, D.A. & Biggs, J.B. (Eds). *The Chinese Learner: Cultural, Psychological and Contextual Influences*. Victoria: CERC & ACER.

3

THE CULTURAL DYNAMICS OF TEACHING

It is well documented in cross-cultural research on learning that learners, whatever their origins, are potentially capable of achieving most learning objectives. Provided certain conditions of learning are met, such as the provision of adequate feedback, sufficient time on task, an awareness of the meaning of the material to be learnt and, where necessary, an appreciation by the teacher of the cultural context in which the learning takes place, most learners have at least the potential of realising their goals. However, what is not so well documented is how learners approach the learning task, and the teachers' roles in the intensely intercultural dynamics of pedagogy.

For instance, information about what styles, methods and idiosyncratic patterns learners and teachers employ (often together) to solve problems can tell us more about the context of learning and teaching than just knowing the learner has been successful in getting the correct answer. Even less well documented is how content, and especially specific approaches to learning content, needs to be considered an essential component of a pedagogy that addresses cultural needs, and how teachers should be trained to implement such a pedagogy effectively.

The lack of information on cross-cultural pedagogy is due firstly to insufficient research on the subject (Thomas 1997b), and secondly, little attention has been given to melding well-established research findings on cultures of learning, together with studies that already exist about teaching strategies and styles used in different cultural contexts. These are major tasks facing educators and particularly teacher educators. Educators must convince those who make the ultimate decisions about educational policy, that improving pedagogy for the future needs to be balanced between providing the basic learning competencies, and ensuring that socio-cultural values and traditions remain a part of a learner's experience. Cross-cultural as well as educational research, carried out mostly in developing countries, into different learning and teaching cultures, discussed in Chapters 1 and 2, has shown how meaningful and effective culturally rooted pedagogy can be (Aikman 1994; Nunes 1994; Teasdale & Teasdale 1994).

Research which identifies different cultural pedagogies, and describes the impact they may have on improving educational quality, will be a welcome antidote to the possible unifying excesses that educational change in the context of modernisation and globalisation is likely to bring. Through a melding process, it should be possible to provide a meaningful and interesting pedagogy that bridges new values with the old, and sets former knowledge and skills in the context of the new. In order to understand the desire to develop pedagogies which can be sensitive to the needs of children growing up in an age of rapid change and increasing multiculturalism, it is necessary, at first, to briefly examine the changing nature of pedagogy itself; and secondly, to investigate cultures of teaching and learning and their future prospects within the framework of classroom praxis.

This chapter will be structured around three main questions:

1. What is the nature of pedagogy, and to what extent can it be considered a set of cultures?

2. What models of pedagogy can be applied in multicultural classrooms, which will help teachers understand the cultural dynamics of teaching?
3. How do different interpretations of the nature of pedagogy lead to better praxis and professionalism within multicultural classrooms?

THE NATURE OF PEDAGOGY AND CULTURES OF TEACHING

In this part of the chapter we will address two themes which are included within the first question posed above. The first relates to the changing nature and traditions of pedagogy, while the second refers to the notion that teaching may be viewed as a set of cultures.

The Changing Nature and Traditions of Pedagogy

The subject of pedagogy is not recent, its origin can be confidently traced to the time of the Greeks and probably before that. The notion of pedagogy both as an art and a science has provided its students over recent years with plenty of these ideas. The source of many of the ideas have come from psychologists such as Piaget (1971), Bruner (1966), Olson & Bruner (1996), Shulman (1986) and Gagné & Driscoll (1988). More recently the work of educationists such as Schon (1983), Zeichner (1983a) and Bennett (1993) have added further insights into developments in pedagogy, with particular reference to teacher education.

While little has emerged in the way of a workable theory (or theories) of teaching, it is possible to discern three different theoretical traditions relating to research into teaching and teacher education that have arisen in the 1990s (see Figure 3.1). Two of these traditions have been termed by Zeichner (1992)

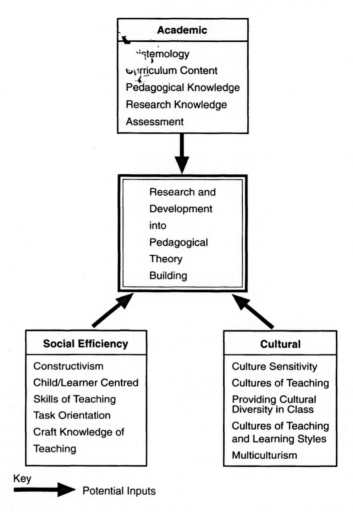

Figure 3.1: Pedagogical theory building and inputs from three traditions of teaching

as "academic" and "social efficiency" respectively, while the third tradition which refers to teaching as a "cultural process" has been investigated by Olson & Bruner (1996), Kruger & Tomasello (1996) and discussed by Thomas (1997a,b) in the context of teacher education.

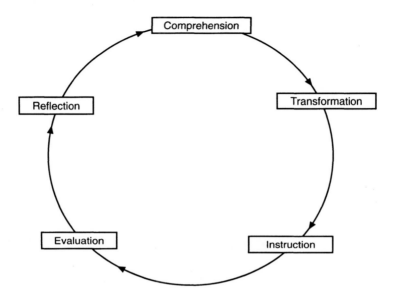

Figure 3.2: Shulman's (1987) model of pedagogical reasoning

The "academic tradition" draws on evidence which emphasises the need for teachers to have a sound knowledge base,
in order for them to promote comprehension among students.
The work of Shulman (1987) on pedagogical reasoning is
at the cutting edge of this particular tradition, in which he
delineates seven knowledge bases. These include content
knowledge, general pedagogical knowledge, curriculum
knowledge, pedagogical-content knowledge, knowledge of
learners and their characteristics, knowledge of educational
contexts and knowledge of educational ends. Shulman's
pedagogical reasoning model (see Figure 3.2), which builds
on these knowledge bases, identifies the skill of a teacher's
understanding which is so necessary to develop comprehension among the learners.

The "social efficiency" tradition draws on research evidence
from studies on teaching and learning in classrooms, which
take a constructivist view of learning. Learning and teaching

in terms of this tradition view children as being actively involved intellectually with learning which accompanies the development of teaching skills and teacher knowledge to promote this involvement. Bennett (1993) in the UK has formulated a five-stage task model of teaching (see Figure 3.3), which emphasises not only the task at hand but teacher intention to involve learners in the process of teaching.

The third tradition views teaching as a "cultural process" reflecting different cultures of teaching, one or more of which may match particular contexts at different times. As the focus of this book is about culture and praxis in schools, let us therefore examine the next theme, which is about how the various cultures of teaching might inform and stimulate practitioners, to develop pedagogies that would provide learners with more meaningful guidance, and improved forms of explanation in class.

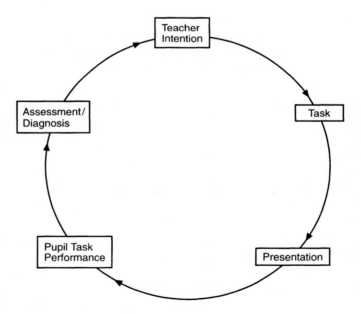

Figure 3.3: Bennett's (1993) model of task processes

Teaching as a Set of Cultures

The act of teaching is increasingly being perceived as a culture or set of subcultures. It is interesting to note that the third edition of the American Educational Research Association *Handbook on Research on Teaching* (Wittrock 1986), space was given to a chapter on "The Culture of Teaching". Since then, although not necessarily related to this event, interest has intensified in the subject and there has been a considerable amount of research generated on teaching as a culture or set of subcultures.

The research on teaching as a culture should also be seen against a universal need to improve teacher quality by providing better opportunities for teacher development. During the 1980s, the work of Schon (1983) and others on the concept of the *reflective teacher*, has added further interest to the debate on viewing teaching not just as an activity but as a culture. Strategies on teacher development, and the outcome of current research into the cultures of teaching, are now closely related activities. As a result, a duality of purpose arises which on one hand underlines the need to understand how teachers transmit their skills and knowledge, and on the other, how a teacher can further his or her personal development. This duality of purpose on the part of the teacher would be an important factor in the effective transmission of knowledge, values, attitudes and skills in education, as it would lead to improved teacher motivation and commitment.

The extensive review of the subject by Feiman-Nemser & Floden (1986) indicates a growing number of research studies which identified a variety of cultures of teaching. These authors came to the conclusion that it is no longer tenable to hold the view that teaching has a uniform culture. They cite the work of Little (1982), Metz (1978) and Zeichner & Tabachnik (1983). Teaching, it appears, is a complex and varied process, not just a uniform set of encounters and traits. The process of teaching is both rich and diverse, so we can speak of cultures of teaching rather than a culture of teaching. This is contrary to the early work of Waller (1932) and that of Jackson (1968) and Lortie (1975), who perceived teaching to have a uniformity which is typified by a certain number of generic features. More recently, David Hargreaves (1983) has spoken of the term "teacherish" being used as one of several universal descriptions of teacher behaviour. Hargreaves also advocates the need for pedagogical space and even professional possession, both features being included as pervasive and generic features of a teaching culture.

Andy Hargreaves (1992) takes the view that teaching cultures might be better explained if we distinguish between the content of a culture of teaching and its form. The *content* according to Hargreaves includes substantive attitudes and values, habits and ways of doing things shared within a particular group. Academic cultures, pastoral cultures and subject cultures therefore predominately reflect the content of a diverse teacher culture. *Form* includes pervasive features such as *individualism* which emphasises the isolation of teachers in the classroom, *balkanisation* in which teachers work in separate groups, often in competition with one another, *collaborative* cultures which emphasise professionality between teachers with a tendency to have compatible initiatives improving practice, and finally *contrived collegiality* binding teachers in time and space to meet certain demands from their superiors.

From the above, it appears that teaching is a suspension of subcultures having a common matrix of pervasive features like individualism, a need to have pedagogical space, and a need for collaboration and collegiality among practitioners. Teaching is in the main an intentional process, but cultural contexts may influence the nature and degree of intention in different teaching situations. For instance, a mother who teaches her child to use eating utensils correctly at the table might be cooking or cleaning while she is instructing the child. The child is likely to register the non-intentional cooking and cleaning behaviours for use in later life, as well as the intentional task of learning to use a knife and fork. In this case, we have a mix of both intentional and non-intentional teaching behaviour, all of which add to the child's behavioural repertoires.

In this example there are different intentional levels of teaching with different pedagogies being used by the mother. However, the child is far from passive to both the forms of instruction, as he or she is building up "shared experiences" (a term used by Bruner & Olson) with the mother. Intention is the principal driving force behind the act of teaching, and which distinguishes much of teaching from learning. However, all three main traditions, the academic, social efficiency and the cultural, have an important stake in the essential task of building and developing sound working theories of teaching, and as Figure 3.1 shows, features from each tradition, e.g. curriculum content, constructivism, cultural sensitivity, play a vital part in the theory-building process. Let us now examine the second question posed earlier in this chapter, which addresses the problem of how different pedagogical models may be applied to the cultural dynamics of the classroom, and how praxis and professionalism may be improved.

MODELS OF PEDAGOGY AND THE CULTURAL DYNAMICS OF CLASSROOMS

Multicultural classrooms help to concentrate the minds of teachers on how to manage their teaching and learning strategies in class. The sheer complexity and cultural variety that we often find in multicultural classrooms provide a stiff challenge for any teacher. The multicultural classroom may consist of different ethnic groups, each group often having their own languages, dialects, different religious persuasions and holding a diversity of cultural traditions. In order to help teachers meet this challenge, it may be necessary to identify

models of pedagogy that are able, in the first place, to meet
the basic requirements of formal education and in the second,
allow children the opportunity to maintain their socio-cultural
identity, wherever and whenever possible, during their years
of schooling.

A model may predict, explain, initiate ideas or act as a framework for action (Thomas 1997a). In the five models of pedagogy to be discussed, all exhibit these features in varying
degrees, yet each reflects a different emphasis and approach
to the act of teaching. The five models to be discussed are as
follows:

- Folk
- Culture-sensitive
- Integrative
- Instructional objectives/rule following
- Intercultural

The *folk* model examines teaching from the standpoint of the
child's mind and its interaction with the instructional process,
while the *culture-sensitive* model looks at how key pedagogical components relate to each other, and to the cultural sensitivities of different contexts. The *integrative* model examines
how two or more approaches and traditions to teaching may
be closely integrated into a whole, providing learners with the
benefit of two or more perspectives to learning and understanding. The *instructional objectives/rule following* model
examines the value of having a set of rules and principles
within the framework of instructional objectives. This model
enables teachers to structure, plan and make decisions about
how learning can be made more effective and efficient.

The *intercultural* model aims to provide teachers and pupils
with a better understanding of the various cultural interfaces
which exist in multicultural and multi-ethnic classrooms. It
aims to promote an ethos of understanding between the
teacher and the learner, so that all concerned can learn from

each other. The intercultural model is essentially proactive, progressive and socio-cultural in nature.

Before we examine the five models further, it may be useful to distinguish between the use of context and situation, for the purposes of clarity in the discussions that follow. Context refers to relevant circumstances surrounding something under consideration, while situation is a position in which a person finds him/herself, and in the case of teachers having to act upon events. Let us now examine the first model of pedagogy.

Folk Pedagogy as a Model

Teaching which puts the learner at the centre of the process is far from being a new idea. It is at the heart of the child-centred approach in education, and has been pioneered over the years by figures such as Rousseau, Dewey and Piaget. Jerome Bruner in the 1960s elaborated upon Piaget's somewhat clinical approach to the subject, by making the links between child development and education more relevant to classroom practice. Bruner also attempted to link instruction with the child's ability to understand the world around him (Bruner 1966). In collaboration with Olson, Bruner has more recently again provided educators with further challenges about making teaching and learning more relevant and effective, by exploring the relationship between children's minds, and the instruction they receive not only from teachers, but from parents and significant others in the immediate world of the child.

The kernel of Bruner & Olson's approach is based on shared experiences, beliefs, goals and intentions, which to these workers mean that teaching and learning behaviour is a dynamic cultural process. The notions of so-called *folk psychology* and *folk pedagogy*, which refer to the use of intuitive theories of how our mind and the minds of others work, is a central tenet of Bruner & Olson's approach. They also argue that by applying a culturally oriented psychological approach to exploring childhood experiences and explanations of their world, the emphasis is put not only on what the child does, but on what the child thinks he or she is doing and why. The work of Tomasello, Kruger & Ratner (1993) on cultural learning, and Rogoff (1990) on apprenticeship, enriches further the "folk" approach to learning and teaching. Olson & Bruner provide us with four perspectives of how children's minds function, and how this functioning relates to the adoption of a particular form of pedagogy. We will briefly examine all four below.

The *first perspective* emphasises the way children may be perceived as *doers*, imitating the behaviour of adults and peers by being socialised into a cultural way of doing some activity. This imitation would include anything from learning how to utter sounds, to speaking a language or performing a skill such as holding a pen or brush to paint with. It is a type of demonstrational apprenticeship which is common among young children before and after they enter school.

The *second perspective* views the child as a *knower*, in which he or she acquires information either informally or formally (i.e. being taught). The information is built up over time and acts as a basis from which new knowledge fits into the context of existing knowledge. A pedagogy which serves to recognise the fact that children know more than what is credited to them is in contrast to the stance taken by most psychologists and many teachers, that the child's mind starts as a *tabula rasa*. In this perspective to pedagogy, the teacher not only recognises how the child's knowledge capacity increases, but actively tries to match instruction to that capacity in order to enrich the child's cognition.

A *third perspective* emphasises children as *thinkers* in which they not only develop theories about the world around them, but have ideas about the mind and how it works. The pedagogy which accompanies this view would emphasise the importance of discussion, collaboration and argument between the teacher and the child, as well as among other children. A *fourth perspective* sees the child as an *expert* by virtue of the fact that he has acquired objective knowledge and expertise, and is able to contribute to the culture. The role of pedagogy in this situation is to act as a means of assisting the child to evaluate and construct his or her understanding of the world. This form of pedagogy is one that emphasises facilitation and consultancy rather than didactism.

A Culture-sensitive Model of Pedagogy

Indicators from educational research point to the fact that pedagogy is no longer considered just an instructional process, with broadly accepted methods of delivery and predictable learner–teacher interactions. Pedagogy is far more complex. The author's view of pedagogy (Thomas 1997b) is that there are four main components which interact with one another (see Figure 3.4). The first is the *epistemological* component and refers to the knowledge base which all teachers need; a second is the *process* component which includes activities, such as planning, instruction, managing, evaluating and reflection. The third is *contextual* which includes language, religion and cultural traditions, while the fourth is a *personalistic* component and refers to the part played by a teacher's personal development.

Six main factors may affect one or all of the four pedagogical components; these include political, economic, societal, research and innovation, teacher professionalism and finally, cultural. The effect cultural factors may have in developing a pedagogy is particularly pertinent to our discussions in this chapter (see Figure 3.5).

In many developing countries, cultural heritage has suffered some neglect and even rejection (Thomas 1994) – this is the result of a drive to modernise educational systems and look elsewhere (mainly to the West). However, developing countries are starting to realise they have a rich cultural store

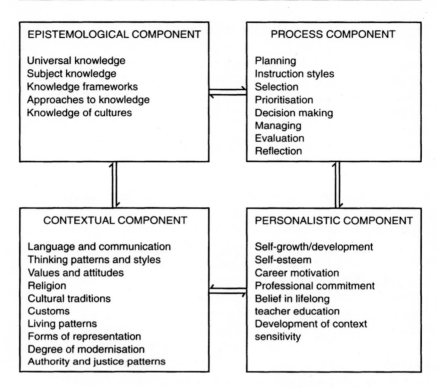

Figure 3.4: A culture-sensitive pedagogical model

of traditions, ways of communication, discourse, values and beliefs that continue to endure, irrespective of change. These attributes have a stabilising role for the future of such societies. Making teaching more sensitive to cultural contexts and the factors that determine these contexts is what the task of developing a culture-sensitive pedagogy is about. It must be emphasised, however, that a culture-sensitive pedagogy is one that should complement existing pedagogies. It is unlikely that it would replace modern methods of teaching and learning.

The essence of a culture-sensitive pedagogy would incorporate the best ideas and practices from all types of teaching, but

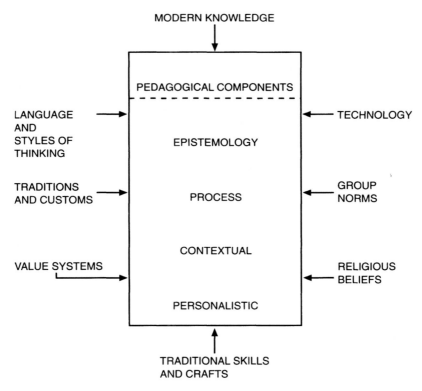

Figure 3.5: Cultural inputs into a culture-sensitive pedagogical model

at the same time it would ensure that the cultural context of teaching and learning would be pivotal. Let us explore the pivotal nature of cultural context in more detail which can be such an important ingredient of a culture-sensitive pedagogy for many cultures.

A pedagogy that is culture sensitive can be perceived as one in which each of the four pedagogical components discussed above are so integrated with one another that they actively reflect culture-specific knowledge, behaviours, attitudes and skills. These culture-specific attributes should complement the basic learning requirements common to all schooling.

However, two prerequisites need to be considered before a culture-sensitive pedagogy can become a reality. The first relates to an analysis of the cultural context of a particular situation and involves the identification of needs and goals, this we will term *cultural analysis*. The second prerequisite involves the selection and processing of the information obtained from a cultural analysis, and is in reality what we call a process of *cultural selectivity*. Let us examine these two processes further.

A *cultural analysis* is an extensive examination of the cultural context of a community, small group or even an individual. A cultural analysis which involves schoolchildren would probe in depth what each pupil would bring in cultural terms to the classroom, e.g. language skills, type of dialect, making wire toys and other skills learnt at home. It would seek to find out as much as possible about cultural interactions, between pupils during the school day, e.g. friendship patterns, or rule following in games and play. The outcome of a well-conducted cultural analysis, should ultimately enrich curriculum planning through the adoption and adaptation of ideas and practices specific to a particular cultural group. A cultural analysis would also explore whether the cultural patterns established are necessary to fulfil the needs of developing more effective teaching.

Cultural selectivity, the next stage after a cultural analysis has taken place, should provide appropriate knowledge and experience for making the pedagogical components discussed above more sensitive to the cultural needs of learners and teachers. The task of selecting appropriate data, for possible use in developing the knowledge and instructional base for a culture-sensitive pedagogy, is formidable. For instance, let us examine the case for developing a school curriculum for the early primary-school years.

The rationale for including numeracy, literacy and writing is relatively easy to establish. However, the way children engage in different learning styles and strategies to achieve success in the 3Rs as their preferred culture-specific route to this achievement is more complex and time-consuming. The work of Carraher, Carraher & Schliemann (1987) and Nunes (1994) with Brazilian street children concerning the learning of mathematical operations, and discussed in Chapter 2, gives testimony to the arduous task of combining careful analysis and selection from a particular cultural context. What follows are a number of possible exemplars of how each component of the pedagogical model discussed above may be developed as part of a wider culture-sensitive pedagogical process.

Developing the Epistemological Component

Causality and Causal Thinking in African Schools and Society
We will examine two instances of causality, namely social and physical. The author found that while working in Nigeria and Malawi as a teacher educator in the 1970s, most teacher trainees were able to explain and discuss, often quite eloquently, their notions of *social causality* from their day-to-day life experiences among the family and community. For example, the origin of family quarrels, marriage difficulties and causes of debt and petty theft are often the subjects of many problems that need to be resolved from time to time, and which trainee teachers are familiar with in their homes. Such discussions are common in family and community discourse, involving the resolution of family feuds and disagreements.

At the level of *physical causality*, trainees were often able to determine what went wrong if a transistor radio did not work, or a bike needed repairing or how they would trace in stepwise manner the causes of crop failure in their gardens at home. Building on this knowledge and experience proved to be invaluable in explaining causality, and developing problem-solving strategies during pre-service training of science teachers. However, textbooks and teacher guides that the students used rarely tapped this resource but included instead, references to almost entirely Western sources. There

is a need for educators from developing countries to completely revamp school curricula, and include within them as
much of their own culturally relevant knowledge and skills as
pos-sible, but alongside the modern-day requirements of technology and other disciplines.

*Incorporating Knowledge about Cultural Values into the School
Curriculum*   We will examine below both family and business
values in our discussions. The knowledge and experience
gained over the centuries, about respect for family and community through the enduring principle of filial piety in CHCs,
had until recently not been included in most social studies and
civics curricula. It was only in the mid 1980s that knowledge
about Confucianism and Mencius was being considered to be
part of values education in secondary schools in Singapore,
and more recently for ethnic Chinese pupils in Malaysia. This
was introduced to counteract the perceived dangers of
Western influences.

Family discussion about business ventures, profit making and
profit sharing, the hierarchical nature of family decision
making and prioritising targets, is another salient area which
contributes to the rich and fascinating epistemology of the
culture of South and North East Asia. It might be argued that
these areas of cultural knowledge are so well known among
the family and the community, that it is unnecessary to include
them in school curricula. On the other hand, however, their
inclusion would alert pupils to the merits of their own traditions, alongside those values external to their own culture
such as individualism and competitiveness that are promoted
by the school system.

Developing the Pedagogical Processes Component

Pedagogical processes include managing, decision making
and instructional activities common across all cultures, but
there are also culture-specific elements within each activity

which are emphasised in different cultures. Let us examine a culture-specific pedagogical style, which has been proved to be an effective way of getting pupils to learn their first language, namely the teaching of Mandarin.

Teaching and Learning Styles Involved with Learning Chinese Mandarin   Teaching styles can often be very culture specific as in the case of teaching Chinese alphabetical characters. Most teachers of Chinese Mandarin favour a strongly didactic approach, in fact it is well-nigh impossible to teach Chinese in any other way. Learning Mandarin pictographs not only requires rote learning for recognition, but the application of rote learning in teaching pupils how to write each line and curve of a pictograph in a definite sequence so that it constitutes a final symbolic representation. A dot or a line in the wrong place can result in a totally different meaning.

Rote learning also extends to the mastery of the Mandarin phonic system, with its four different tones which pupils need to identify in order to express the correct meaning. Awareness on the part of teachers that teaching and learning styles suited to a particular form of cultural learning, play a valuable part in making instruction more effective in a particular teaching situation. In the example cited above, teaching various parts of a language like Mandarin, which directs pupils to learn by rote, is the only effective method of language learning, and as a result, the method constitutes an aspect of an established and well-tried cultural pedagogical process.

However, the work of Kwan-Terry (1994) in Singapore has shown how culture-specific teaching styles associated with rote learning of Mandarin could transfer negatively across to other subjects of the curriculum. While rote learning may be necessary for learning a language like Mandarin, it becomes, according to Kwan Terry, difficult for children to engage in more creative, original and analytical thinking in other disciplines like literature and science, due to the over-dependence on inflexible learning strategies, and the rote memorisation associated with learning Mandarin. Teachers, therefore, need to be sensitive to the effect of negative transfer at certain stages in the teaching process, and be able to develop a cultural flexibility in their teaching styles, so that different teaching styles can be adopted. What this means is that cultural flexibility needs to become part of a culture sensitive pedagogy which alerts teachers to both the positive and negative attributes of certain cultural norms.

However, it would be a mistake to think that the rote basis for the learning of a language like Mandarin has an entirely negative side. In Chapter 2 we examined the work of Marton & Saljo (1976) on surface and deep approaches to learning, and discovered that the apparent surface learning typified by much of rote procedures can provide learners with a basis for deeper approaches to learning. The development of deeper learning approaches is a function of several factors, the cultural context, the nature of the task and how learners are able to encode both. In other words, there are important cognitive consequences to the memorising of Chinese characters for the later development of deeper learning approaches (Tang & Biggs 1996). The discussion about surface and deep learning structures is explored also in Chapter 4, when we will address the issue of assessing these forms of learning structures.

Developing the Contextual Component

Knowing and selecting the appropriate context is the key to the development of a culture-sensitive pedagogy. The contextual component refers to the dynamics between knowledge about customs and traditions, use of local languages, ways and modes of thinking, styles of communication through drawing, different forms of social discourse, specific kinship agendas and ways of judging and evaluating group members. The role of spiritual and religious beliefs as part of a community's value system, and a school values education programme, would be another crucial focus of this component.

However, there are several issues that need to be addressed when assessing the part context may play in developing a culture-sensitive pedagogy. The first refers to the extent to which knowledge exists about a particular context. In other words, has an adequate cultural analysis been carried out? The second issue relates to what form of cultural selectivity has been used. A third is about who selects, is it the teacher or are those decisions made by curriculum writers who are not themselves teachers? A fourth issue relates to how the selection of one cultural context may transfer across to other existing contexts, and which context in particular would enhance a child's cognitive performance.

A final issue relates to the question of acceptability, especially as far as parents are concerned. For instance, it might be seen as unnecessary to include the teaching of traditional values and other culture-specific knowledge, as it may be perceived as a distraction from those aspects of the curriculum which promote academic achievement. Parents may even hold the view that most homes already provide a sufficient cultural and religious base for their children. Let us examine two instances in which selecting cultural context could promote more meaningful and even enjoyable teaching and learning, one example coming from Malaysia and the other from the Ivory Coast.

Tapping Traditional Malaysian Storytelling and Dance Routines for Enriching a Cultural Curriculum Among the ethnically diverse school population of Malaysia, the author has noted the lack of "take up" by curriculum planners from a rich aesthetic and artistic cultural context which typifies all three main ethnic groups which make up Malaysian society (i.e. Chinese, Indian and Malay). There is an extremely rich endowment among the Malay, Indian and Chinese communities in art, storytelling, dance and music.

This endowment is given every opportunity to flourish outside school in evening clubs and during the many public festivals held throughout the year, but this only actually engages relatively few pupils and the focus is ethnic specific, that is Chinese, Malay and Indian cultural events are in the main attended by each ethnic group respectively. Curriculum planners, for the most part, tend to downplay the important contribution that could be made to the study of art, drama and aesthetics from this rich multicultural heritage. As a result, there is an overemphasis on examination-focused curriculum subjects, like history and geography, so depriving pupils of a curriculum which could bring a strong element of cross-cultural aesthetic enrichment to the learning process.

Informal and Formal Planning Strategies Used in Weaving and Learning Transfer in the Ivory Coast A study by Fabienne Tanon (1994) compared the influences of formal education and informal education (weaving) on planning skills. She also investigated how the practice of a complex activity such as weaving impacts on cognitive ability, as far as learning transfer is concerned. The research took place in the Ivory Coast where there is a combined influence of a strong weaving tradition and a formal Francophone educational environment. Two tasks were given to 110 male subjects from a rural area, and the sample was divided into weavers and non-weavers, schooled and non-schooled. The first task involved weaving, while the second required subjects to load and unload passengers with luggage, using a taxi travelling between five different villages.

Both tasks require planning strategies to be developed. The results showed that planning and learning transfer is enhanced by activities which require children to engage in informal tasks such as weaving. Such activities combined with schooling open up greater opportunities for making formal schooling more relevant and effective. It would be the role of teachers in these instances to make themselves familiar with the nature of informal activities such as weaving, fishing, construction of toys from junk materials, and select planning sequences which characterise these informal activities into their own teaching regimens. The above shows how a reciprocity between different contexts (i.e. the informal and the formal) can provide a useful teaching strategy, which reinforces the value of cultural sensitivity in pedagogy.

Developing the Personalistic Component

The role of teachers, their commitment and their motivation are particularly important in the development of a more culture-sensitive teaching regimen. A major problem which the author has met in training teachers in many developing countries is to get trainees to recognise that much of which they already have in their cultural context is as important as what is necessary to import from others. The answer partly lies in the way teachers are trained, and partly in the ways society values its cultural traditions. However, on the other hand, both teachers and society at large should be open and critical about some of the constraints produced by a culture, in situations where adaptation to change is slow. It is unlikely that the views of Kwan-Terry on the disadvantages of learning Mandarin in Singapore would be welcome to diehard Chinese Mandarin scholars. However, the government of Singapore does recognise the fact that what Kwan-Terry says about over-zealous didactic teaching, can be a barrier to more analytical and open learning.

The quality of an educational system is only as good as the quality of its teaching force. In order for teachers to be active, credible and effective, they need to feel that their context matters and that developing more sensitivity to the needs of their learners is an integral part of that context. The role of teachers acting as a "cultural bridge" has been previously discussed by the author (Thomas 1994). This analogy of a "bridge" is intimately linked to the recognition that the personalistic component of the pedagogical model plays a

vital part in raising the expectations of pupils, as well as initiating and maintaining high levels of motivation during their
years of schooling. It is only through constant encouragement
by teachers in enhancing a sense of self-esteem, and a sense
of competence, that children will come to terms with the
requirements of living in a fast- and ever-changing world.
Teachers who are "in tune" with the old and the new cultures
will be able to help children adapt and adjust to such change,
and meet the cross-cultural challenges of globalisation
(Thomas 1998).

Before we move on to examine the integrative model of
pedagogy it might be useful to add that developing cultural
sensitivity through teaching is also the hallmark of so-called
indigenous pedagogies, which arise from an indigenous culture-
based curriculum. Like our discussions of a culture-sensitive
pedagogy, there is a need for an indigenous pedagogy to have
its own theory and practical basis. Aikman (1999) points out
that in Peru, while trainees may receive Western-type training
in child development and other education disciplines, they
can also be given the opportunity to study indigenous child
development among their own ethnic group. Aikman also
quotes several instances from Canada and the Pacific region,
where indigenous teachers who may have less education
than their non-indigenous counterparts are developing their
own successful pedagogical and evaluative strategies. Both
culture-sensitive pedagogy and its near neighbour *indigenous
pedagogy* underline a constant theme of this book, namely the
importance of cultural relevancy in the classroom.

Integrative Pedagogical Models

The third model of pedagogy examines how different
approaches to teaching can be integrated. Integration is understood in the present context as a mechanism which involves
identifying and melding together certain aspects of content

and process that are common between two or more curriculum subjects. The objective of developing an integrative pedagogy, would be to provide a means of enabling the transfer of key concepts through the instructional process.

An integrative pedagogy would draw on various cultural contexts to make teaching and learning more effective and relevant. We will examine three examples of an integrative pedagogy; the first is used in bilingual education, the second example discusses the integration of different pedagogical approaches to learning, and the third examines integration embracing an indigenous–religious approach and a Western secular one.

An Integrated Pedagogy for an Effective Bilingual Education

Linguistic theories have had more influence on first-language (L1) acquisition research, whereas their influence on second-language (L2) acquisition has had less impact. Nevertheless, there are parallels between L1 and L2 acquisition. Researchers such as Roulet (1980, 1995) have proposed an integrative pedagogy based on the assumptions that learning an L1 does provide a point of reference for analysing the process of L2 learning. This is particularly evident where L1 and L2 are similar as in French and Spanish, which are both Romance languages. In these languages, learning strategies, errors and order of acquisition in L2 development parallel quite closely those for L1. By developing an integrative approach to bilingual teaching, the teacher is not only involved in the acquisition process of learning two languages, but he or she is a key agent in the intercultural transmission associated with the languages concerned. This means that teachers who practise an integrated pedagogy, especially in a multicultural society, are not only involved in teaching two languages, but are actively engaging pupils and themselves in acquiring two cultures.

Integrative Pedagogy That Embraces Different Pedagogical Traditions

The recent academic successes of secondary-school pupils in CHCs like Singapore, Taiwan and Japan reflected their top positions in the international league tables in subjects like mathematics and science (*The Ecomomist* 1997), and have prompted educationists to examine the reasons for this success. Factors such as close interest and supervision by parents of their children's homework, and the fact that high school achievement is prized above all else, may be responsible. Another observation has been the emphasis in the classrooms of these countries on full-frontal or whole-class teaching, featuring a strongly didactic pedagogical approach to classroom learning, and put forward as a reason for this success story.

One cannot but be struck, when visiting classrooms in any of the countries mentioned above, by the strong simularities to classroom climates that were typical of those in the UK and other European countries before the 1960s. A strong feature of these schools is the dominance of the teacher's role as an instructor rather than as a facilitator. This pattern of pedagogy is the result of a historical development which accompanied the growth of Western educational traditions, in which the didactic process was formalised, and instruction gradually became a large group affair, with the attendant matching of instruction to the age of the learners.

Features such as moral perfectability, emulation (imitation of role models), diligence and effort which typify CHCs have been integrated into the former didactic European model of pedagogy, so giving the teacher more control over the learning process. While this integrative pedagogy has probably been a key factor in delivering impressive success rates for pupils in the subjects mentioned above, it has been achieved at a cost: namely the neglect in developing creative and intuitive abilities among these pupils (Hatano 1990; Inagaki 1986).

Integrative Pedagogy Embracing the Religious with Secular Western Traditions

The nature of teaching is not only influenced by folk psychology, folk pedagogy and being sensitive to cultural context; comparative education and cross-cultural studies show that a complex relationship exists between the influence of religious values held by a particular society, and the increasing incidence of secularism. This complex relationship is often reflected in the way education and schooling are delivered. For instance, in North Africa, sub-Saharan Africa, and some countries in South East Asia, it is often possible to observe how Islam and Christianity have fitted successfully into indigenous cultural contexts, and how methods of imparting religious messages have been reflected by schoolteachers who had themselves (and their recent forebears) been influenced by a religious faith. Pedagogy is, in fact, part of an ongoing process of *cultural melding*, involving Western-type schooling, a set of religious values, e.g. Islam or Christianity (coming from outside the indigenous group), and the superimposition of both upon an existing value system.

Let us examine a case of this type of integrative pedagogy from West Africa. Koranic tradition aims to educate the whole person, but according to Serpell & Hatano (1997) in view of the pressure to expand the formal school system in a country like the northern Cameroon, the focus has narrowed considerably. Two parallel systems of education exist, the Koranic tradition and the Western tradition, exemplified by the French system of education. Koranic education involves a group of students gathered around a master teacher or *mallum*, usually in his own home. The curriculum is fixed in content, but flexible in terms of age of enrolment and pupil progression. The *mallums* are mature and strongly engaged with the community from which their pupils come. The *mallums* are also persons with high prestige, by virtue of their own indigenous socialisation and standing in the community (Santerre 1971). This is in contrast with the French style of schooling, with its emphasis on the school as a separate entity, and with teachers who may come from outside the immediate community.

For as long as both Koranic and French systems exist side by side, children will experience two patterns of pedagogy which are integrated in an informal manner. Both forms of instruction are of benefit to the pupils. Koranic pedagogy provides a strong feature of individualised instruction, which emphasises the moral and social development of the learner. It also provides access to schooling, which is both adaptable and flexible. The French system enables pupils to have a window on the outside world, and this has implications for these pupils to be exposed to more modern approaches to learning and teaching. It is a real and worthwhile challenge, if a pedagogical integration could be developed between the two approaches, in which the strengths of both traditions could be used by the teacher; this would benefit all pupils, making their schooling not only more relevant and effective, but possibly more enjoyable as well.

An Instructional Objectives Pedagogy That Emphasises Principles and Rules

The models of pedagogy discussed so far have emphasised two key factors, namely the central position of the learner and the importance of cultural context in teaching. Folk pedagogy (which is related to folk psychology) developed by Bruner & Olson emphasises the status of the learner who is at the centre of the teaching process, while the culture-sensitive pedagogy emphasises the role of cultural context in developing knowledge and process in teaching pupils in multicultural classrooms. However, much of pupil learning is also concerned with the mastery of concepts and principles that form the building blocks within each subject discipline. From these building blocks, higher-order mental operations can be developed and applied to various forms of problem solving.

When Benjamin Bloom (1956) wrote his now famous *Taxonomy of Behavioural Objectives*, its impact on teaching and learning in the classrooms of the USA was immense. The effect was also felt in many countries throughout the world as a blueprint curriculum design. The so-called curriculum objectives model was not only a blueprint for pupil learning, it was soon to affect the way instruction was to be delivered in class. Behavioural objectives were set out in pupil learning guides and accompanied by teacher guides and training manuals, which contained sets of instructional objectives that dovetailed the behavioural objectives found in pupil learning materials. The instructional objectives covered most aspects of lesson planning and presentation, including the teaching of concepts, rules and principles of disciplines such as science and geography.

The instructional element of any model of pedagogy will naturally be a key factor, as it provides the framework and driving force behind the intention to teach. Therefore, pedagogies that emphasise concept learning, and the subsequent development of rules in particular subjects like mathematics, language learning or science, need to take account of the aims, rationale and esoteric nature of these disciplines. It is therefore necessary to include in our discussions about models of pedagogy a model that not only enables teachers to lay the foundations and principles of understanding a particular subject discipline, but one that allows teachers to develop these principles, so they can be used to further the learner in his or her pursuit of the subject within the wider framework of instructional objectives. The author has termed this model of pedagogy an *instructional objectives pedagogy*, emphasising principles and rules, and is an amalgam of two perspectives of behavioural psychology.

The first perspective includes the instructional model put forward by Gagné and Driscoll (1988) which underlines the need to have a framework that melds learning processes with instruction. Gagne's model satisfies the need to have a pedagogy that not only emphasises the close interface that exists between learning and teaching, but that knowledge and skills acquisition is ultimately achieved when the learner is able to learn and apply rules and principles competently. The second behavioural perspective uses Bloom's notion of the behavioural objective to structure curriculum content and the activities of teaching, learning and ultimately pupil assessment.

However, we have seen from discussions in previous chapters that there are many instances where children from different cultures have been able to bypass the formal teaching of rules and principles of curriculum subjects altogether. This is because pupils had not attended school or had dropped out. In spite of this situation the children were able to exist successfully, making a living out of selling things. The research of Nunes (1994) and Schliemann, Carraher & Ceci (1997) is well known in this area (and has been referred to in earlier chapters), where they studied child vendors making a living on the streets of Brazilian cities. These children used everyday mathematics to sell their wares. It seems that from this research in Brazil and other countries, that street children can perform quite complex calculations more effectively than their counterparts in school, without having to be taught the appropriate mathematical rules. These observations are explained in terms of the importance of the "immediacy" of situation in which these children operate.

Surviving on the street by selling things teaches the child vendor a lot about the everyday use of mathematical operations which they learn very quickly. These children are also resilient and are constantly making decisions about their day-to-day lives. Some educators have advocated that classroom activities should be redefined and reflect what goes on out of school. It is argued that everyday activities such as buying, sharing and bartering should be more closely simulated with school mathematics, making the subject "situation specific" and therefore more meaningful. However, Schliemann (1995) has warned that mathematics (and other school subjects), should not be over-supplemented with reproductions and imitations of "out of school" situations, as they focus too narrowly on an immediate application to a particular problem, rather than give students a set of principles that can be applied more widely in the long term.

There is, therefore, on one hand a need for teachers to be made more aware of the advantages that everyday cognition brings to a child's understanding of his or her environment. On the other hand, the teacher has the responsibility to expose pupils to the rules and principles underpinning all curriculum subjects, and getting the pupils to master and apply these principles to problems they may meet later in school, or when they enter the world of work.

A pedagogical model that emphasises concept learning, rule following and the use of principles to enrich and explain the "out of school" world of children is necessary for three reasons. Firstly, it provides the foundation from which more knowledge is gained; secondly, it results in the acquisition of higher-order skills; and thirdly, contributes ultimately to the development of critical thinking. When these aspects are set alongside an approach to instruction that favours the use of aims and objectives, the teacher (some educators would argue) has a pedagogy that provides much needed structure to pupils' learning in class from which logical thinking can be developed further.

Nevertheless, the appreciation on the part of teachers that pupils' everyday cognition has an important role in the preadolescent years must not be disregarded, as it supplies the context with which most children are familiar. The challenge for teachers who may adopt this pedagogical model, will involve making decisions about where and when children's everyday activities can be usefully included or omitted from the instructional process, so that they will enrich rather than hamper the learning and development of higher-order concepts and principles.

An Intercultural Pedagogy as Part of Multicultural Education

Few societies nowadays can be insulated from the influences of foreign cultures. Schoolchildren especially in many developing countries experience very marked cultural changes even on a daily basis. For instance, a child leaves his or her "home culture" at one part of the day and enters the very different culture of the school sometime later. The child is confronted with different value systems and organisational procedures, different styles of learning, and is often taught in a different language.

An intercultural model of pedagogy aims to assist the teacher to understand the cross-cultural interface which pupils experience in the complex cultural dynamic of the school. Intercultural pedagogy, unlike the other models we have discussed, is mainly socio-cultural in nature. The model attempts to develop a better understanding among different cultural groups, hopefully engendering positive attitudes and resulting in a more effective and meaningful multicultural education. The teacher has a pivotal role in fostering cross-cultural interaction through the medium of an intercultural pedagogy in multicultural classrooms.

There are many forms of and approaches to multicultural education. Eldering & Rothenburg (1997) distinguish between four perspectives, *disadvantage, enrichment, bicultural competence* and *collective equality groups*. The *disadvantage* perspective has a built-in assumption that different cultural groups are in educational arrears, and there is a need to catch up with the dominant culture. Multicultural education for *enrichment* relates cultural diversity with enrichment, and so enrichment could be aimed at either a particular ethnic group, or for all the school population.

Multicultural education that emphasises *bicultural competence* refers to situations in which pupils coming from two different

cultures have the strong likelihood of being doubly accultur-
ated. Where multicultural education emphasises the *equality
of groups*, the aim is to develop a collective equality between
cultures, ironing out the cultural gap between school and
society. This issue will be discussed further in Chapter 6 in
which the cultural dynamics of school–society relations will
be addressed. A flexible intercultural pedagogy would be able
to address all these perspectives, depending on the society's
policy towards multiculturalism. Let us examine the use of an
intercultural pedagogy for two approaches to multicultural
education, namely *biculturalism* and *enrichment*.

Biculturalism as Part of an Intercultural Pedagogy

Teaching foreign languages is a common feature of most
secondary-school curricula, and in many countries foreign
languages are also taught at the primary-school level. However, in countries like the USA and the UK being bilingual or
multilingual is often seen as overburdening the rest of the
curriculum and unnecessary. However, in most developing
countries many children are taught in a language that is
culturally and linguistically different from the one they experience at home. This imposes many disadvantages on children, one of which would be a barrier to better academic
achievement.

Another negative outcome would be that the indigenous language is perceived to be second best, and would not figure
very much in teaching. However, it has been discussed in
Chapter 2 that bilingual teachers are in effect bicultural agents
in the classroom because of the close link that exists between
language and culture. There is also growing evidence that
being bilingual confers considerable advantages on pupils,
not least providing a greater degree of authority and empowerment (Serpell & Hatano 1997; Mohanty & Perregaux 1997).

Learning even one's own language is a significant cultural
event for a child, learning two or more languages provides an

even greater cultural enrichment, as well as a challenge for both learner and teacher. Bilingual teachers are able to act as a bridge between two cultural systems. The analogy of the bridge allows for an intercultural flow to take place between children who come from different cultural traditions, enabling them to experience both their own culture and that of others. This opportunity for bicultural exposure, through bilingualism, is a key element in an intercultural pedagogy, which could result in a well-balanced bicultural integration within the school.

The work of Gumperz (1982) has shown that language used by multilingual individuals in multilingual societies often results in different forms of psychological integration. Such integration entails different types of socio-linguistic interaction between people from different cultural backgrounds. These interactions often result in the adoption and adaptation of language use and cultural traditions across communities. Such studies and more of their kind will be able to promote the development of an effective intercultural pedagogy, and hopefully a better understanding among different cultural groups in the future.

Facilitating Enrichment as Part of an Intercultural Pedagogy

The assumption behind enrichment as a basis for multicultural education is that cultural diversity is closely related to societal enrichment, and that education should reflect this as far as possible. Enrichment, in this context, means it could be aimed at specific cultural groups, or at all pupils. In the former case, enrichment is about what a particular group has contributed from its culture, whereas in the latter case, the approach is one of sharing cultures with the ultimate aim of improving human relations and is the essence of intercultural education. We will focus on the latter intercultural dimension of enrichment here, because of its pertinence to our discussions about intercultural pedagogy.

Bartolome (1994) has found from his research that, however well meaning teachers are towards promoting enrichment in multicultural classrooms, they often employ teaching strategies that are inappropriate for students who come from different cultural backgrounds, and who have specific learning requirements and styles of study. These inappropriate teaching strategies actually impair the enrichment process. There are several ways in which enrichment can be facilitated in the pedagogy that teachers might employ. For instance, how *visual learning cues* might be used with students from minority groups. At another level there is a need for teachers to be aware that most students seek a *structure and organisation* in their day-to-day life in classrooms, and desire opportunities for better means of shared communication.

Let us first examine some aspects of *visual learning cues* that would assist pupils in their learning. The considered use of visual symbols, pictures and images facilitates comprehension of written material significantly. If the visual cues originate from the student's own culture, such images or literature of the countries in which they or their parents were born assist the learning process even more so. Knowledge about students' culture-specific visual learning cues by teachers would assist learning markedly, especially if teachers were able to organise classroom activities around students' cultural backgrounds, which reflected some of these visual stimuli.

An aspect of behaviour related to visual learning cues is eye contact. An appreciation by the teacher of different cross-cultural patterns of eye contact between persons is often helpful. For instance, in CHCs and several African cultures, direct eye contact between older and younger people is avoided where possible, often as a mark of respect for the older person. A teacher who insists on making direct eye contact over a protracted time period may find the pupil's attention decreases and often accompanied by some withdrawal behaviour. For pupils who come from a non-direct eye contact culture, learning becomes a distinctly uncomfortable process, when confronted with teachers who do not balance their patterns of direct eye contact in the interactions with these children. In the early phases of acculturation by newly immigrant pupils who have specific cultural visual learning cues including eye contact behaviour patterns, the more the teacher is made aware of these features, the smoother will be the adjustment of these pupils to a new cultural classroom climate.

In turning to pupil adjustment to different patterns of classroom *structure and organisation*, it is important for teachers to be aware that many immigrant pupils have been used to a highly structured and formal classroom regimen. For example, children from different cultures are used to starting the school day by standing up in class and entering into an exchange of greetings with the teacher, often lasting over 15 minutes. The classroom seating arrangement is usually in the form of rows of desks which also facilitates a disciplined start to the school day. Pupils from these situations who are thrust into less formal classroom climates need time to adjust to the new environment. The teacher, therefore, will need to develop strategies that can combine the formal with the more informal interactive classroom management approaches to learning. The use of group learning or dyadic partnerships for practical work, as well as well-planned field studies which would explore various cultural backgrounds, would make enrichment relevant and effective as well as interesting, provided they were introduced by the teachers in a planned way.

PEDAGOGY, PRAXIS AND PROFESSIONALISM

In concluding this chapter, we will examine a number of issues which relate to the third question posed earlier, of how various interpretations of the nature of pedagogy might improve praxis and professionalism in multicultural classrooms. Firstly, however, we need to establish what may constitute good praxis in multicultural classrooms, and how the quality of teacher professionalism can be developed in concert with improvements in praxis. In essence, good praxis in multicultural classrooms is about teachers being sensitive to cultural diversity, and enabling the value of this diversity to be shared by all concerned. Praxis is also about the intentions of teachers to be as fully informed as possible about the cultural context of their pupils, and to develop teaching and learning strategies that draw on that context, where appropriate, so that it will benefit all pupils from whatever background they come from.

Linked closely with good praxis is the provision of sound policies for teacher development, so that a teacher's professionalism can be enhanced to meet the challenges of cultural diversity in the multicultural classroom. Teacher development begins during the years of pre-service training and continues throughout a teacher's professional career. It is imperative for teachers who work with different cultural groups to be given every opportunity to develop their knowledge and skills to assist them to understand the nature of cultural diversity, and to expose them to relevant cross-cultural research that may assist their professional development. In Chapter 7 we will discuss further the need for teacher training and development within the framework of cultural diversity; however, at this juncture we will outline some of the implications of the research on teaching in cross-cultural contexts, discussed in the course of this chapter.

Pedagogical Traditions and Cultures of Teaching

It is clear that there have been substantive changes in the nature and development of pedagogy over the last 50 years which reflect, in general, an emphasis away from didacticism to a more shared approach to learning between teachers and learners. The three traditions set out by Zeichner (1992), namely "academic", "social efficiency" and "cultural", are to be found in varying degrees in many educational systems, depending on the emphasis which teachers are required to put on a pupil's development (see Figure 3.1). All three traditions have important implications for teaching pupils in multicultural classrooms.

The need for all teachers to have a sound training in knowledge and comprehension of curriculum subjects confirms the fact that academic content is equally important when teaching children from other cultures. To allow teachers to actively engage their pupils in learning tasks which help them to construct meaning and experiences about the world around them introduces a strong element of social efficiency into pupil learning, whether it takes place in monocultural or multicultural classes. Whatever the cultural profile of the classroom, the social efficiency tradition of teaching is beneficial to all pupils.

The recent research and writing about teaching as a set of cultures has important implications for teaching in multicultural classrooms. One implication is that the tradition of teaching, being a cultural process, is greatly strengthened by the fact that teachers are part of a mosaic of cultural processes related to the act of teaching in different situations and contexts. Teachers are not only concerned with academic learning and social construction in the classroom, but they are also operating within an intercultural dynamic involving the cultural contexts of teachers, their pupils and the culture of the school.

The second implication refers to how the notion of teaching as a set of cultures provides a useful basis for teacher development and the promotion of professionalism. The analysis by Andy Hargreaves (1992) of teaching cultures having both *content* and *form* is useful from the standpoint of developing professionalism among teachers who are directly concerned with teaching pupils from diverse cultural backgrounds. The *content* which Hargreaves discusses includes developing attitudes and values and ways of sharing ideas within and between groups. Teachers who wish to acquire a better understanding of cultural diversity within their classrooms, would be well advised to develop this type of content in their day-to-day interactions with their pupils. The *form* of teaching cultures which include the pervasive features of *collaboration* and *collegiality* are particuarly important for teaching in culturally diverse situations, as it is necessary that teachers who are engaged to do so are able to share ideas with colleagues. It is important that those teachers who are already successful in understanding that cultural diversity leads to better social interaction, should also be able to share their expertise with younger and less experienced teachers.

Models of Pedagogy and the Melding Process

The five pedagogical models discussed in this chapter provide sufficient choice for teachers, whether they are teaching in a monocultural or multicultural classroom climate. There are cases where the application of one model may be sufficient to meet the needs of the school curriculum. The *instructional objectives/rule following* model is such a case, and modifications to this model have been widely used in both developed and developing countries. There is little doubt that this model is an adequate one to use, if the main aim of teaching is to match learning objectives with learning outcomes. The model is also valuable insomuch that it emphasises the importance of rules and principles in learning subject matter. For many developing countries after the granting of independence, most curriculum planning used this type of model, for it provided a meaningful structure and feedback for learners and teachers alike, which previously was by and large absent.

However, some of the other pedagogical models discussed earlier have become more high profile in recent years, because schooling is increasingly seen as a social preparation for adulthood as well as a process of skill and knowledge acquisition for the workplace. Of particular concern to the interests of the present book, the *folk, culture-sensitive* (including an indigenous pedagogy) and *intercultural* models of pedagogy provide teachers with the possibilities of developing teaching strategies which emphasise the socio-cultural development of pupils during their years of schooling. While the *integrative* model is in the first place a skills model for language acquisition in two or more languages, by virtue of the fact that bilingual teachers are also promoting biculturalism, the application of an integrative pedagogy also provides considerable socio-cultural input into teaching and learning.

It is unlikely in multicultural education that any one of the five models used alone would meet the demands of cultural diversity, so teachers will need to be able to make choices about which specific teaching strategy might be used and under what circumstances. Figure 3.6 shows that culture-specific teaching strategies may be developed if such choices need to be made.

In many cases two or more models may need to be melded together in order to meet certain cross-cultural classroom situations. For instance, it may be necessary to harness parts of the epistemological or process components of a culture-sensitive pedagogy with the intercultural model, in order to realise intercultural enrichment with reference to visual learning cues or developing partnerships for class practical work.

Melding is not an easy task. It requires considerable teacher knowledge, experience and sensitivity towards the cultural contexts in question. It also requires teachers to be good at selecting which pedagogical model would be the most appropriate to meld with another, and how the meld can be delivered in the classroom. Successful melding is, however, only achieved when teachers have been given adequate training

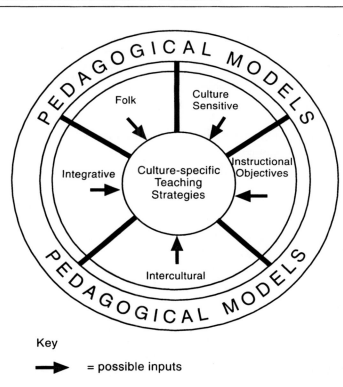

Key

➤ = possible inputs

Figure 3.6: Pedagogical models and the development of culture-specific teaching strategies

and are able to apply their training when the opportunity arises.

SUMMARY

1. Three main questions were posed in this chapter relating to (i) the nature of pedagogy and cultures of teaching, (ii) models of pedagogy and their application to the cultural dynamics of teaching in multicultural classrooms, (iii) intercultural interpretations of pedagogy leading to better praxis and professionalism.

2. It is possible to discern three different theoretical traditions in an analysis of the nature of pedagogy; these are academic, social efficiency and cultural, emphasising the importance of content, process and cultural context respectively.

3. Teaching is increasingly being perceived as a set of cultures of which *content* and *form* underpin a valid analysis of the process; *content* includes attitudes, values and interpersonal approaches, while *form* refers to pervasive features such as individualism, balkanisation, collaboration and collegiality.

4. Models of teaching help to explain, predict, initiate ideas and hopefully act as frameworks for the further development of theory, resulting in sound praxis.

5. Five pedagogical models are discussed, including *folk, culture sensitive, integrative, instructional/rule following* and *intercultural,* all of which have an underpinning from cross-cultural research studies.

6. Each of the five pedagogical models have valuable strengths in explaining the cultural dynamics of teaching and learning in multicultural classrooms, as various case studies from different countries discussed in the chapter show.

7. The five models also provide teachers and teacher educators with many ideas, some of which can be melded together if necessary, for developing teaching and learning strategies, to meet the needs of praxis in the classroom.

SUGGESTIONS FOR FURTHER READING

Bartolome, L.I. (1994). Beyond the methods fetish: towards a humanising pedagogy. *Harvard Educational Review,* **64**(2), 173–194.

Bennett, N. (1993). Knowledge bases for learning to teach. In N. Bennett & C. Carre (Eds), *Learning to Teach.* London: Routledge, pp. 1–17.

Eldering, L. & Rothenburg, J.J. (1997). Multicultural education: approaches and practice. In K. Watson, C. Modgil & S. Modgil (Eds), *Educational Dilemmas: Debate and Diversity.* Volume 1, *Teachers, Teacher Education and Training.* London: Cassell, pp. 306–316.

Hargreaves, A. (1992). Cultures of teaching: a focus for change. In A. Hargreaves & M.G. Fullan (Eds), *Understanding Teacher Development*. London: Cassell, pp. 216–240.

Olson, D.R. & Bruner, J.S. (1996). Folk psychology and folk pedagogy. In D.R. Olson & N. Torrance (Eds), *Handbook of Education and Human Development: New Models of Learning, Teaching and Schooling*. Oxford: Blackwell, pp. 9–27.

Thomas, E. (1997). Models of teacher education and their role in educational planning. In J. Lynch, C. Modgil & S. Modgil (Eds), *Education and Development: Tradition and Innovation*, Volume 3, London: Cassell, pp. 106–121.

Zeichner, K.M. (1992). Conceptions of reflective practice and teacher education. In G. Harvard & R. Dunne (Eds), *Westminster Studies in Education*, 15.

4

CULTURAL CONTEXT AND EDUCATIONAL ASSESSMENT

In this chapter we will continue to examine the relationship between learning and cultural context from the perspective of educational assessment. In the second half of the 1990s, research comparing the achievement scores of secondary-school children from different parts of the world in science and mathematics has shown how performance of pupils from CHCs such as Taiwan and Singapore have been superior to children of similar age ranges in Western countries like the USA and the UK (*The Economist* 1997). Why is this so? What is it about East Asian school systems that can produce such a level of attainment? Is the high level of attainment due to the style of classroom teaching that is used with these pupils? Is it the motivation of the pupils? Are there specific cultural factors that are at play which promote this high level of pupil commitment and success?

These are some of the questions that educationists, politicians and economists especially from Western countries are asking themselves. Questions relating to the nature of cultural context and assessment of pupil learning have been among the most frequently posed, not only in the West but across the globe. The way children are taught in these societies, the type of assessment used by teachers and the effect these two factors have on academic attainment have also been among the most commonly addressed questions. In this chapter, we will examine four key questions relating to learning and assessment in the context of cultural differences:

1. What are the assumptions about learning as far as educational assessment is concerned?
2. What are some of the key issues and problems in cross-cultural assessment that educators need to be aware of, to develop better ways of assessing pupil learning?
3. To what extent do cross-cultural differences in learning affect pupil assessment?
4. What assessment strategies can teachers develop to enhance learning, while accommodating the cultural background of the student?

As a general background to discussing cultural context and educational assessment, it is necessary to examine the relationships between learning, teaching and school assessment, as they are so closely linked as far as schooling is concerned. In the section that follows we will address these relationships within the context of the first question posed above.

LEARNING, TEACHING AND ASSESSMENT

As is well known, learning, teaching and assessment are closely related, but in order to understand their relationship within different cultural contexts, it is important to examine some of the key assumptions that underlie the current thinking about assessment and learning in general, and how teachers can accommodate the role of learners in different cultural contexts. Learning in school is no longer thought of as an accumulation process in which the "good" learner knows more. This is the quantitative tradition, of which the behaviourist learning theories are the main theoretical bases and from which learning and teaching can be planned within the framework of behavioural objectives (Bloom 1956).

This tradition emphasises the possibility that knowledge and skills can be categorised into discrete units and packaged into a set of competencies. Cole (1990) describes this as a quantitative approach to learning, and compares it with the qualitative approach which encourages learners to understand, interpret and incorporate new learning into existing learner knowl-edge and skills. The quantitative tradition draws its ideas from Skinner, Watson and, more recently, from researchers into information processing such as Schmeck (1988) and Blumenfeld (1992). There is much emphasis on the study processes of students, as if there were no other situational variables such as school, home environment, and the affective and emotional world of the student. Entwistle & Waterson (1988) and Biggs (1993) are among the main critics of this approach, and Biggs in particular has raised the importance of motivation as a key variable that must be accounted for in the whole process of learning.

The *Student Approaches to Learning* paradigm (SAL) pioneered by Biggs (1993) focuses on the learner and particularly on the role of situational variables in explaining learning. The seminal work of Marton & Saljo (1976) on approaches to learning, in which they distinguished between students who used "surface" and "deep" strategies to solve a task, has been a key stimulus to the formulation of the SAL paradigm.

Students who tackled a particular task from a surface perspective were characterised as using memorisation of facts and detailed knowledge drawn from the task materials. However, students who use the deeper learning approaches to tackle a task prefer a wider view of the problem, aiming at an in-depth understanding of the total problem to be tackled. The work of Biggs, Marton & Saljo and others represents Cole's *qualitative* approach to learning, which assumes that students learn cumulatively, incorporating what they learn with the experiences they already have. It is the role of the teacher in this tradition to help students construct meaning and explanations, building on their own experiences and learning to transfer the knowledge and skills to other similar tasks.

Assessing the quantitative approach to learning relies heavily on criterion reference testing, which indicates to the learner whether or not a correct response has been obtained. This is the principal basis for assessing whether learning has been effective or not. Measurement is a total outcome of a binary system (i.e. correct or not correct), the correct answers being given an item score, which is then added to other item scores, forming an aggregate. Assessment of qualitative learning takes a longer-term perspective, and aims to give students an understanding of their status in the development of a set of concepts or principles. One method to link learning and qualitative assessment in a more meaningful way, would be to establish a hierarchy of understanding for each concept or principle. By situating the test in a developmental and authentic setting, assessment of qualitative learning is made more relevant to what students are likely to meet in everyday situations.

The so-called "backwash effect" in which changing student learning can be produced by changing the examination system is a well-known factor in educational assessment. There are two perspectives to this effect: firstly, the role of teachers and institutions in setting examination tests, and secondly, the student's perception of the institutionally constructed test. Research shows that teachers tend to assess for low-level outcomes and then often produce test items that are too difficult for the students (Marso & Pigge 1991; Reid 1987). The student perspective as far as "backwash" is concerned varies considerably between students. So-called cue seekers are students who are adept at recognising what areas of the course are most likely to be examined. Levels of understanding of a particular subject are often created by the examination itself, these levels being different from what the course originally set out to achieve (Entwistle & Entwistle 1992).

Teacher approaches to learning are also related to the "backwash effect". For instance, Biggs (1979) found that when students were instructed to learn for detail, those who had a predisposition towards a surface approach performed well on tests that assessed facts, compared to those students who were much more attuned to a deeper approach to learning. But deep learners did better on abstracting information from the main text than did the surface learners. In these cases, deep or surface instruction gave rise to the "backwash" rather than the examination itself. While "backwash" is seen to have a somewhat unfavourable effect for meaningful learning, it does motivate students to get to grips with their course content, and may even stimulate them to employ more demanding learning strategies, especially if the assessment is based on qualitative criteria (Tang & Biggs 1996).

The above discussion has attempted to trace the relationship between learning and assessment from two main traditions and the key assumptions that lie behind the use of these traditions. The first tradition that was discussed was the established behaviourist or quantitative tradition, and the second was the more recent constructivist or qualitative approach to learning. The focus of the discussion on the two traditions centred on school learning, as the school is the venue where a substantial amount of experience has been gained over the years about learning, and where research into both learning traditions has been most intense, especially as far as the constructivist approach is concerned. Apart from the work of Biggs and Watkins, research carried out by the other workers referred to above has not focused strongly on cross-cultural contexts. Furthermore, even the valuable work of Biggs and Watkins has not only been rather recent, but it concentrates mainly on Asian societies, and particularly those Asian societies that have a dominant Confucian heritage. Let us therefore continue to consider question two, and examine in more depth the cross-cultural perspective to learning and assessment, and explore what part, if any, cultural context plays in assessing learning.

KEY ISSUES AND PROBLEMS IN CROSS-CULTURAL ASSESSMENT

Psychological testing and assessment have a long tradition in America and Europe, and are a well-established part of mainstream psychology. A major issue has been whether the fruits of this tradition can or should be transferred to other cultures. The transfer of psychological measures developed in Western countries either in the original or modified form has been known to cause serious problems relating to validity and relevance of the measure. Cross-cultural psychologists such as Sinha (1983) working in India and Lonner (1990) in the USA have argued strongly that unless tests are developed within a particular country, they may miss concepts that are significant for that country. While many tests may be successful for Western contexts, it must not be assumed they will be suitable in situations where they have not been initiated.

Psychological assessment helps to categorise people so that their behaviour can be profiled, which assists employers in finding the most suitable employees for a job, it also places students for academic study, or helps to instruct remedial and clinical intervention to be taken. On the other hand, assessment of personality, values or attitudes may be needed at the level of the group rather than at the level of individuals, in order to have a profile of a community. In either case a psychological test, according to Anastasi, needs to be an objective and standardised measure of behaviour (Anastasi 1988). Anastasi's definition applies to objective and formal psychological measures of behaviour for all cultures. The work of Kulkarni & Puhan (1988) in India and Zhang (1988) in China shows how these researchers are working towards psychological measures that are strongly reflective of their own cultural contexts, and yet attempt to meet the rigorous demands described by Anastasi.

Lonner & Berry (1986), Lonner & Ibrahim (1989) and Lonner (1990) among other cross-cultural psychologists have written extensively about the proper development or modification of psychological measures for application in cross-cultural contexts. Walter Lonner, in particular, has identified five recurring methodological issues in cross-cultural assessment and testing, which need to be addressed if we are to have valid measures of behaviour across cultures, and especially when we need to develop such measures for use in schools and colleges. Figure 4.1 shows the five methodological issues in company with a number of socio-cultural and psycho-cultural determinants which may influence the nature of educational assessment devised within specific cultural contexts, and which are discussed later in this chapter. Let us firstly examine each of the issues, followed by a discussion of the determinants in the next section of the chapter.

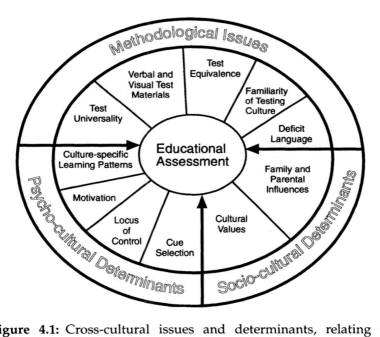

Figure 4.1: Cross-cultural issues and determinants, relating to educational assessment

Familiarity of the Testing Culture

Tests and assessments in school and work are common occurrences in Western countries and many of the so-called Asian
tiger economies, but there are still many developing countries
where testing is much less frequent. In adapting tests from
Western contexts to parts of the developing world, it is important to take this issue of familiarity differential into account.
As Trimble, Lonner & Boucher (1983) have pointed out, there
are at least three assumptions which the tester and researcher
make when using a psychological test. The first assumption is
that individuals can rank order stimuli along a linear scale,
e.g. 1 to 5; a second assumption relates to making judgements
about certain stimuli which may be unfamiliar to people from
other cultures, e.g. sorting and categorising tasks; and thirdly,
that individuals are able to make self-assessments – if a person
is asked to make a judgement on his or her superior, in some
cultures this would be thought of as unthinkable and so the
question would be avoided.

How Universal Are Psychological Tests?

The issue here is to what extent can a test of a concept developed in one culture be or should be transferred to another
culture, as if the features of that concept were the same, and
would not change as a result of the cross-cultural change?
For instance, many Western psychology testing regimens rate
speed and accuracy as key attributes for assessing successful
performance, while in African and some indigenous Latin
American cultures, accuracy is only achieved by quiet con-
templation and thoughtfulness. It is therefore highly danger-
ous to transfer psychological tests to other cultures without
carefully considering the effects of transfer and the outcomes
for construct validity. The way forward is to develop the test
from the cultural context in question, examples of which are
discussed in the later part of this chapter.

How Equivalent Are the Comparative Bases of Tests across Cultures?

Valid comparisons across cultures cannot be made unless the bases for such comparisons are equivalent. For instance, if we were measuring conformity across cultures, it is important to be sure what conformity means to both the cultures being compared. To one culture, conformity may mean total acquiescence to the rules of a society, to other cultures it could mean being selective with the rules in the way they might be interpreted. There are several procedures that need to be controlled for when trying to ensure that tests are equivalent. Firstly, the need for an equivalent translation of the concepts that are being tested is extremely important. Secondly, the cultural familiarity of terms being tested is a crucial factor to be established. For instance, where tests or interviews require people to compare extremes such as poverty and affluence, it is important to establish how culture loaded these terms are in a particular culture. As Brislin (1986) has pointed out, many careful hours of translation and back-translation are required to make tests and other forms of assessments as equivalent as possible. Thirdly, who administers the test or interview is often crucial, for unless the interviewer is familiar with the nuances of the culture being investigated he or she may mislead or even scare the respondent.

Verbal or Visual Test Materials, Which Are Better for Testing across Cultures?

It has been assumed that in some cases comprehension of language is a more variable medium to use than using the visual mode to explain the same phenomenon. The use of pictures and diagrams can often provide a clearer means of communicating a particular task. The argument runs that by removing as much written language as possible from a task or test, one may be a step nearer to achieving "culture fairness" in a cross-cultural situation. However, caution needs to be observed, as some research studies show that just getting rid of verbal material for assessment purposes will not always give clearer and rapid results to the problem of stimulus equivalence. It seems that as previous experience is mostly verbal, it tends to have a marked influence on a person's interpretation of a visual test, as both Bagby (1957) and Deregowksi (1980a) have shown in their respective research work on visual perception.

Use of Deficit Language and Test Result Interpretation across Cultures

Testing different individuals on the same test means that comparisons can be made between Joan and Martha who come from the same culture. In this situation, it is often the case that teachers will make deficit statements such as Martha did less well than Joan, because Martha has poor motivation, is less able or she attends a school in a deprived area. In a cross-cultural situation, where Joan is being compared to Aziza, who comes from a different ethnic and religious background, deficit statements need to be made with great care or even avoided, according to Lonner (1990). The main reason is that unless test items are sufficiently developed to ensure conceptual equivalence, what is being tested may not be what is intended, and will therefore be both invalid and biased culturally. Let us move from a discussion of the main issues and problems connected with cross-cultural assessment, to research that has been carried out into cross-cultural differences in learning and assessment, to see how some of these issues have been addressed and in turn how they influence praxis.

CROSS-CULTURAL DIFFERENCES IN LEARNING AND EDUCATIONAL ASSESSMENT

The conventional wisdom that has emanated from researching learning environments in Western countries is that quality learning is characterised by teachers who encourage their pupils to aspire to the use of deep approaches over surface approaches, when they engage in learning. The use of deep approaches to learning means that students can abstract essentials from detail, use frameworks in conceptualising knowledge and are encouraged to assess their own learning outcomes. In other words, teachers who encourage their students to develop deeper approaches to their studies are in effect improving the quality of thinking by the use of higher-order cognitive skills and strategies. It follows, therefore, that educational assessment will need to reflect the intended outcomes of the use of deeper learning approaches. The development of various forms of assessment, intended to measure the outcomes of deep learning, will pose a particular challenge for teachers. For instance, the construction of appropriate feedback mechanisms including tests and student profiles will have to be developed in tandem with the development of teaching strategies, which will stimulate the greater cognitive demands of a deeper approach to learning.

Research into the impact of educational assessment on learning in cross-cultural contexts has received considerable attention in countries that make up the Asian Pacific rim. In particular, countries like Japan, Korea, China, Taiwan and Singapore, which are included within the Pacific rim, have populations which share a fundamental Confucian heritage; although there is a substantive cultural and linguistic diversity between these nations, they nevertheless hold a set of common cultural values, sometimes referred to as Asian values. Ho (1991) has in fact coined the term for a shared Confucian culture in these countries, namely Confucian Heritage Cultures (CHCs), and referred to in earlier chapters. We will continue to use Ho's term for the remainder of the book. In view of the more recent and substantive research carried out in several CHCs, much of the discussion that follows will refer to findings from this part of the world, but with some reference to assessment and learning in non-Confucian societies in Asia and Africa.

Learning and Assessment among CHC Students: a Success Story with Paradoxes and Misperceptions

We will examine below in the context of cross-cultural differences, and in particular those among CHCs, the proposition that the use of deeper approaches over surface ones is preferable for the qualitative development of thinking. We find that a number of Western researchers such as Murphy (1987), Bradley & Bradley (1984), Samuelowicz (1987) and Purdie & Hattie (1996) record that students from Confucian heritage societies like Singapore and Hong Kong are in the main, exposed to strategies that emphasise rote learning, and that assessment reflects this, by employing measures that rely heavily on recall. In other words, both the teaching and learning strategies that are employed in schools in these countries show a predisposition to surface learning rather than a deeper approach to learning tasks. These observations have fuelled half-truths about the low quality of learning in this part of the world, which has given the impression, critically coined by Biggs (1996), that the student is merely a "tape recorder". Such observations have led educational researchers such as Watkins & Biggs (1996), in their illuminating account of *The Chinese Learner*, to question such assumptions about learning in these cultures.

This is particularly pertinent in the light of contrary evidence mentioned above, which has shown Singaporean and Korean students outperforming their counterparts from Western countries in subjects like science and mathematics. Not only have students from the CHCs outperformed those from Western countries, but when these students continue their studies in Western countries like Australia, the UK and the USA, they continue to outperform their Western counterparts. An even more interesting observation is that the children of Asian migrants (which would also include those from the Indian subcontinent as well as CHCs), who may be born in a Western country, also perform well, some of whom are regularly at the top of their class.

There is clearly a paradox here; on one hand, many Asian students are successful academically, yet on the other, the teaching they receive is mainly characterised by an emphasis on more surface approaches to learning. How, therefore, can this be explained? According to Watkins & Biggs (1996), what we have here is a strong case of misperception, and in this case, a Western misperception of learning and thinking among CHCs. Reports about misperceptions by Westerners relating to the behaviour patterns of non-Western cultures are not new, as has been discussed by other contributors to this series on Culture and Professional Practice. Misperceptions (i.e. misplaced observations) and even misconceptions (i.e. unjustified explanations) are all too common when research findings from cross-cultural studies are interpreted in fields such as child care, communication and legal practice as well as education.

It is argued here that many misperceptions and misconceptions about learning and its assessment in other cultures arise from an ignorance on the part of many professionals about the role played by context, and of the cultural determinants on the behaviour of individuals that belong to a particular cultural group. We will examine two sets of determinants that are likely to shed light on why misperceptions and misconceptions arise, when we try to understand cultural differences in assessing learning. The two determinants are *socio-cultural* and *psycho-cultural*, and they will be discussed mainly in the context of misperceptions of learning in Confucian heritage societies. However, our discussions will also be extended to cover cases of misperceptions of pupil learning from different parts of Africa and Australasia.

Socio-cultural Determinants and Educational Assessment

We will consider two key socio-cultural determinants in the discussions that follow, the first being the *cultural value system of Confucianism* and the second, *familial and parental influences*.

A discussion of these two determinants will hopefully throw light on why many students having roots in a CHC are so successful academically.

The Confucian Ethic as a Determinant   The economic success story of the so-called Asian tiger nations is often associated with high academic success of students from East Asia, as well as those South East Asian countries with ethnic Chinese populations. This association has fuelled intense interest and attention in the underlying cultural ethos of these societies throughout the world. The assumption is that economic and academic success must, in part, be due to the cultural ethos of Confucianism and its close link with Buddhist philosophy.

The Confucian ethic has been compared to the Protestant ethic, with its emphasis on hard work and the high value which is put on education. It was not long, therefore, before people from Asian societies witnessed the strong pervading influence of the Protestant ethic which may have been a key factor in the successful development of Western capitalism. The similarities of retaining an ethical system such as Confucianism alongside that of Protestantism may be important in explaining the scholastic success of East and South East Asian students. This contention is given further credibility when many oveseas students from these parts of the world outperform their Western counterparts. The diligence and positive attitude of Asian students towards education, coupled with a high level of achievement motivation, are consonant with the fundamental Confucian conceptions of learning. These conceptions include a striving for perfectibility and educability for all, and the application of effort to fuel a high level of achievement motivation.

It is no wonder, therefore, that Asian students who possess a strong Confucian heritage with a breadth of skills and attitudes are so successful when they are assessed on a variety of learning tasks. Their high levels of extrinsic motivation follow on naturally from their efforts to succeed. However, on the other hand, the concept of Confucian perfectibility confers a special form of individualism, in which there is a striving for inner peace, and the love of learning something for its intellectual, spiritual and social value. This provides a framework from which a more intrinsic motivation can be developed. Going hand in hand with the quest to achieve perfectibility is the development of a more reflective attitude to learning, and this is sometimes confused by Western educators as a sign of docility, when in fact the student may be approaching a problem in ways that are reminiscent of deep learning strategies.

From the above discussion it is clear that an understanding of the Confucian ethical system, which is so much part of the socio-cultural background of many Asian learners, provides a valuable insight into explaining their scholastic success. It also follows that ignorance on the part of Western observers about the deep-seated value system which surrounds the life and work of those who come from Confucian heritage societies, will give rise to the misperceptions and misconceptions that we have referred earlier in this chapter. While it is obvious that the Confucian philosophical and ethical influence is a major determinant in explaining examination success, we need to examine other factors that may also have a role in the process. Let us examine, therefore, the second socio-cultural determinant, namely that of familial and parental influences.

Familial and Parental Influences as Determinants   Anyone who has worked in the education sector in one or more of the so-called Asian tiger economy countries will have noticed the intense support that parents give to their children's education. This support takes several forms. Perhaps of greatest importance is the issue of homework. Not only is there more set homework on average for Asian students, compared to that given to British and American children, but most Japanese and Korean parents (mostly mothers) spend a substantial amount of time assisting their children with that homework. This is particularly the case for primary-school children. A similar situation relating to pupil perceptions of parental concern involving supervision of homework was also found by the author in Singapore (Thomas 1989). Parental support also takes the form of hiring tutors to coach children in essential subjects like mathematics, language and science, and this may also happen for students attending secondary school.

In Thailand and Vietnam, expensive home tutoring in learning English and computer studies is also quite common. Parental influence is often manifested in the form of strong positive support for institutional schooling and for the status of teachers. This positive attitude towards the teaching profession and to learning in general is a strong Confucianist feature, which is not only part of the learner's cultural make-up, but pervades the home and society from which the learner comes. The work of Fan (1993) in Hong Kong on students writing at home and writing for examinations found that home conditions were more relaxing and amenable. In fact writing at home seems to engender more openness and adaptability in the children's writing. These findings suggest that although homework can be a chore, it seems that home conditions can make the task more enjoyable in some circumstances, so providing us with further evidence of the positive influence of the home on educational attainment.

Finally, the principle of *filial piety* is also likely to figure prominently as part of home influences on educational attainment. Much energy and time (as well as money) are spent by parents on the education of their children, and this in turn is perceived by the sons and daughters as a parental sacrifice to ensure that, they the children, will have a secure future. In response to this perceived sacrifice, the children feel a strong sense of filial duty to succeed in their schooling at all costs. The filial principle is an exceedingly strong determinant of academic success among most Chinese and Japanese students (Thomas 1990), and is closely bound up with the Confucianist ethic discussed earlier.

Psycho-cultural Determinants and Educational Assessment

We will examine a number of psycho-cultural determinants, in order that we may be able to explain further certain aspects of the academic success reported above for Asian students. Four determinants to be discussed include *locus of control, motivation, culture-specific learning patterns* and *cue selection.*

Locus of Control and Motivation   The observation that CHC students are passive and imitative learners, initially at least, displaying the so-called "docility syndrome" has led several workers to investigate the nature of the locus of control and its ramifications on learning among Asian students (Parsons & Schneider 1974; Samuelowicz 1987; Lee 1996). An in-depth treatment of Confucian views about education will reveal that learning is not approached as a surface phenomenon, it can be shown that a deeper approach to the learning process is nearer the truth. The role of reflective thinking in the process of learning is very much part of Confucian tradition, as the following quotation from Confucianist writing shows:

> ... studying extensively, enquiring carefully, pondering thoroughly, sifting clearly, and practising earnestly ... The Mean XX.19 (Lee 1996, p. 35).

A learning process, therefore, that goes through these stages is far from being just a surface affair. It is, however, recognised that initially students may pass through a receptive stage in their learning, in which the locus of control is strongly external, and is the result of authoritative teaching styles. However, it is clear that research from Hong Kong and other CHC societies shows that students are capable of switching from an external to an internal locus of control, in which an emphasis on taking instructions, receptivity and memorisation is followed by periods of analysis, interpretation and "thinking through" ideas (Watkins & Biggs 1996). The later stages of a student's internal locus of control are characterised by an ability to fit new concepts and principles into existing frameworks, thereby improving levels of understanding and meaningful application.

A well-known outcome of a strong external locus of control is its effect on extrinsic motivation, and the way in which CHC students perform in class tests and end-of-term examinations. However, the fruits of an internal locus of control are to be seen in the way students begin to show preferences for understanding and initiating new ideas, rather than just deploying surface strategies to their learning tasks. Watkins (1996) has in fact shown that when Australian students were compared with Asian students, the latter report a higher preference for learning strategies that emphasise understanding other than surface approaches. This shows that Confucian traditions do not only judge success in learning by high levels of test performance, but the tradition also emphasises intrinsic motivation as a key factor in the pursuit of learning as part of personal development. The learning model of motive/ strategy for learning put forward by Biggs (1993) adds the constructs of surface and deep motivation to surface and deep learning respectively. He also includes achievement motivation as part of achievement strategy. Bigg's model therefore puts a strong emphasis on the role of motivation which assists in illuminating the importance of both extrinsic and intrinsic motivation within the Confucian tradition of learning.

Culture-specific Learning Patterns, and Cue Selection Gardner (1989) reported that during his first visits to China to observe art and music teaching, much of the teaching was mimetic (or directive) as opposed to being transformational (student centred). Like many Western observers before and since, Gardner quickly realised that his observations had not taken account of the deep-seated cultural Confucian tradition that pervades much of Chinese pedagogy. Chinese educators believe that, in the first place, emphasis should be put on skill learning which is characterised as being a repetitive and con-tinuous process. This type of learning is a cultural as well as an educational necessity, for it is perceived to be the "right way", and is a pedagogy that stresses careful supervision of learning, by "holding the hand" of the student, which will hopefully lead to more creative and innovative learning.

This type of pedagogical approach is not only found to be a feature of Chinese students; Hess & Azuma (1991) in a comparative study of Japanese and American mothers, teachers and children found a phenomenon known as "sticky probing", in which a particular problem is endlessly discussed by teachers and students until there is agreement on how the problem may be solved. This somewhat public treatment of a problem which a student or teacher has identified is analysed and reconstructed so that the correct solution is eventually reached. It is important to emphasise that this approach to problem solving, together with repetition learning, is a way of laying down the basis for better quality thinking, and should not be seen as rote learning.

Linked to the above culture-specific learning patterns is the ability of students from CHCs to seek out cues – this is espe-cially evident when students prepare for examinations. It has been shown that many students from CHC societies plan much of their learning and prepare for assessment through being highly cue conscious (Biggs & Watkins 1996). That is, students learn to perceive what their teachers will demand of them in a test or end-of-year examination, and they will con-sciously seek out as many cues as possible that will bring them success.

There is, however, always a gap between what teachers say they want from the class, and the tasks that are set by the teachers. This incongruity is especially marked in construct-ing examination questions. Students glean through past examinations papers to spot questions and items, which encourages rote memorisation and discourages critical analy-

:adth of knowledge and skills. However, stu-
ng and Singapore are very adept at "playing
;ame of cue spotting. When surface learning
, the type and content of the tests are much
than for assessment of deeper learning, since
nd answers for the latter approach are far
ıd more discursive. Nevertheless, cue spot-
ting and selection of various sections of subject matter that are
likely to be assessed in a test or examination, are extremely
well practised and certainly contribute to the academic success of many students from CHC societies.

Learning and Assessment in Cultures Other than CHCs

The research carried out on learning and assessment on students from CHCs has shown two discernible trends; firstly, the
propensity to apply surface or deep approaches to learning
seems to be reflected across all CHCs, and secondly, assessing
learning produces a fairly consistent pattern of high academic
achievement. When it comes to explaining these trends,
both socio-cultural and psycho-cultural determinants appear
to play key roles. The influence which these determinants
have on learning and assessment underlines the pivotal role
that context plays in understanding learning and its assessment, especially in cross-cultural studies of behaviour. Let us,
therefore, examine learning and assessment in cultures other
than the CHCs, with reference (where appropriate) to socio-
cultural and psycho-cultural influences, in order to find out
more about the cultural dynamics of learning and assessment
during the years of schooling.

Assessment of Rote and Repetitive Learning as Part of a Learning Culture

The work of Santerre (1975) with Islamic African schoolchildren referred to in Chapter 3 has shown how vital it is to

recognise that there is a strong need for pupils to learn by rote. The role of recitation of passages from the Koran must not just be seen as an automatic mnemonic exercise. The whole act of recitation within the Islamic context is a preparation and an initiation of the young into the value system of a world religion. This is an example of a high-profile socio-cultural determinant of how a certain type of learning is prescribed, and how it may be assessed. Recitation is an essential first stage in preparing the mind for a deeper understanding of Islamic values.

The same argument also applies to students being exposed to Christianity and the teachings of Buddha. The repetitive nature of learning within the Islamic Madrasahs and Buddhist monastic schools is a stage further on from rote in the process of learning, for it allows teachers and peers to correct errors as they go along, and thereby begin to understand the substantive nature of a system of values and beliefs. Feedback in the form of oral and/or written tests is a common mode of pupil assessment in these cases.

In the Northern Nigerian state of Kano in Nigeria, which is predominantly Muslim, rote and repetitive learning are still the norm in the Koranic schools. In the years before WW2 there were no formal examinations; however, in Koranic schools today, examinations are set to test the pupils' ability to learn and remember key passages from the Koran. Even within the state schools, it is not only scholastic attainment that is desired, but parents and teachers require pupils to be respectful and obedient, and this begins by exposing children early on to the teachings of the prophet.

Making Assessment More Applicable to Culturally Relevant Situations

Construction of examination test items should not only probe a student's ability to apply his or her knowledge and skills to school-based tasks, but there should be opportunities for students to apply their skills to situations outside school. In other words, examinations need to account for problems that are likely to be met in everyday life, such as in the home, in the market place, in the shop, playing games and on the sports field. Not only would these examinations make the student focus on application as a necesssary cognitive skill, but they would also use situations and materials that are familiar to the student. Assessment would also be a means of enriching curriculum content as well as assisting in improving the pedagogy.

Educators who take the opportunity of using examinations to improve education provide encouraging prospects for making the curriculum, the pedagogy and the examination system itself more meaningful and culturally relevant to all learners. Kellaghan & Greaney (1992) describe examples of items from the Kenya Primary School Certificate Examination, which provide instances of everyday out-of-school problems. Two of these items appear in Figure 4.2. In the two examples, the content and the location are very well known to Kenyan

---

Item 1

Diarrhoea is a disease that kills many babies in Kenya.
When babies have diarrhoea they lose a lot of water and foods. One correct way to treat babies with diarrhoea is to

A. keep them wrapped up and warm so that they sweat out the sickness
B. give them drinks of boiled cold water containing some sugar and a little salt
C. give them very little food or water until the diarrhoea stops.

Item 2

Wangari lives in a village with many people. From which one of the following sources can Wangari collect the best drinking water?

A. a big river nearby
B. the rain from her mabati roof
C. the dam near the village
D. a swamp on her farm.

Figure 4.2: Two items from the Kenya Primary School Certificate Examination in Health Science (Kellaghan & Greaney 1992)

primary-school children and particularly reflective of their urban or rural cultures. The questions are also requesting the pupils to apply their knowledge and skills about the health issues to everyday situations. In both cases, therefore, socio-cultural and psycho-cultural influences are playing a determining role in the assessment process.

Before we proceed to address the fourth and final question posed in this chapter relating to assessment strategies, it would be valuable to examine what implications cross-cultural research relating to CHCs and non-CHCs may have for the praxis of assessment in multicultural situations. There are three implications that emerge from the experiences and research discussed in this section that could be relevant for successful teaching in multicultural classrooms.

The first implication concerns early recognition of cultural misperceptions and misconceptions. It is clear from the work of Biggs, Watkin and Tang in CHCs, and Santerre in Africa, that teachers should not over-generalise about pupil comprehension on the basis of superficial observations and perceptions. In many cultures, deeper approaches to learning may develop slowly, after pupils have been given a substantive grounding in surface and rote forms of learning. It does not mean that surface learning is the dominant or only mode. An early recognition of such misperceptions, especially where teachers are confronting pupils from several cultures in their class, would certainly not only benefit the learner, but it could also allow teachers to think through pupil assessment strategies more carefully.

A second implication relates to a number of socio-cultural determinants of which two emerge with some prominence from the research reported in Hong Kong and Nigeria. Firstly, the role of a strong philosophical and religious background and secondly, the home and family support of school learning. In considering the socio-cultural determinant of a religious/philosphical background, it is clear that children from CHCs are already on a strong motivational pathway to success, reflecting the strong Confucian ethic with its emphasis on hard work, and the value of having a good education.

Similarly, Nigerian Muslim children who are being instructed in learning passages from the Koran and are constantly being tested for accuracy are provided with a disciplined respect for a religion as well as a firm grounding in surface learning. An appreciation by the teacher of such religious and cultural backgrounds would provide valuable clues about how to manage learning and teaching more effectively in multicultural classrooms. Turning to the influences of family and home, the strong interest of the family and the home in a pupil's schooling is a recurring feature of the cross-cultural research that we have been discussing. Teachers may need to be aware of how much pupils are assisted at home by their parents, e.g. helping them to complete homework tasks. In some CHCs, e.g. Taiwan, Japan, Korea and Hong Kong, as we have seen, the mother is a key person in assisting her child to produce homework on time for the teacher. However, in other cultures the family influence may not be so strong, or it may even be non-existent. It can be valuable for teachers to know whether or not their teaching is being supported at home, so that those learners who receive little home support may be surveyed and given more help in class.

The third implication relates to psycho-cultural determinants, of which the role of pupil motivation, the ability of students to switch between deep and surface approaches to learning depending on the cultural context, and the value of cue selection in determining examination performance, are among the areas that have been recently researched. Knowledge about the importance of these psycho-cultural determinants on the part of teachers, would be most helpful in situations when they wish to know how to control pupil motivation, when the development of deeper learning approaches might be best introduced, and the limited use of cue selection in preparing students for examinations. Let us now examine how various assessment strategies have been developed to meet cultural needs in a variety of countries, including Myanmar (Burma), China, Nepal and Nigeria.

ASSESSMENT STRATEGIES TO ENHANCE LEARNING IN CROSS-CULTURAL CONTEXTS

From the above discussions on learning and assessment, it is possible to improve the process of pupil learning and thinking by developing more meaningful and imaginative assessment strategies. This, in turn, could influence the curriculum content and design, as well as the pedagogy. Let us therefore examine in the final section of this chapter some examples of assessment strategies that have been used to improve the quality of learning within different cultural situations.

Using Continuous Assessment for Improving Levels of Basic Education in Myanmar (Burma)

In the framework of the Myanmar–UNICEF country programme of co-operation, a Continuous Assessment and Progression System (CAPS) has partially replaced old-fashioned teaching and learning approaches to schooling, as part of a policy to achieve universal primary education and to reduce school drop-out to 80% by the early years of the next millennium (Grauwe & Bernard 1995). CAPS is used with children undergoing their early years of primary schooling, and includes the use of teachers' guides, assessment exercises, booklets for children to use in the Myanmar language, English and mathematics. Teaching aids and learning materials include references to local knowledge and skills, and there are manuals for multigrade and remedial teaching when required. A modified competency approach is used in learning, with a type of formative assessment taking place at designated intervals during each term.

CAPS is a major departure from previous practice in Burmese primary schools in at least three ways. Firstly, newly introduced planned and varied assessment procedures aim to improve the level of learning and secondly, learning and assessment activities have been made more relevant, by reinforcing curriculum subjects with a measure of local knowledge and skills. Finally, assessment is now based on a formative system, which monitors pupil performance over the whole time they spend at school. This is in stark contrast to the former summative assessment, and its effect on the quality of learning and teaching.

How School-based Assessment Is Being Used to Enhance Moral Education in China

In the People's Republic of China, abilities are assessed through the school-based assessment system, a much broader approach than that used by the external examination system. The school-based approach embraces moral, intellectual and physical aspects of a student's personal development. There are also varied forms of assessment that are used in appraising student achievement in these domains.

The origins of this form of education come from the days of Mao Zedong, in which the "three goods" concept was introduced for the youth of China. The "three goods" were "good in health, good in study and good in work". The main objective of this form of education was to motivate students to achieve all-round development. Assessment procedures include a considerable amount of student self-assessment, peer appraisal and an ethos of peer learning. These forms of assessment are also used for assessing moral education, the five loves being the main focus of the programme. The five loves include "love motherland, love people, love labour, love science, and love socialism". Moral education continues throughout the period of formal education for all Chinese students, even up to and including the tertiary level (Wang Gang

1996). Ideology is also included as a subject within the moral education curriculum, and is characterised by similar assessment procedures.

Once again we see that various forms of assessment are being used to judge the effectiveness or otherwise of a course of study which is highly cultural in both a Confucian and political/ideological sense. Assessment therefore, appears to have a key role not only in the intellectual development of students, but in their socio-cultural development as well.

Pupil Self-assessment as Part of a Culture Shift in Asian Schools

Increasingly, pupil self-assessment is being added to the repertoire of other measures which profile a student's scholastic attainment. Japan, Malaysia, India and Nepal are among those countries in Asia that have begun to use self-assessment on a wider scale since the end of the 1980s. This is perhaps, a somewhat unexpected observation, in view of the fact that so much school learning in Asia is still teacher centred. However, the use of self-assessment in these countries is still somewhat limited, and the idea of introducing this form of assessment has arisen with the increase in multiple-class or multigrade teaching, where one teacher teaches several grade levels in one class (APEID/UNESCO 1988).

Pupil self-assessment allows children to assess their own performance at certain intervals, either weekly, monthly or longer. The rationale of any form of self-assessment is that the learners are able to recognise strengths and weaknesses themselves, and with guidance from the teacher, they will be motivated to improve upon their weaknesses and build further on their strengths. Self-assessment has become a feature of Japanese education, and the *Japanese Methodological Guidebook for Teachers* contains several exemplars which teachers may use directly, or modify themselves. The exemplars show how self-assessment can be structured for the child's use. A rating scale is used to assess a series of items such as planning work, consultation with teachers and use of tools. Structured self-assessment schedules are also provided for children to comment on their classroom activities, such as getting opinions over to others and their participation in discussion.

These are still early days for self-assessment to become widely used as an established mode throughout the schools in Asia. However, the die has been cast, and learners are being made more responsible not only for their own learning but its assessment as well. From our previous discussions about certain myths and misperceptions surrounding learning and assessment among Asian students, student self-assessment is not likely to be a problem at least for students; whether teachers and educational administrators will perceive it as an issue remains to be seen.

Developing Higher-order Culture-based Cognitive Tests for Improving Pedagogy in Nigeria

Assessment instruments, as we have discussed above, should aim at trying to get a balance between assessing both surface and deep learning. However, research evidence has shown that all too often assessment in many countries targets the relatively easier surface learning tasks, especially where the language of testing is not the mother tongue. If the central aim of education is to foster the development of deeper learning approaches, assessment modes should therefore be developed to realise this aim. By emphasising deeper approaches to learning, teachers should be encouraging students to apply principles to untaught problems and situations, and be innovative and creative about possible solutions to difficult problems. Following this strategy will mean that teachers will have to develop more demanding learning situations in class, therefore putting a greater emphasis on higher-order cognitive skills.

Ogundare (1988) provides evidence from Nigeria, in which primary-school students were taught social studies using a problem-solving approach to the subject, which encouraged students to develop skills of observation, analysis, interpretation and application. Ogundare found that when students used such approaches to their studies, not only did they acquire more facts, they understood them better. They also became adept at using higher cognitive skills such as application and evaluation in other problems.

EDUCATIONAL ASSESSMENT, CULTURE AND PRAXIS

The phrase "cultural bridge building" not only appears in the title of this book, it is also a constant theme running throughout all seven chapters. Nowhere more apt is the need for bridges to be built than in the area of educational assessment. The era of cultural bias and the unfavourable reputation this has had on educational testing especially during the days of Biesheuval and other workers in Southern Africa, are now well known. Since that time, there have been many attempts to make educational testing, and assessment as culture fair as possible. The contribution of recent developments in cross-cultural research into educational assessment, has shown that the quest for culture-fair assessment continues to be taken seriously.

However, it is clear that bridges need to be built between the recent research findings from cross-cultural studies on testing, and their possible use in school assessment. In the light of what has been discussed in the present chapter, there are four main implications for educators who are engaged in developing sound, fair and effective educational assessment in different cultural contexts. These refer to (i) changing views about assessment and learning, (ii) the need to be aware of mis-perceptions of pupil learning and assessment, (iii) research findings of methodogical issues relating to assessment, and (iv) the effect of socio-cultural and psycho-cultural determinants. We will examine each of the four below.

Changing Views about Assessment and Learning

Firstly, the relationship between assessment and learning has been highlighted in recent years by the trend to de-emphasise the cumulative view of learning in favour of a more inter-pretative approach, in which learners incorporate what they learn into experiences they already have. This has particular significance for developing modes of assessment for pupils who come from different cultural backgrounds. Including cultural experiences in the learning process, which will be assessed by measures that reflect these experiences, brings educational assessment several steps nearer to a culture-fair testing regimen.

Misperceptions of Pupil Learning and Assessment

A second implication of the recent cross-cultural research discussed in this chapter as far as teachers are concerned are the issues surrounding misperceptions (and misconceptions) of the abilities of certain ethnic groups. The research by Watkins & Biggs with CHCs in Hong Kong draws attention to the fact that hearsay, unreliable anecdotal evidence, or research that omits to control for cultural context, lead to false stereotyping of certain ethnic groups as far as their cognitive capacities are concerned. It was shown that by probing the complex cultural background of pupils from CHCs, school learning is far from being a surface phenomenon.

Methodogical Issues Relating to Assessment

The research associated with cross-cultural methodological issues examined at the beginning of the chapter (see Figure 4.1) has implications for educators who are concerned with developing appropriate assessment procedures, including classroom tests. Teachers or educational researchers who intend to use tests developed outside their cultural context (etic), but which may need to be modified for a particular context (emic), will find the research relating to test universality, test equivalence and verbal/visual test item preferences particularly valuable in meeting the need for construct validity. Also the nature of test materials, and especially the language in which the tests are presented, would be areas where recent research by Brislin and others has shown how crucial these variables are in contributing to effective and valid forms of pupil assessment.

Socio-cultural and Psycho-cultural Determinants

Finally, educators will find that by being aware of both psycho-cultural and socio-cultural determinants of educational assessment, provides them with a wider picture of learning and assessment within different cultural contexts. Clearly, teachers need to be tuned into any culture-specific background effects that are related to parental and other family influences, which may or may not provide support to school-age children. For instance, to what extent are a pupil's high test scores a function of parental pressure? In the case of CHCs we see that cultural values play a key part in the climates of home and school which are highly conducive to high pupil achievement. The importance of psycho-cultural determinants (see Figure 4.1) is well known in the way they can influence educational assessment universally, but knowledge about culture-specific learning patterns, and an obsession by pupils in some cultures to develop high incidences of cue selection, indicates how a knowledge of the dynamics of a particular cultural context may improve not only praxis but a better understanding of educational assessment as well.

SUMMARY

1. Four main questions were addressed in the chapter which included the following: (i) the relationship between learning, teaching and assessment, (ii) general issues and problems relating to cross-cultural assessment, (iii) how cross-cultural differences in learning affect pupil assessment and (iv) developing assessment strategies that accommodate different cultural contexts.
2. The relationship between learning and the development of new forms of assessment, is being increasingly influenced by the move towards a greater acceptance that learning is more than just a *quantitative* process involving knowledge and skill acquisition; it is also cumulative, *qualitative* and a process in which situational variables such as motivation play an important part.
3. Teachers play a pivotal role in developing forms of assessment that will strike a balance between the use of *deep* and *surface* approaches to learning, which will accurately reflect well-constructed learning and teaching strategies.
4. The *transfer of psychological measures*, to other cultures that have been developed in the West, has caused serious problems relating to validity and cultural relevance; this has resulted increasingly in the construction of tests which are more reflective of cultural contexts, as in India, China and other developing countries.
5. In developing culturally relevant forms of assessment, it is necessary to ensure that the following factors are controlled for as rigorously as possible: *familiarity* of the testing culture, test universality and the *dangers of cross-cultural transfer*, that the concepts being tested are *equivalent*, the use of *verbal or visual* modes in test construction, and the measured *use of deficit language* across cultures.

6. Research on the impact of educational assessment on learning in cross-cultural contexts has been carried out in many parts of the world, but interest in the remarkable academic success of pupils from the Confucian heritage cultures (CHCs) has spawned particular attention on how this has been achieved.

7. Contrary to what has been stated about the preponderance for most CHCs to favour surface approaches to learning and teaching and the effect this has on assessment, the evidence shows that many CHC pupils have a deeper understanding of what they learn at school, and that this is related to both *socio-cultural* and *psycho-cultural* determinants.

8. The influence of *Confucian ethics* and the strong interest of the *home* in children's scholastic achievement are among the most important socio-cultural determinants, while *locus of control and motivation,* and *culture-specific learning patterns* including *cue selection* constitute the key psycho-cultural factors.

9. Research on learning and assessment in cultures other than CHCs has shown that *rote and repetitive learning,* which is an integral part of the learning culture in many Afro-Islamic societies is an important part of learning, as it prepares pupils for a deeper understanding of higher cognitive concepts, leading to the development of tests which approach culture fairness and are reflective of the curriculum.

10. *Innovative assessment* strategies are being introduced into many countries in order to improve teaching and learning; these include the use of *continuous assessment in* Myanmar (Burma), *school-based assessment* in China, *self-assessment* in Japan and *culture-relevant assessment* focusing on problem solving in Nigeria.

SUGGESTIONS FOR FURTHER READING

Biggs, J.B. (1993). What do inventories of students' learning processes really measure? A theoretical review and clarification. *British Journal of Educational Psychology,* **63**, 3–19.

Cole, N.S. (1990). Conceptions of educational achievement. *Educational Researcher*, **19**(3), 2–7.

Fan, F. (1993). How examinations affect students' approaches to writing. In J.B. Biggs & D.A. Watkins (Eds), *Teaching and Learning in Hong Kong: What Is and What Might Be*. University of Hong Kong. Education Papers No. 17.

Marton, F. & Saljo, R. (1976). On qualitative differences in Learning. 1: Outcome and process. *British Journal of Educational Psychology*, **46**, 4–11.

Lonner, W.J. (1990). An overview of cross cultural testing and assessment. In R.W. Brislin (Ed.), *Applied Cross Cultural Psychology*. Newbury Park, Calif.: Sage, pp. 56–76.

Sinha, D. (1983). Human assessment in the Indian context. In S.H. Irvine & J.W. Berry (Eds), *Human Assessment and Cultural Factors*. New York: Plenum, pp. 17–34.

5

THE CULTURAL DYNAMICS OF SCHOOL ORGANISATION AND MANAGEMENT

The concept of management is part of a greater organisational whole, which includes work-related values and attitudes, motivation, job satisfaction and leadership styles as well as different forms of managerial behaviour. To understand organisation and management from a cross-cultural perspective, one needs to have an insight into the cultural goals, values, working practices and challenges faced by managers and their teams, whether in industry, commerce, health management or in education. These insights also hold for school organisation and management, since the drive to provide a better quality education has become equated with good management practice.

Those responsible for education systems in most developing countries have found that not only is it important to improve the level of teaching and learning, but the proper management of resources and the infrastructure of schools and classrooms are equally necessary. However, in most countries education management has only recently become a priority issue, along with curriculum development and teacher education. In fact management forms a necessary and pervasive underpinning to successful schooling.

In developing countries, however, there is a special need to develop management practices that do not blindly emulate the West, from which most models originate. It has already been shown elsewhere in this book that culture has a strong influence on schooling. It has also been shown how culture shapes and melds activities like learning and pedagogy, often resulting in marked changes in educational practice. Similarly, culture has a key influence on how schools and classrooms are managed.

Therefore, the more we know about the nature of management practice as part of the wider cultural context, the more educators working with multicultures will be able to deliver better managed schools and, hopefully better quality education. However, while there is already a large body of knowledge available from cross-cultural research in organisational and industrial psychology (Hui & Luk 1997), alas there is little in the field of cross-cultural educational organisation and management to date. Nevertheless, we will attempt in this chapter to address some of the key issues facing education managers and teachers, who have the task of managing schools and classrooms that are predominately multicultural.

We will examine three key questions relating to the cultural dynamics of educational management:

1. To what extent can recent findings from cross-cultural research into organisational behaviour provide new insights for education managers and teachers?
2. In the light of recent cross-cultural research into organisational behaviour, can education management training models be effectively transferred to different cultural contexts?
3. What are some of the more effective cross-cultural strategies which are being used to manage multicultural classrooms?

Let us therefore examine the first of the above questions.

CROSS-CULTURAL RESEARCH INTO ORGANISATIONAL BEHAVIOUR, AND EDUCATION MANAGEMENT

The major exporter of organisational theory to both Western and non-Western countries has been the USA (Hofstede 1980). Therefore claims that management theories are predominantly Western-centric (Trompenaars 1993) provide no surprises. A review by Adler & Bartholomew (1992) of studies on organisational behaviour and human resource management showed that the concept of culture figured prominently in well over 60% of the studies. They also found that almost 94% of the studies reported that cultural determinants played a salient part in management practice.

Many of these studies have highlighted the fact that unless there is an awareness about the effect cultural influences have on the transfer of certain management strategies to other situations, cross-cultural misunderstandings may arise. On the other hand, a knowledge about cross-cultural mismatches and misunderstandings also provides valuable information for adopting and adapting particular management innovations. In other words we should also learn from the mistakes.

Nevertheless, recent developments in cross-cultural research show that by developing a mix of emic and etic approaches to various cross-cultural problems, we could avoid the excesses of Western-centric dominance, while at the same time taking advantage of the benefits of indigenous practices. For instance, Japanese management practices are showing less deference towards status and age factors than hitherto, and encouraging more open discussion between all team members (Shaw & Welton 1996). In this section of the chapter, we will first discuss some of the pertinent research that has been carried out into areas closely related to management in general, and this will be followed by examining some specific cross-cultural issues relating to educational management.

Cross-cultural Research into Areas of Organisational Behaviour Relating to Management

We will examine research into a number of areas of organisational behaviour relating to management, which may help us to understand the cultural dynamics of managing schools and classrooms. The areas to be discussed include *work-related cultural values and motivation, job satisfaction* and *leadership styles*.

Work-related Values and Motivation

These areas are chosen not only because of their importance in developing good management practice in any school system, they are processes which can be considerably influenced by the cultural context in which educational management is being practised and developed. Most societies recognise, for different reasons, that work is not only necessary but may be good and honourable as well. The Protestant ethic of hard work is rewarding for the individual and allows him or her to worship God at the same time. The Protestant work ethic is not confined to Western countries, for it has its expression in many non-Western cultures as well. The Meaning of Work (MOW 1987) project found that two clear and distinct traits emerged, *entitlement* (in which people hope to gain something as a result) and *obligation* (in which people feel that they are working for something called society). These traits parallel the I–C dimension that will be discussed later in this chapter. The two most common work-related values in East Asia, namely the Confucian and the Japanese style ethic which is derived from it, have been associated with economic success among the Asian tiger countries.

However, in contrast to present-day versions of Protestant individualism, familial and other socio-cultural values are at the core of the value systems in this part of Asia. The Chinese Culture Connection (CCC 1987) identified the factor of Confucian work dynamism (Cwd), which showed that thrift, persistence, respect of authority and status emerged as positive features. It was shown that Cwd ranked high with workers from Hong Kong, Japan and Taiwan, but low with workers from Nigeria and the Philippines (Hofstede 1991). In Japan the work ethic was particularly strong where workers perceive their values in terms of a workspace which fosters character building and spiritual training, as well as relaxation through management-organised sporting activities.

However, the work values of the West are more job specific, embracing features such as the intrinsic worth of the job itself and the material benefits it gives to workers. In general, for many workers in Western society, there is also a strong separation between work and home, where little intrusion into home and leisure is allowed at the end of a working day. But it could be argued that attitudes among Western managers towards working conditions are beginning to change, with the advent of Japanese management practices promoting a more East Asian work ethic.

Much of the cross-cultural research on work-related values has tended to use the I–C dimension as a basis for comparison, but Hui (1988, 1990) has suggested that Hofstede's I–C dimension may be too simplistic. It assumes that collectivists or individualists treat other people all alike. Hui argues that collectivism is target specific, that is people feel solidarity with some people and not others. The way time and attention are distributed among members of a group will differ as a function of kinship, friendship, where they live, and the degree of commonly held values that exists among the group. In other words, it is not whether an individual is concerned with the collective group, but the way the psychological involvement is distributed among individuals and some group members. This is known as target-specific individualism, and influences to some extent the nature of work-related values held by certain cultural groups.

Work-related values are closely linked to motivation and work goals (Ronen 1986). Ronen (1994) found similar work goals for a number of diverse cultural groups which included British,

German, Chinese and other nationalities. He discovered that
the I–C dimension was related to another dimension which
he called materialism–humanism (M–H). He then assigned
each work goal from each culture and proposed that an underlying universal structure of needs could be identified. By
reformulating the Maslow (1954) and Alderfer (1972) cate-
gorisations, Ronen suggested that physiological, safety and
existence needs are equivalent to materialistic collectivism, in
the sense that goals are common to a paid group of employees. Social needs are related to non-materialistic collectivism,
while self-esteem needs are equivalent to materialistic individualism, and self-actualisation and personal growth are
related to non-materialistic individualism. Ronen's work is
an interesting meld of the two dimensions, which could
throw light on how work-related values are influenced by
motivation.

However, Nevis (1983) has pointed out that while the structure of needs may be universal, their relative strengths are
different. In a country like China the notion of "belonging" is
very important and self-actualisation is seen as a service to the
group, the community and the nation. In countries where the
Confucian work ethic is predominant, non-material rewards
are expected and valued. However, in recent years the
Western concept of autonomy has become ranked quite highly
among some Chinese workers (Shenkar & Ronen 1987), so
there is evidence for a degree of mixed motives driving the
workforce.

Job Satisfaction

Successful management is enhanced considerably if workers
derive favourable satisfaction from the job they are doing. Hui
(1990) has shown how important it is to recognise the complex
relationships that exist between the antecedents of job satisfaction. It is obvious from previous discussions that societal
values are a strong determinant of work-related values, and
together with motivational influences will have a significant

effect on the level of job satisfaction. However, job expectations are also a key factor in the realisation of job satisfaction.

Much of job dissatisfaction is related to perceived discrepancies between actual outcomes of the job and the person's expectation of that job. Unrealistically high expectations can lead to low job satisfaction, and this can happen in both Western and non-Western societies as de Boer (1978) found in his research comparing Western and non-Western countries. A person's expectation of a job will also be determined by factors such as personal goals such as prestige, and the cultural values in which that person has been socialised.

There are, however, no conclusive data bearing on the relationships between cultural values, work values and job satisfaction; even so there are important implications for education management as all three areas are integral to good management practice. In almost all developing countries where there is a strong cultural base to their value systems, it is easy to develop a bridge between these values and their interpretation as part of the value system that underpins a school culture. This is because most teachers are likely to hold similar values to those of the society and of the school in which they work, making the task of school management easier.

Alas, in many Western societies the value systems of society, school and those held by teachers are often at variance with each other. It may be that cross-cultural research has important lessons therefore not only for developing countries but for developed countries as well, but for different reasons.

Leadership Styles

Clearly leadership style has an important bearing on the type of management that exists within an organisation. The question of what makes a good leader has had many answers in the past. It is possible to summarise some of the more useful responses provided by social psychologists into three categories. The first set of answers would be those emphasising *personality* characteristics, the second category may be described as *behavioural* which examines observable behaviour patterns, and the third category is called *contingency approaches* which focus on the interaction between the leader and the environment.

More specific details about leadership style will be discussed later in the chapter, in the context of power/distance dimensions and managerial leadership. However, all three leadership categories mentioned above are key components in the development of an effective leader that also have implications for educational management. The research carried out by Nik Hishun (1998) with Malaysian residential secondary-school students, showed how even young pupils recognise these categories as important in developing leadership abilities among educators as well as politicians.

The discussion about work-related values, job satisfaction and leadership needs to be seen further within the context of cross-cultural research into issues concerning dimensions such as I–C, power/distance, uncertainty/avoidance dimensions, and the need for more emic forms of management especially in developing countries. Recent research into each of these issues provides valuable insights into the cultural dynamics of school organisation and management, helping education managers to become aware of the problems of multicultural school management, and to develop strategies to solve some of these problems. It is to a discussion of these issues that we now turn.

Key Cross-cultural Issues and Their Impact on Educational Management

We will examine five current and important cross-cultural issues that pervade both the theory and practice of cross-cultural research, and which are likely to have an important

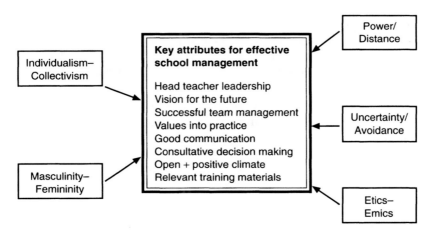

Figure 5.1: Key cross-cultural dimensions involved in the development of effective school management

bearing on the cultural dynamics of school management, especially in multicultural settings (see Figure 5.1). The five issues to be discussed include *individualism and collectivism (I–C), power/distance (P/D), uncertainty avoidance (U/A), masculinity–femininity (M–F) dimensions*, and the *emic–etics* of developing school management strategies.

Individualism and Collectivism (I–C)

To understand culture and cultural differences, workers such as Bhawuk & Brislin (1992), Hofstede (1980) and Hui (1990) have cited the distinction between individualism and collectivism as being among the most important concepts in the more interpreting interactions during intercultural encounters. The distinction between the two concepts is based upon the different goal priorities which a person wishes to pursue. As far as the more, individualistic societies are concerned, e.g. the USA, Canada and the UK, persons have been brought up to put themselves and their ambition before anything else. Generally, the group goals are of a lower order of priority than those of the individual.

In more collectivist societies, e.g. Malaysia and Zimbabwe, individual goals tend to be less important than those of the group, and great value is put on conforming and honouring group norms before self-interest. The seminal work of Hofstede provided a view of culture which consisted of five categories, of which individualism–collectivism was a key category; the other categories included power/distance, uncertainty/avoidance, masculinity–femininity and Confucian dynamics. Trompenaars (1993) also included within his seven categories of culture, individualism–collectivism, like Hofstede.

Kagitcibasi (1990) has pointed out that the most important distinction between I and C is the emphasis which is placed on the feeling and opinions of group members, and the "psychological closeness" between a person and others. Again in collectivist societies, there is more concern about how decisions made by one member of the group will affect others. Decision taken by individualists is much more of a personal affair, and apart from immediate family (in some circumstances), they are not worried about if and how decisions will affect others.

As far as international management is concerned, a key factor in trying to understand the nature of management in a collective society is that persons will tend to treat the company as a collective, and often in the same way as they treat the collective culture at home. This is quite common in Chinese and Japanese companies. However, this is in stark contrast to the individualist, who pursues his own goals, and makes decisions independent of the organisation.

Sharing of knowledge, skills and materials, and a strong measure of conformity are also typical collectivist characteristics. Sharing of rewards on an equity basis (i.e. rewards are distributed on the basis of a person's contribution) is more favoured by individualists, whereas equality of rewards (i.e. all persons receive the same) is more common among collectivist cultures. Data from the research quoted above are mostly obtained from persons working in the world of business, commerce and industry, but their observations about cultural differences have implications for educational management. Let us now briefly examine some of these.

Educational managers such as head teachers and college principals pursue two levels of goals; firstly, those goals laid down by the government and local governing bodies (i.e. the curriculum, budget allocation, teacher pay and rewards), and secondly, those goals which the manager may be able to set (i.e. day-to-day running of the school, extra-curricular activities, fundraising). In collectivist societies, meeting the first goal level is mandatory, with strong central control to ensure its achievement. In meeting the second level goal, the manager has more latitude. However, goals that put the school as the priority mean the staff will tend to act in line with the ethos of a collective culture. This, in turn, is reflected in the type of management style which puts collegiality before individuality. The "psychological closeness" referred to earlier plays a key role in promoting a school ethos among the staff, so enabling decisions to be taken by the head teacher with little dissent from the staff.

Where both managers and their staff come from collectivist societies, collective-style school management practice is often a natural extension of home collectivist culture, and so the cultural transition is smooth. The strong familial ties of persons from collectivist societies, labelled *familism*, transfer naturally across into the group as shown by research carried out in India by Sinha (1994) and by Negandhi (1984) in Uruguay. However, group affiliations tend to be strongly based on obligation between group members, a dominance of group decision making leaving little opportunity for any form of individualism.

In all this, the goals of organisational effectiveness and efficiency may be compromised. Although there is little research on the effect of familism on management practice in education, from the author's experience of working in Singapore and Malaysia certain familistic attitudes do filter through into interpersonal relations among school staff; for instance, obligation and pooled decision making are common on a day-to-day level.

However, it is difficult for teachers and managers under these conditions to show openly their individualist ambitions, e.g. to aspire to become a head of department, or perhaps a school head. However, by developing training programmes which would include the advantages of both individualistic and collectivist approaches to school management, it would be possible to develop an acceptable level of individualism among "budding" managers, as it would be part of the training programme.

For highly individualistic cultures, where it is thought desirable to achieve the goals of collegiality, staff co-operation and sharing of ideas and practices among staff, school management training will need to reflect these collective attributes in much the same way that would be planned for collective-centred school organisation and management. All in all, characteristics of individualism such as self-reliance, autonomy, independence and confidence relate well with head teacher leadership and future vision, while collectivist characteristics such as shared goals and beliefs, and group dominance fit in with school management attributes like team management and translating values into practice (see Figure 5.1).

Power/Distance (P/D) Dimensions and Managerial Leadership

In company with individualism–collectivism, P/D is perhaps the next most important cultural dimension to consider when we discuss the cultural dynamics of management practice, and particularly the dynamics of educational management. This is because so much of educational management in non-Western countries has yet to be influenced by management ideas which regard top-down decision making as being coun-terproductive for effective human resource development. Hofstede included P/D as one of the five cultural dimensions that can assist us to distinguish between different cultures, as far as work practices are concerned.

Power/distance is the amount of emotional distance between employers and employees. In high P/D cultures, employees prefer managers to lead, and to answer to leadership styles that are paternalistic, caring and authoritative. In low P/D cultures, employees will express themselves more openly. They will also expect to play an active part in decision making. The concept of P/D is closely linked to the notion of leadership, and as the usual management functions such as planning, organising, staffing, directing and control are subsumed under the broad category of leadership, then fulfilling these functions will also be closely related to P/D.

We will continue to discuss cross-cultural perspectives to the P/D dimension within the notion of managerial leadership, in which the features that constitute good leadership are dove-tailed where necessary and where possible into those charac-teristics that make for sound and effective management practice.

Cross-cultural Perspectives to Models of Managerial Leadership
There are several approaches to managerial leadership that have been researched cross-culturally and which may have implications for better management practice in different cultural contexts. We will examine four approaches which are internationally practised, and in which a certain amount of cross-cultural research has been carried out. The four approaches are *two-dimensional*, *situational*, *participative* and *team arrangements*.

Two-dimensional approaches to managerial leadership include the Ohio State leadership theory, which postulates the importance of "initiating structure" and "consideration" as key dimensions of leadership. In "initiating structure", the leader serves a distinct set of functions to subordinates, such as task structuring, role clarification and task requirements. "Consideration" includes mainly providing socio-emotional support to subordinates. Western data suggest that the more a leader shows the characteristics of these two dimensions, the more successful the leader is likely to be (Tjosvold 1984).

Another two-dimensional analysis of leadership is labelled transactional and transformational (Bass 1985; Burns 1978). Transactional leadership has a strong emphasis on contingent rewards, whereas transformational leadership includes charisma and individualised consideration. Misumi (1985) in Japan has a two-dimensional view of leadership, which includes an emphasis on the subordinates' performance (P) and consists of pressure to work hard as well as planning the work. The other dimension is an emphasis on maintenance (M) of work group solidarity, harmony and good interpersonal relationships.

It is argued by Misumi that this PM theory is superior to other styles of leadership, especially in collectivist societies. For the PM theory to work in Chinese societies, however, Peterson (1988) suggests that a third dimension is needed called C, which includes a moral dimension, so giving us the PCM model.

In the context of both the P/D dimension and the cultural dynamic of educational management, the range of two-dimensional approaches discussed above would have implications for developing school management strategies in different cultural contexts, if they were to be considered. However, a key consideration will be the form the P/D dimension takes in various cultural contexts. In schools where the culture is supportive of strong paternalistic but authoritative characteristics, PM and PCM models would be suitable. Where contexts are more supportive of participation and consideration, transformational models are likely to be more successful.

The *situational* model of Blanchard, Zigarmi & Zugarmi (1985), which is closely related to Fiedler's (1967) contingency theory of leadership, is a tailor-made approach to leadership management. Each member of a team is catered for in order to meet his or her specific needs as a manager. The most appropriate leadership style is selected (such as directing, coaching, delegating, supporting), to match the manager's motivation, commitment and competence. These styles are selected for a particular individual, and for a particular set of tasks. The effective use of this model would result in better task sharing, a stronger sense of ownership among the team, together with improved levels of management skill of the team members.

The model is well suited to low P/D, highly individualistic cultures, and if it were to be used on collectivist and high P/D contexts, considerable adaptation would be necessary. Shaw & Welton (1996) suggest, however, that cultural differences should not be used as an excuse for not experimenting with this model of leadership. The use of the various leadership styles, e.g. coaching, delegation, should be discussed to see how suitable they may be for a particular context. In the main, directing and delegating leadership styles are easier to promote in collectivist, high P/D cultures, whereas coaching and supportive styles are treated with suspicion and generally go against the grain.

Nevertheless, in countries like Singapore, Malaysia, Thailand, South Africa and Nigeria, management training which encourages the use of a mix of managerial leadership styles, typical of both low and high P/D cultures, is starting to take effect. It appears that the success of employing various leadership styles at the school level depends upon a thorough cultural analysis of a particular context (see Chapter 3, p. 94). For instance, in Singapore there has been since the late 1980s an

impressive attempt to develop a more supportive management style among teachers.

The school principal and his or her deputy, having themselves
been trained previously in new management techniques, then
pass the appropriate knowledge and skills on to their staff.
While the P/D dimension is still relatively high in Singapore,
compared to the situation in the 1970s and early 1980s, it is
probably lower and more amenable to exploring new ideas
and practices, in view of government policies that encourage
a more open style of school management.

Participative management, it has been argued, depends not on
cultural values, but on managers' perception of the need to
ensure quality, and on team members' acceptance of, and
commitment to, the decision. This has been supported by
the work of Bottger, Hallein & Yetton (1985) in Australia,
Africa and some Pacific islands, who showed that cultural
explanations for differences in management practice were
de-emphasised. However, it has been shown by other
workers that participative management practices, especially
in collectivist societies, have an adverse effect on performance, because subordinates are not prepared to act without
direction (Tannenbaum 1980; Whyte 1983). Sinha (1973),
working in India, discovered that when subordinates were
asked to participate in decision making by their employers,
the subordinates perceived them as weak.

Team arrangements have different effects on management
practice, especially within the constraints of the P/D and I–C
dimensions. For collectivist cultures, working with the in-
group is motivating for most members, while for individualists, working alone is more so. It has been shown that for most
Japanese personnel, teamworking has a positive effect on the
quality of team management, where the responsibilities are
shared. This is later reflected in a greater degree of work
commitment and improved levels of performance (Kalleberg
& Reve 1992).

As far as education management is concerned, both participative and team management approaches have considerable merit, as they seek to engage all the significant players in meeting the goals of effective school management. The two approaches emphasise sharing of responsibilities, and in essence, therefore, should find accord with collectivist cultures. However, school organisation and management in most developing countries are still typified by a top-down approach, which favours high P/D between the head teacher and the teaching staff.

In most cases, high P/D and a collectivist culture go hand in hand, and the strong hierarchical features of high P/D will mitigate against group decision making that is perceived by the head teacher to override authority. It is, however, possible that where there are strong common goals between the school head teacher and staff, team and participative practices are likely to become part of management practice. For instance, the management of the Harambee schools in Kenya, and the community schools pioneered by van Rensburg (1978) in the 1960s and 1970s in Botswana, showed how participation and team arrangements can work inside and outside schools. The unifying concern as far as these African schools were concerned was to get school and community working together, so that shared responsibilities were delegated in such a way that parents (who often provided much of the money) and the staff and pupils had a common goal; namely the creation of effective and efficient schooling for their community.

Uncertainty/Avoidance (U/A)

The amount of emotional distance between managers and those they manage constitutes Hofstede's U/A dimension. People with a high U/A index prefer predictable situations so they know what to expect. For instance, such persons perceive a manager to have a certain status and prefer that his or her roles are clear and well established. Persons who have high U/A are usually not high risk takers. On the other hand,

persons with a low U/A index are happier with role diffuse-
ness, prefer taking risks and are more willing to challenge
authority. Head teachers who encourage low U/A are more
likely to get their staff involved in team management as well
as taking part in group decision making.

However, in most developing countries, education management is characterised more by high U/A, in view of a long-
established hierarchical cultural tradition, which is highly
resistant to change. Clearly, an effective education manager
will have to balance the needs for both degrees of emotional
distance, depending on the situation.

Masculinity–Femininity (M–F)

This is another of Hofstede's original work value dimensions
which he actually labelled masculinity (Hofstede 1980). This
value dimension is related to the degree to which achievement
orientation is part of a certain culture. It particularly refers
to gender expectations, in which high-masculinity cultures
value status, challenge and high achievement, while high-
femininity cultures value good working relationships and
co-operation. Since Hofstede's work in the early 1980s, much
has changed concerning the role and status of women in
many Western societies, but to a much lesser extent in developing countries. Gibbons, Stiles & Shkodriani (1991) compared gender and family roles among Dutch people, and
those recently arrived from developing countries who were
now living in the country. They found that those from the
second group showed more traditional attitudes towards
gender roles, but that girls responded less traditionally than
boys.

There is a real danger that the M–F dimension leads to stereotyping of gender roles, and that this can be extended into
school management especially in developing countries.
According to Best & Williams (1997), the strength and activity
differences between male and female stereotypes were greater

in developing countries, where levels of literacy and basic education were low, and in countries where the number of women with university education is sparse. To reduce these effects, better economic conditions and improved access to education clearly need to be high on the agenda. Best & Williams also commented on the current research into gender stereotyping. They conclude that female stereotyping appeared more favourable and less weak in Catholic countries than in Protestant countries, and this may be due to the greater role of women in the Catholic tradition.

The research on gender roles, and especially that relating to sex trait stereotypes, self-esteem and culture-specific practices, has clear implications for the development of education managers who will obviously have both male and female personnel to manage. All the key attributes for effective school management discussed in the next section, and appearing in Figure 5.1 (middle box), need to be developed irrespective of gender status. However, in school cultures where there exists a strong tendency towards masculinity (in developing countries many head teachers are male), it is important to involve women teachers as much as possible in team and consultative management. An increase in the numbers of women being promoted to headships would be another measure to ensure balance, less stereotyping and the provision of more representative role models for female pupils.

The Emics and Etics of School Management Practice

It may be useful at this juncture to remind the reader about the meaning of the terms "emic" and "etic" in our discussions about the cultural dynamics of school organisation and management. The term "emic management" refers to the use of strategies that derive from a particular culture's approach to managing people, while "etic management" refers to the use of management strategies that arise from outside a specific cultural context, but may be prescribed for use within that context. For instance, an emic management strategy would be the continuous use of debate among parents about areas such as pupil access or what pupils are taught. This form is common among certain indigenous Peruvian groups who have a debate with the head teacher who then makes a particular management decision relating to the pupils. An etic management strategy would be the introduction of a situational or two-dimensional type of managerial leadership into a local context where top-down autocratic styles have previously been the dominant pattern.

The emics and etics of school organisation and management are perhaps the most difficult to write about in view of the paucity of information that exists on the subject, yet it is becoming an ever-important subject in view of the reports of failure of the cultural transfer of Western management models to developing countries (Rodwell 1998).

The previous discussions about models of managerial leadership, and the research derived from these models, suggest that outside the education sector there have been developments taking place to make management more accountable to local conditions. For instance, the work of Bottger, Tannenbaum, Whyte, Sinha and Kalleberg (cited earlier in this chapter) provide plenty of evidence of the success, or otherwise, of participative and team arrangements for management practice in commerce and industry. What emerges, however, from much of the findings is that the failure to change management and leadership styles among institutions in non-Western contexts is mostly linked to the fact that insufficient "cultural homework" has been done on the part of overseas advisers, about how people can be prepared to accept, and actively engage in, change that affects them personally.

However, the cultural dynamics relating to school management and organisation that typify the situations encountered by managers of the Harambee schools in Kenya (Hill 1991), the non-formal education Sorowe brigades in Botswana (van Rensburg 1978), and the Australian Aboriginal schools described by the Teasdales (1994) in Australia's outback provide valuable information on how culture-specific management strategies can be used in these societies, to ensure the type of schooling they think is most appropriate. Another cross-cultural instance would be the way partnership decision taking, relating to school access and the need for curriculum relevancy, is accomplished among the Peruvian indigenous peoples of the Amazon region (Aikman 1994). The research by Aikman shows how tricky contextual problems concerning preferred language use, and the ownership of their indigenous form of education, can be maintained by employing their particular style of management, in the face of more aggressive etic practices.

It is clear that emic management strategies would be often desirable so that management and leadership styles characterise a particular cultural context. This is particularly pertinent where a policy exists which advocates closer school–community relationships, or where there is a need to make the school curriculum and organisation culturally relevant to both pupils and teachers, as in the Peruvian and Aboriginal cases.

However, culture-specific autocratic management practice results in a lack of commitment among staff and also low morale, so there is a need for etic strategies that advocate greater staff participation in school management, with opportunities for more teamwork to promote staff collaboration and collegiality. More shared decision making, and a greater use of two-dimensional management leadership, which have been successful in other cultures, could also be part of a repertoire of ideas and should be on offer for education managers in any culture.

From the cross-cultural research into organisational and management practice discussed so far, it appears there is a place for both emic and etic management strategies in different cultural contexts, and this applies to school management as it does to other sectors such as industry and commerce. In many instances, the successful interchangeability or reciprocal use of emic and etic management strategies is likely to be the result of well-planned cultural transfer as part of effective management training.

In conclusion, cross-cultural research reported above in a number of areas does provide some valuable insights and direction for developing more effective management practice in schools and classrooms. The research on work-related values and motivation has shown how having a strong set of values, as in the CHCs, provides a sense of belonging and sharing, which can be a valuable asset in making management a participative process in school. The research on I–C provides useful insights into the way management decisions may have to be made about group issues, as well as factors that influence an individual's personal career development.

Understanding how the P/D dimension in various cultures works is also important, when introducing ideas about shared team decision making. The value of being able to assess the impact of U/A, and M–F factors which may emerge in the course of day-to-day school management, will also enable education managers to make more informed decisions involving high risk and gender sensitivities respectively. The research discussed above points to the need for more in-depth cultural analyses of a particular cultural context, before radical practices are introduced, if failure is to be avoided.

Finally, by examining different management cultures, it is important to develop a balance between retaining emic or culture-specific elements alongside incoming etic influences and experiences, as experienced in our references to the Peruvian and Australia aboriginal cases above. These cases and others discussed later in this chapter provide insights into how a balance may be achieved. It may be that training head teachers to develop a balance in their application of different management practices, should figure prominently in future management training programmes. It is to the subject of education management training and cultural transfer that we will now turn.

EDUCATION MANAGEMENT TRAINING, AND THE ISSUE OF CULTURAL TRANSFER

In this section we will examine the second question posed in the introduction to this chapter, of how education management training may be transferred to other cultural contexts, in the light of recent cross-cultural research into organisational behaviour and management practice. In recent years, there have been considerable developments relating to the field of educational management in Western countries, where management has increasingly been perceived as being not just an organisational adjunct to the process of education, but an integral part of it. The adoption of effective and efficient management practice is now recognised to be at the heart of implementing policies that promote effective teaching and learning, providing valid modes of pupil assessment, the enhancement of a favourable school ethos, and the professional development of all grades of staff.

Many examples of successful school management in countries such as the UK, Sweden, Australia and the USA have been taken as models for improving educational management in Asia and Africa, some with a reasonable measure of success, e.g. Singapore, Malaysia and Kenya, but others with serious problems relating to adaptation and transference. We will first examine in outline some of the more recent ideas in educational management training, and the cross-cultural problems associated with the transfer of ideas and practice.

Recent Ideas in Educational Management Training

As Rodwell (1998) has pointed out, the importance of educational management development is now recognised throughout the world. However, educational management is not just about applying particular models and theories to school organisation and administration, and ultimately to classroom practice. It is also about developing a positive ethos in the school. Working for a positive school ethos goes hand in hand with the aim of developing an effective and efficient management strategy.

Management is concerned with many aspects of school life, it is about working conditions for staff and students, it is about aims and objectives of the school and how the outcomes are assessed. Management is also about the extent to which there are shared values between staff and students, and between them and society, including politicians who ultimately control the education system. In other words, the success of developing and applying sound principles of educational management will depend upon key players such as head teachers, their staff and students all playing their part, so that effective management results in the development of a favourable school ethos.

According to a recent study about effective school management in the UK (DFE 1992), high levels of head-teacher leadership, a clear vision for the future of the school, and the existence of successful team management emerged as key factors in the development of educational management. In the same study consistency between espoused values and practice, effective means of communication and consultative decision making, coupled with an open and positive climate within the school, also appeared to be important determinants in making schools easier to manage.

In recent years, there have been significant changes in the thinking behind developing new alternatives to areas such as traditional teaching and learning, school improvement and school effectiveness, and how schools are managed and administered. The approaches to educational management have increasingly focused more on knowing about actually engaging in management practice, as well as knowing about the theories which underpin various management strategies. Where schools have been given greater autonomy to run their own affairs, there is a need for head teachers to have a training that is mainly school based, and with a strong emphasis on "management self-development" (MSD). This approach to management training requires considerable initiative on the part of head teachers.

In the UK, the School Management Task Force Report (DES 1990) predicted a shift from tutor-directed training to school-based self-directed learning in groups. The emphasis for school managers to take full responsibility for running their schools is extended further, whereby the school manager takes more of the decisions about his own training. Several models of MSD are based on a set of ideas derived from the reflective practitioner (Schon 1983), experiential learning styles (Kolb 1984) and job-related problem solving (Revans 1982). Some of these ideas are starting to filter through to school management styles in many parts of the world. Another trend is to develop mentoring for school heads as a key management skill, and to bring in a more competency-based approaches to training managers. These ideas would be the bases for further innovations to management training in schools.

There is a growing trend not to advocate one particular model of MSD, or any other new approach to educational management. According to Rodwell, the need for a mix of models is gaining greater support, in view of the fact that selecting a particular training model for one situation, and then discarding it for another later on, due to policy change, reflects an *ad hoc* approach to planning and policy formulation (see Figure 5.2).

The use of one particular management training model, or a mix of several in one culture, has implications when the need arises for their transference to a different cultural context. For instance, in countries like Sri Lanka and India management training has been mainly tutor driven and based at an insti-

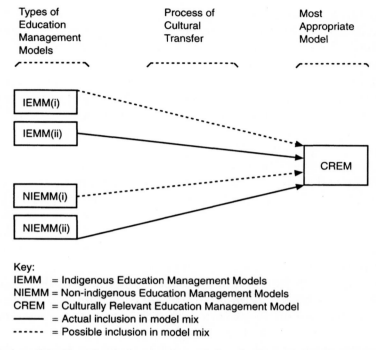

Figure 5.2: Developing mixed models of education management through cultural transfer

tution of higher education, providing an element of prestige to the training. Relocating training to a primary or secondary school, situated near a Malaysian *kampong*, may look like a good idea to an outsider, but would be perceived by most head teachers as having less importance than if the training was carried out at an education faculty or government training institute. This example reflects a contextual problem of cultural transfer among others which will be discussed below.

Problems of Cultural Transfer

In the 1980s and 1990s there has been a substantial demand in developing countries for better management strategies, not

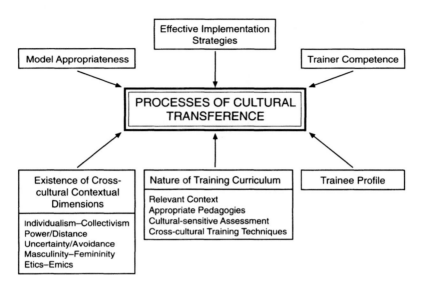

Figure 5.3: Factors influencing cultural transfer of education training models

only in education but in sectors such as health and industry. Many developing countries have looked to the USA, Australia and the UK for assistance in management training. Agencies such as the Commonwealth Secretariat (1994) and UNESCO (1986) have also been active in promoting materials for innovative practice in managing schools and colleges. However, there have been many problems and factors concerning the transfer of ideas and practices about educational management from Western countries, to less developed societies (see Figure 5.3). The main problems include lack of materials for training, poor expertise of trainers, lack of commitment by governments to implement changes, and in many cases the cultural inappropriateness of the models that were advocated by the overseas experts.

In view of some of the failures relating to transfer, educational researchers such as Johnson (1995) in South Africa and Kulasena (1992) in India and Sri Lanka have begun to develop approaches that seek to combine both traditional and innovative ideas into strategies that match the culture of management needs in a country or region.

It appears that the common occurrence of uncritical transfer has been responsible for many failures, both now and in the past. Nevertheless, internationalisation continues apace in many developing countries, reinforcing ill-considered innovatory transfer, which is undesirable in the long term. However, there are moves afoot to explore the possibilities of making more vigorous adaptations to selected Western models, coupled with a search for indigenous strategies, from commercial and industrial sectors (Kirkbride & Tang 1992), and from the education sector in Peru (Aikman 1994) and in Australia (Teasdale & Teasdale 1994).

There are several constraints that operate during the process of cultural transfer:

- The nature of context
- The personnel receiving training
- Psychological profile of the trainees
- The curriculum for management training

We will briefly examine each below.

The Nature of Context

This constraint is about the essential need to get an accurate picture of the context into which new ideas will be put into action. The use of techniques that emphasise the value of thorough *cultural analysis* of the situation, coupled with a careful process of *cultural selectivity*, are likely to give the transfer process a good start. Issues such as the degree of collectivism or individualism, an accurate picture of P/D relationships, and an assessment of the status of the U/A dimensions together with the nature of the value system that underpins the socio-cultural fabric of the society, would need to be explored as part of the contextual analysis (see cross cultural dimensions box in Figure 5.3).

The Personnel Receiving Training

This constraint refers to the personnel that will be trained, such as school principals and their deputies, senior teachers, office managers and sometimes teachers. Factors such as age, qualification, length of service and experience in management are likely to affect the transfer of new ideas and practices. For instance, where a principal has been using a particular management style for most of his or her career, attitude and especially behaviour change that are associated with cultural transfer become more difficult to achieve in these circumstances (see Trainer Competence box in Figure 5.3).

Psychological Profile of the Trainees

A psychological profile refers mainly to the cognitive and personality characteristics of the personnel being trained. Clearly if the personnel are well motivated, have a high self-esteem and self-concept, the chances are that such persons are likely to be more sympathetic to the take-up of new ideas. From the cross-cultural research referred to earlier in this chapter on work-related values and motivation, there are distinct differences in the way people from different cultures are motivated, as far as their work practices are concerned. Transferring new management practices from the British or American school system to countries like Taiwan or Japan would require a careful cultural analysis as to whether the new practices could embrace notions such as "belonging" and "sharing" and service to the group (see Trainee Profile box in Figure 5.3).

The Curriculum for Management Training

The training curriculum includes subject content, the skills and techniques associated with an innovation, as well as the modes of delivery. To tackle these issues satisfactorily, it is necessary that the curriculum is designed to reflect as much cultural relevance as possible, and that teaching and learning strategies are "culture sensitive" (Thomas 1997b),

otherwise the credibility and validity of adopting and implementing new ideas about educational management will be
seriously questioned by those experiencing the transfer (see
Training curriculum box in Figure 5.3). Considerable cultural
barriers are set up, not only if the training content is perceived
as irrelevant, but is delivered in such a manner that the
trainees cannot locate the management concepts and principles within their own specific cultural context.

In addition to these constraints can be added a lack of
resources for training, poor expertise of trainers and the
inappropriateness of the management models advocated by
overseas experts.

Cross-cultural training has been the subject of much research
in recent years. Studies by Hofstede (1980, 1991) and Brislin
(1994) on cross-cultural differences in organisational behaviour have drawn attention to the fact that it is important to be
aware of cultural differences when interpreting management
practices in different societies. These issues are discussed
further in Chapter 7.

The discussion above which attempts to answer the second
question posed earlier has shown that the existence of a core
of value-free managerial concepts that can be transferred
across cultures (Sims & McAulay 1995) is being increasingly
questioned by those who seek effective and relevant management practice, more suited to local conditions (Safavi 1992). It
is argued that better adapted versions of existing Western
models that incorporate certain cultural ideas and skills,
might be the beginning of polycentric management development (Shaw & Welton 1996; Rodwell 1998).

However, a search for more indigenous strategies that will
address psycho-cultural and socio-cultural issues related to
the cultural transfer of management practice might be a better
way forward for many developing countries (Bajunid 1996).
However, even if the search for more indigenous strategies

proves to be successful, educators would be well advised to examine in some detail to what extent the constraints identified above may need to be considered before cultural transfer is finally implemented. Let us now turn to some case studies of cross-cultural management strategies that are being used in multicultural classrooms in different parts of the globe.

MANAGEMENT STRATEGIES IN MULTICULTURAL CLASSROOMS

In this final section of the chapter, we will move our focus from educational and school management in general to class-room management, as we address the third question posed earlier in the introduction. Classroom management varies across different cultural contexts in terms of its strategies and ideology, and it also differs between and within countries. Most variations relating to class management may reflect the culture and ethos of the school, teacher culture and the community. Management strategies will differ as to whether the school is a primary or secondary institution, or whether it is situated in a deprived area or one of affluence, and will also depend on the cultural profile of the school population, i.e. to what extent it reflects one or more cultures. It is clear from the above that not only is classroom management a complex subject, but because of its complexity there is no particular strategy that can be adopted by all teachers.

Nevertheless, classroom management is needed in order that teaching and learning are able to take place as effectively as possible in whichever country that classroom is situated. The need for order, control and the realisation of certain academic and social goals which are laid down by the school are universal prerequisites, irrespective of cultural factors. However, in situations where the pupil composition of a classroom is predominantly multicultural, knowledge and understanding about the different cultural backgrounds from which these pupils come are not only desirable but essential. Let us examine a number of strategies that reflect different approaches to class management from different cultural and international perspectives.

Classroom Management Strategies for Diverse Cultural Contexts: Some American Challenges

Carol Weinstein (1998) has discussed at length the shift in the nature of classroom management practice in the USA since the 1970s. She has also commented on the cultural mismatches that happen all too often, when white American middle-class teachers try to manage pupils who come from different cultural backgrounds.

There has been an increasing recognition that managerial strategies developed by white American middle-class teachers for their selfsame social class do not meet the needs of children from other cultures (Grossman 1995). Lisa Delpit (1988) has examined issues of power and authority in the classroom where so-called progressive teachers use indirect statements or veiled commands, when speaking to black children, instead of using direct demands. Delpit records that black children expect teachers to act as authority figures, and when the teacher does not, by being too friendly, the trust is lost in the teacher.

In a case study of an African American second-grade teacher (reported by Noblit 1993), who taught that caring is not about democracy but about the ethical use of power, instruction was teacher centred, rules were prescribed and penalties imposed where violations occurred. The teacher acted out of a sense of moral authority, and a willingness to take responsibility for providing a context in which children could participate fully for their own good, and for the good of their own culture.

In another case Ballenger (1992), an experienced early childhood teacher, had considerable behavioural problems with

Haitian pre-schoolers. She describes how she learned from the more successful Haitian teachers how to tackle these children's behavioural problems. Ballenger listed the Haitian teachers' questions relating to the pre-schoolers' bad behaviour. Questions included "Does your mother let you bite?, Do you kick at home?" Invariably answers by the children were "No". The Haitian teachers would also say to the badly behaved children that "they were not bringing to school, the good ways of their home". Ballenger's analysis of the interactions shows that Haitian teachers stress collectivist values of the group, to appeal for better behaviour. Haitian teachers also refer to the act of biting or kicking as bad and explained the consequences afterwards, unlike American teachers who tend to do the opposite.

Finally, the use of rhetorical questions by the Haitians implies the children already know it is wrong to misbehave, in contrast to the American teachers who seem to be presenting new information to the children. It soon dawned on Ballenger that by adopting the above cultural-specific strategies to manage the children's behaviour, she was able to be much more successful at managing these types of cross-cultural dilemmas.

The case studies above show that different cultural contexts faced by many American teachers in day-to-day classroom situations are providing interesting but difficult challenges for effective class management. The combination of authoritative and caring approaches to form a new paradigm for the development of class management strategies is the result of meeting the rigorous demands of teaching in cross-cultural situations.

Culture-Specific Management Strategies for Developing a Classroom Community: Realising a Japanese Goal

There are a number of tenets which are associated with the development of management activities in Japanese classrooms. Firstly, in Japan schooling is primarily a group concept and the objective of classroom management is to socialise children into the group. Secondly, a principal task of classroom management is to develop a sense of community where trust, emotional security, empathy and *kokoro* (or heart) are essential ingredients of good management practice. *Kokoro* is a central concept in Japanese education, and is about developing the child's sense of well-being and his or her relationships with peers, teachers and others.

Thirdly, developing an effective classroom community is based on the notion that children's participation in self-management is a priority for teachers. Self-management means setting goals, performing classroom duties and signing up to all sorts of classroom duties called *kakari*. This particular interpretation of self-management tries to ensure that pupils have as much shared experience as possible and learn how to be responsible for what they do. The teacher is a full participant in this process, offering advice and help where necessary.

Finally, classroom management is about developing, for each child, the notion of a total education, which attempts to meld individual uniqueness within the group collective. The role of the teacher in ensuring that these tenets are upheld is pivotal, for if the child shows disruptive behaviour, lacks participation and is unable to concentrate on a particular task, this is perceived as poor teacher management of the class.

A classroom management programme, implemented by a small school in northern Japan called the Midorigaoka elementary school and discussed by Shimahara (1998), shows how both teachers and pupils work together to produce a classroom management plan for the benefit of all participants. A set of goals was agreed upon, which included improving interpersonal relationships within the school, nurturing the concept of *kokoro* or heart, and strengthening self-awareness towards group attachment.

The programme is interesting in the context of the present chapter, because the staff at Midorigaoka are attempting to forge a workable relationship between emphasising the development of individuality and self-realisation, in the context of managing collectivist group activities. The Midorigaoka teachers develop a pupil's distinctive abilities through the usual pattern of lessons, class meetings, lunchtime activities, classroom cleaning and attending sports festivals and going on visits. In developing the collectivist agenda, teachers organise some of the instruction in class through two types of *han* or small groups, one dealing with an academic project, the other being concerned with life management tasks such as peer assistance, leadership and group decision making. The groups number around six members and get reorganised periodically. The fact that teachers share many management decisions with their pupils also raises a question about the nature of the P/D dimension in this school programme, and about this dimension within the wider Japanese culture.

The Impact of Socio-cultural Background on Perceptions of Classroom Management: a Dilemma for Israeli Teachers and Pupils

In recent years, Israeli teachers have been confronted with the issue of improving their teaching strategies in the face of increasing problems of class discipline and student violence. The influx of Jews from countries as diverse as the former Soviet Union and East Africa has also presented teachers with additional pressures on their form and style of pedagogy. The expectations of students from diverse cultural backgrounds do not match what they experience when they attend school in Israel for the first time. The liberal and more open approaches to learning in Israeli classrooms are extremely alien to pupils who have been use to strict classroom discipline, and to a very didactic approach to teaching.

Research by Ben-Peretz & Steinhardt (1996) on 14 immigrant tenth-grade students from the Ukraine and Ethiopia showed that these students could not adjust to the level of classroom noise, and found the relaxed atmosphere of the class difficult to accept. The students tried to act like their Israeli-born peers, sometimes misbehaving even worse than their newly acquired compatriots, but they were also aware that they should respect their teachers at the same time as they had been taught to do so in their previous home country. This gave rise to considerable levels of cognitive dissonance between the beliefs and behaviours of these immigrant students.

There have been a number of programmes organised by the Israeli government to assist teachers to improve their classroom management styles. Most programmes are based on a pluralistic approach, in which teachers are expected to generate and develop their own classroom management strategies, in accordance with their personal knowledge and priorities of the students' needs. There is a common structure to most of these programmes which include viewing films, observations of classroom situations, simulation and analysis of case studies. In dealing with culture-specific problems, teachers are encouraged to examine how effective their communication skills are with immigrant students who have a poor knowledge of Hebrew, and particularly the meanings and nuances of the language.

The conception of classroom management and discipline in Israeli schools has two continua (Ben-Peretz 1998). Firstly, a continuum between mandated and open frames of discipline; and secondly, a continuum between an individualistic and societal (i.e. collectivist) orientation towards discipline and management. This conception of classroom management provides a clear challenge for all Israeli teachers. With their greater degree of autonomy and the implementation of more student-oriented teaching strategies, we are witnessing attempts at finding a *modus vivendi* between the value of having a collective and co-operative school ethos, while encouraging an appropriate degree of individuality among students.

I–C as Part of Changing Classroom Management Patterns: the Case of a Chinese Primary School

Moral education and teaching content usually from textbooks are a principal function of Chinese education; the former takes place both inside and outside school, while the latter is firmly located in the classroom. Classroom management is not visibly represented as a subject as such, because a teacher's classroom management strategies are in reality centred on teaching, and therefore the term "teaching management" is used in China for what would be termed elsewhere as classroom management. This underlines the fact that teaching and class management are one and the same thing. In the Chinese context, the teacher's personal judgement is the main factor in classroom management, and this judgement reflects the collective norms of most teachers throughout China. The collective norm in turn is the expression of both socio-political and socio-cultural contexts (Mak 1998).

Since the late 1970s there has been a radical change in Chinese economic and social policy, and this has affected education throughout the country. Teaching models after 1950 were mainly ones that were developed along Soviet lines, with their strong emphasis on strict classroom discipline and didactic teaching styles. After 1978, attempts have been made to introduce Western models, drawing on the theories of Dewey and Bruner. Teachers are encouraged to become more like facilitators, and pupils to be more active and responsible for their own learning. In other words, there is a move to introduce measures of individualism into both teaching and learning, but within the context of the group collective.

Research carried out by Grace Mak (1998), in a primary school situated in the newly industrialised city of Shenzhen near Hong Kong, showed that her observations of teaching and learning in primary classes 2–5 provided an interesting blend of collectivist group teaching with carefully planned injections of pupil-centred activities. Teachers in the Shenzhen region also receive in-service (as well as pre-service) training, with supervisors from the local normal schools. Packages are being developed, which include CD-ROMs and video material, to improve children's learning and to make it more self-active. The training also aims to give teachers opportunities to show their individuality by developing more innovative teaching and classroom management strategies.

While the general approach to classroom management in China is still traditional, developments along the lines described by Mak and other researchers, show that introducing new approaches to teaching and class management is beginning to produce changes in the cultural dynamic of schooling. In this case the dominance of collectivist approaches is being slowly counterbalanced by an increasing emphasis on individuality, of both teacher and learner.

The case studies from the USA, Japan, China and Israel show how different classroom management strategies that have been used in these countries reflect some of the cross-cultural issues, e.g. I–C, P/D, discussed earlier. By relating some of the research findings connected with such issues, teachers in these and other countries faced with similar classroom problems might be able to develop even more effective means of dealing with classroom management. In other words, the country case studies could in effect act as models for improved organisational and management praxis.

SUMMARY

1. The chapter attempts to address three key questions relating to the cultural dynamics of education management:

(i) Can recent findings from cross-cultural research provide new insights for education managers and teachers? (ii) To what extent can education management models be effectively transferred to different cultural contexts? (iii) What strategies exist for effective management of multicultural classrooms?

2. Culture plays a crucial role in organisational and management practice, and although Western influences predominate, there is a growing volume of cross-cultural research illustrating that a mix of ideas from different cultural contexts enriches practice and avoids misconceptions.

3. In view of the paucity of studies into cross-cultural education organisation and management, we need to look at appropriate findings from cross-cultural studies carried out in industry and the business world, to help us understand the cultural dynamics of education management, and to develop ideas for better practice.

4. Work-related cultural values and motivation, job satisfaction, and leadership are among the key areas of organisational and management behaviour that have been researched in industry and commerce; the findings from studies in these areas provide valuable information for improving education management practice.

5. Research studies embracing five principal cross-cultural issues are likely to have important implications for understanding the cultural dynamics of education management, these issues are *individualism–collectivism (I–C), power/distance (P/D), uncertainty/avoidance (U/A), masculinity–femininity (M–F)* and *the emics and etics* of cross-cultural education management.

6. The cross-cultural research into managerial leadership which addresses the issue of P/D relations has shown that *two-dimensional, situational, participative* and *team arrangements* have many implications for good education management practice, provided the reasons for adopting such models are discussed, and that a thorough cultural analysis is carried out beforehand.

7. There is an increasing awareness worldwide of the need to train education managers in order to develop a positive

ethos in the school; this involves having managers with good leadership qualities, a clear vision for the future, and developing effective team management practice.

8. Management self-development (MSD), which is mainly school based, is being used in a number of Western countries where head teachers have been given greater autonomy to run their schools; transferring such a model across to a non-Western cultural context is plagued with difficulties.

9. Among the principal problems besetting cross-cultural transfer of training are the nature of context, the personnel receiving training, their psychological profile, and the relevance of the training curriculum. In addition there may be problems of lack of resources for training, poor expertise of trainers, and the cultural inappropriateness of management models advocated by overseas experts.

10. There are an increasing number of innovative classroom management strategies being applied in multicultural education settings, in countries as different as the USA and China, where cross-cultural issues such as I–C, P/D and the development of emic approaches to classroom organisation are being successfully addressed.

SUGGESTIONS FOR FURTHER READING

Hofstede, G. (1991). *Culture and Organisations: Software of the Mind*. London: McGraw-Hill.

Hui, C.H. (1988). Measurement of individualism–collectivism. *Journal of Research in Personality*, **22**, 17–36.

Hui, C.H. (1990). Work attitudes, leadership styles, and managerial behaviours in different cultures. In R.W. Brislin (Ed.), *Applied Cross-cultural Psychology*. Newbury Park, Calif.: Sage, pp. 186–208.

Johnson, D. (1995). Developing an approach to educational management in South Africa. *Comparative Education*, **31**, 223–242.

Rodwell, S. (1998). Internationalisation or indigenisation of educational management development? Some issues of cross-cultural transfer. *Comparative Education*, **34**(1), 41–54.

Shimahara, N.K. (Ed.) (1998). *Politics of Classroom Life*. New York: Garland Inc.

Sims, D. & McCaulay, I. (1995). Management learning as a learning process: an invitation. *Management Learning*, **26**, 15.

6

BUILDING CULTURAL BRIDGES BETWEEN SOCIETY AND SCHOOL

So far, most of the chapters in this book have emphasised the key role of cultural context in the schooling process. In some cases, it has been seen that education policy makers have not taken sufficient advantage of the "value added" nature of the cultural background of teachers, pupils and the society from which they come. In other cases, where this background has been recognised as having an influence, policy makers find it difficult to assess its exact role and impact on the total education of children and young adults, and how it can be integrated into the curriculum.

Trying to locate the place of a society's cultural traditions and past developments in a world where the influences of national economic, political and socio-cultural institutions are rapidly being eroded as a result of modernisation and globalisation presents educators with a stiff challenge. Furthermore, the rapid exchange of information through the World Wide Web has accelerated the erosion of the influence of these institutions, resulting in an intercultural flow of new ideas and practices that have both positive and negative effects on all concerned.

These modernising and global changes do not only provide challenges for formal schooling alone, they are also likely to have a strong impact on the nature of the relationships between school and society. Three key components of any society are the family, the community and the world of work. All three components represent cultural contexts that include an important set of stakeholders (employers, religious leaders, parents, other family members and caretakers), who are concerned that the younger generation will obtain the maximum benefits from attending school. Successful school achievement will of course be among these benefits, but the input into a pupil's schooling from his or her socio-cultural heritage should also be an important beneficial factor.

The school plays a key role in the process of socio-cultural reproduction, in which the characteristics of a culture are passed on from one generation to another. Discourse, which includes language and other sign systems, has a key role in the transactions which take place between school and society (Corson 1998), and is an essential part of a society's cultural development. Many cultural discourses which take place during schooling can end up with a "cultural capital" that is often not valued by the community (Apple 1982). In fact according to Bordieu (1971), the school develops a culture of its own, often at the expense of children from marginalised backgrounds. School culture is more often than not perceived as "high culture" by teachers, parents and pupils.

However, all groups have their own cultural capital, and although different from that of the school culture, is nevertheless equally important and legitimate. There is, therefore, a danger that a gulf will develop between school, parents, community and even the world of work, if the culture of the school is not only seen as different but superior to that of the other stakeholders. The existence of a wide cultural gulf raises particular concerns about the relevance of schooling, and the emergence of cognitive dissonance on the part of children as they move daily to and fro between home and school.

In Western countries, the culture of home and school is in the main less differentiated, although children from socially deprived areas suffer varying degrees of alienation, making the cultural as well as the socio-economic gap wider. On the other hand, in many developing countries, the cultural gap between home and school is often highly differentiated. This means that teachers and pupils in deprived areas in Western societies, and in the majority of schools in developing countries, need to develop the means of bridging the cultural gaps for both the short and long term.

This chapter is about how educators may contemplate the building of cultural bridges between school and society, so that an intercultural reciprocity can flow between the two, with the dual aims of enriching the quality of schooling, alongside the task of making education more culturally relevant in all societies. Figure 6.1 shows how a combination of political influences and socio-cultural contexts provides an essential background to the structure and workings of the school system, and societal structures respectively. Political influences are prominent in shaping the role of the school, while socio-cultural contexts such as the family, community and to lesser extent the world of work are more reflective of factors, which would include religious beliefs, language and traditional customs.

In most societies it appears that the weak interfaces are those between the school, the community and parents. It is one of the key roles of a teacher to act where possible as a bridge between these divides. Following on from what has been discussed above, we will examine five main questions:

1. What is the nature of the relationship between school and society in the context of socio-cultural influences?
2. How far do cross-cultural research studies throw light on the nature of school–society relationships?
3. What role should parents and other caretakers have in building intercultural links between school and home?

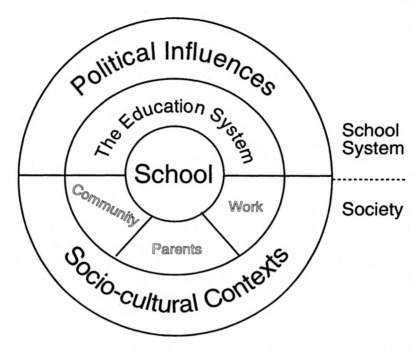

Figure 6.1: Interlinking components and the school–society dynamic

4. How far should community-based education be involved with intercultural inputs into formal schooling?
5. To what extent does a cross-cultural analysis of some selected community-based education programmes, help educators improve their praxis and professionalism through active cultural bridge building?

SOCIO-CULTURAL INFLUENCES AND THE NATURE OF SCHOOL–SOCIETY RELATIONSHIPS

In addressing the first question, we will examine two principal aspects to the nature of school–society relationships in this section of the chapter. Firstly, the part played by socio-cultural factors and their relevance in the school–society relationships and secondly, the nature of cultural reciprocity in terms of the school as a socialisation agent for its students, and for the needs of society. Let us first of all examine the case for socio-cultural relevance.

Strengthening the School–Society Relationship: a Case for Socio-cultural Relevance

Examining the nature of the relationships between school and society is not a new subject. It has occupied the minds of edu-cationists, sociologists and others over the years, the majority of whom agree with the premise that schooling divorced from what goes on the world outside becomes irrelevant and mean-ingless. In a book about cultural influences on schooling, a dis-cussion about the nature of the school–society relationship takes on a particular meaning.

The anthropologist Gearing (1979), and cultural psychologists like Price-Williams (1969) and Schweder (1991), in company with cross-cultural researchers such as Serpell & Hatano (1997), have emphasised the crucial role that cultural context plays in explaining behaviour. For Serpell in particular, who has carried out substantive cross-cultural research on Zambian village schools, there should be a close and endur-ing relationship between the culture of the school and that of the community. This relationship would be strengthened con-siderably if the curriculum was designed to meet the needs of all children, and was perceived by them and their teachers to be relevant to their own cultural context. The poor state of formal schooling in many developing countries is partly due to the fact that curriculum content and assessment procedures are dominated by former (even colonial), Western cultural traditions which had very different cultural agendas.

One of these agendas included the separation of school from society, making the school the arbiter of high culture.

Therefore, acceptance of these former Western-styled attitudes and approaches to teaching and learning, and their
lack of focus on socio-cultural factors, has led to the cultural
alienation of the school from society in many developing
countries.

Recent cross-cultural research in the USA, China and Japan,
carried out by Tobin, Wu & Davidson (1989) on the school as
a socialising agent for the needs of society, showed that society
often identifies the problems and the schools are asked to deal
with them. This research therefore provides another side to the
school–society relationship, for not only is the school a place
in which pupils are being socialised and separated from home
and community, it is also becoming more involved with
society's problems. In other words, the nature of the relationship is becoming truly reciprocal, furthering the cause of cultural relevancy, so let us in the next section explore this
reciprocity further.

The School–Society Relationship: a Case of Socio-cultural Reciprocity

As children get older, more of their socialisation takes
place within the school. Not only are teachers significant
players in this process of socialisation, but peers have a key
role as well. The fact that the school has a certain degree
of independence has both advantages and disadvantages.
An obvious advantage is that teachers can realise the aims and
objectives of formal schooling without much interference
from outside the school. They are able to equip pupils
with knowledge and skills that can be transferred to the workplace for leisure and a pupil's personal development. Children
who attend school are given the opportunities to develop
their abilities in a way that non-schooled children are not.
Schooling trains children to organise and select information,
which opens up immense possibilities for higher cognitive
functioning.

However, the fact that the school is both physically and experientially somewhat removed from everyday living leads to the claim that children may not see its relevance, and as a result may lack the motivation to continue their studies. In other words, the school is conceived as a separate entity in the lives of children and in which teachers may have few formal links with family and community.

The scenario described above is common in the poorer developing countries, but it is beginning to change in some of the middle-income economies. In many Western countries too, the nature of the relationship between school and society has already begun to change quite markedly since the beginning of the 1990s. Parents have a much greater say in their children's education, and are often actively involved in school life. The community represented by the world of work, the police, social welfare organisations, sports bodies and religious organisations are increasingly being requested by schools for their advice and expertise.

However, as the nature of the relationship between school and society is changing (at least in many Western countries), in favour of closer liaison between the two, greater demands are being made upon educators. Head teachers and their staffs are being approached by leaders in society to help identify and solve social problems such as drug addiction, the fall-out from family breakdown and the effects of the growing incidence of crime and violence in society.

In pluralistic societies, there are issues concerning the maintenance of racial harmony and religious tolerance, as well as support for minority groups to have their children taught in their mother tongue, alongside the official majority language. Another issue would be the right of all cultural groups to observe their cultural traditions and customs when and where appropriate. As many educators are intimately involved with these issues on a day-to-day basis, they are again seen as having a pivotal role in ensuring that a child who comes from a minority culture receives an education that meets these demands wherever possible.

However, it could be argued that there are so many demands being made upon the school by society that there may be a strong case for re-examining the balance within this newly developed reciprocity between school and society. There is a danger that school may be seen as the panacea for all society's ills, causing a distraction from its role of training pupils in the knowledge and skills needed for the world of work.

It is clear, therefore, that not only is the nature of the school–society relationship complex, it is made more so by the changing demands of society, and the challenges these demands make on the school and the culture of the school. It appears that cultural relevance and the dynamic process of socio-cultural reciprocity are key factors in understanding the contemporary and changing nature of the school–society relationship. The growing number of cross-cultural studies in this area will throw further light on the cultural dynamics of the school–society relationship. In the next section, we will examine selected cross-cultural research studies, which may help us to understand more about the cultural dynamic that pervades the complex relationship between the school and various sections of society.

CROSS-CULTURAL RESEARCH AND THE DYNAMICS OF THE SCHOOL–SOCIETY RELATIONSHIP

In this section we will address the second question posed at the start of this chapter, in which pertinent cross-cultural research into dimensions such as I–C in the context of family and community is examined. Since the late 1960s, there has been a steady increase in the number of cross-cultural studies of behaviour in cognition, human development, language, social psychology and many other areas. While most studies are still carried out by Western or Western-trained researchers, an increasing number of studies are also being researched by local professionals, who are themselves from non-Western countries.

This trend has strengthened the confidence among many cross-cultural workers to search for ways to explain human behaviour within and across cultures. Many well-known researchers such as Triandis, Berry and Hofstede, have carried out research into a number of areas which will help to provide more enlightened cross-cultural comparisons about human behaviour. In this section we will examine some of these areas, and discuss their value and relevance to cultural bridge building between school and society. Three areas will be investigated that have been the focus of intensive cross-cultural research over the last decade. These areas are the *individualism–collectivism dimension (I–C)*, *cultural values* and *gender issues*.

The Individualism–Collectivism Dimension (I–C)

In the 1990s, there has been an upsurge of interest in the I–C dimension among cross-cultural psychologists, and according to Kagitcibasi & Berry (1989), there may be an indication that it could be a universal. One may ask why I–C has become such a significant feature of cross-cultural interest in recent years. There are at least four reasons. Firstly, Triandis (1988) has suggested from his extensive findings on I–C that it is perhaps the most important dimension of differences in social behaviour across various cultures, thus rendering it a valuable construct for explaining cultural variation. Secondly, the seminal work of Hofstede (1980) showed that an understanding of the I–C dimension has potential for explaining different rates of economic development in different societies. Thirdly, research by Schwartz (1992, 1994) and Hofstede & Bond (1984) on I–C showed that cultural values could also be an important area in which the I–C dimension could supply valid explanations about cultural differences. Fourthly, the I–C dimension is also perceived to be a somewhat simplistic construct, therefore because of this, it has a certain appeal for single explanations to complex issues (Kagitcibasi 1997).

However, like many dimensions (e.g. universalism–relativism), I–C is proving to be far from simplistic, as more research is being carried out in the field. Even in Hofstede's original research I–C was one out of five cultural dimensions. There is a danger that if I–C is seen as a simple and straightforward means of explaining cultural differences, it could be used to explain everything cross-cultural, and in the end explain little. Fijnemam *et al.* (1995) have argued that treating I–C as a high-level psychological concept may be premature. Their research on students from the USA, Hong Kong, Greece, Turkey and the Netherlands showed that applying I–C dimensions did not always indicate strong distinctions between I and C behaviours. However, behavioural features associated with I–C have been identified in the majority of studies, but it might be better to explore their occurrence in different contexts and at different times. For instance, it is possible to be collectivist and individualistic at the same time, depending on the task and on the social setting.

In Chapters 3–5 I–C appeared in our discussions about learning, teaching and assessment across cultures as well as school management. In this chapter we return to the I–C dimension, and examine its value in explaining the intercultural nature of school–society relationships. Most cross-cultural research into I–C has not specifically addressed educational issues. However, this is beginning to change as research carried out by Biggs (1996), Watkins (1996), Baumgart & Elliot (1996) and the present author testifies. These workers have referred to those aspects of the I–C dimension, to try and explain learning and teaching within and across different cultures. We will continue to examine these aspects of I–C in the context of research carried out on home and community which are the two key areas of society that have a direct stake in what takes place within schools. We will first discuss I–C in the context of home–school transfer, followed by an analysis of the value of the I–C dimension with reference to cultural bridge building between community and school.

The I–C Dimension and Home–School Transfer

In cultures that purport to show individualism, it is more likely that independence, individuation and separation will be features of parenting, than in cultures that are more collective. In collectivist cultures, on the other hand, a high premium is put on close-knit relatedness, interdependence between parents and siblings, and a greater incidence for older peers and grandparents to look after the younger children in the family. Collectivist features of parenting also engender attitudes towards having children for security in old age. However, self-sufficiency and self-reliance are strong features of parenting practice in Western countries, while diffuse and enmeshed family boundaries typify Asian and African collectivist societies.

When children in highly individualistic cultures are ready to attend school, they already have the cultural capital to successfully promote their self-esteem, and become competitive in both the academic and social life of the school. On the other hand, when children in collectivist societies are ready to move across from home to school, their socialisation has in the main not prepared them for the change. The emphasis on material and emotional interdependence is at variance with a school philosophy (influenced mainly by Western society) which prizes independence, a spirit of competitiveness and the favouring of individuality. Research by Kornadt (1987) in Japan and Kagitcibasi (1987) in Turkey has shown how intervention during parenting can prepare children for a more individualistic school life.

The I–C Dimension and School–Community Relationships

Triandis, McCusker & Hui (1990) have analysed the main attributes that define I–C in terms of their antecedents and consequents, which is particularly useful for examining the case for closer community–school relationships as part of a wider process of making schooling more relevant. Communities with a high level of family integrity, behaviour regulated by in-group norms, a strong hierarchical structure, an in-group that is homogeneous and distinctive from the out-group, would be a fairly accurate description of a collectivist community. There are communities in which these character-istics are less strongly featured than in others, especially those that are undergoing modernisation. However, the majority of them show most of the features described in the analysis by Triandis, McCusker & Hui.

These collectivist communities also prize values like group obedience and duty, a high degree of sacrifice to uphold group norms, setting common goals and a high degree of social support and interdependence. Communities that have these characteristics are generally able to ensure that their cultural traditions, religious beliefs and their language and other forms of communication are preserved. The chal-lenge for educators is to select and develop those collectivist attributes that can be infused into the life and work of the school, so that in the long term, schooling will be a truly meaningful experience for both pupils and teachers. To facilitate the infusion of knowledge and attitudes which are reflective of the collectivist attributes identified above, cultural bridges will have to be built not only by teachers but also by community leaders and parents. An important factor in building cultural bridges between school and society is an understanding by all concerned of the part played by cultural values in the dynamics of school–societal relationships. Let us therefore examine cross-cultural research into values that is pertinent to our understanding of the school–societal dynamic.

Cross-cultural Research into Values and School–Society Relationships

The study of values in cross-cultural research has received considerable attention since the late 1980s, as values are well suited for examining processes of individual and cultural change, being an integral part of the wider process of change in society. The study of values, unlike that of attitudes and behaviour which tends to be more situation specific, provides better opportunities for abstraction and generalisation, and is therefore more suitable for formulating cross-cultural principles. In a review of recent cross-cultural research on values, Smith & Schwartz (1997) provided a summary of the main features on which most theorists would agree.

Pertinent to our present discussion, Smith & Schwartz in their summary of attributes, included values that transcend individual specific actions, and values embracing wider social situations which we meet at work, within the family, and among friends and other community members. Values act as guides and social frames of reference, and are often ordered in some societies by their relative importance, so providing a system of value priorities. For instance, filial piety is a cardinal cultural value of all CHCs which not only provides a moral framework for society, but is still very stable and enduring (Thomas 1990). This ultimately means that a community and the individuals of which it is composed will reflect a system of value priorities.

There are three main traditions which underpin cross-cultural research on values; the first was stimulated by the seminal work of Rokeach on value rankings and the subsequent cross-cultural applications of Rokeach's work by workers such as Feather (1975) and Zavalloni (1980). This tradition has been criticised subsequently for it provided mainly minimal similarities between cultures in the form of lists of values. A second tradition to the cross-cultural study of values has been the use of the I–C dimension. In this case, researchers have transposed I–C into an individual difference or personality variable, that is the degree to which individuals accept values and attitudes associated with cultural individualism or collectivism. A third tradition, put forward by Schwartz (1992), is based on motivation as the underlying construct. In this tradition, values are distinguished by the type of motivational goal they express.

Schwartz identified 10 motivational types, and 5 of these are directly relevant to our discussion relating to school and society: universalism, benevolence, tradition, conformity and security. All 10 motivational types are organised along two bipolar dimensions, namely openness to change versus conservation, and self-transcendence versus self-enhancement. The five types mentioned above emphasise goals which put a premium on welfare for others, commitment to religious customs, safety and societal stability and restraint of individual actions for the good of the community. These are highly relevant attributes in our present discussion about school–community relationships.

All three traditions are valuable when it comes to developing cultural bridges between school and society. The Rokeach tradition provides educators with a *profile* of what a community perceives as its most important values, e.g. filiality in Confucian heritage societies, or individual freedom in Western societies. This would be an essential first step in building meaningful links between school and society. The I–C tradition provides educators with a valuable *framework*, which could help them understand how a school with its emphasis on individualism and achievement can meet the need of a community that prizes collectivist values. Values within a system of motivational goals, the third tradition discussed above, address a key issue in education and schooling, namely how to develop *motivational strategies* that will enable students to be *selective* about the values they have inherited from family and community, while embracing the newer and possibly different values which most pupils will encounter during their years of schooling, for instance developing more intense competitive and self-assertive values.

Cross-cultural Research into Gender Issues and School–Society Relationships

We now turn to the third area of cross-cultural research, namely that on gender issues which will provide another insight into the dynamics of school–societal intercultural relationships. The use of the term "gender" in the present discussion refers to the distinction between male and female members of the human species, in terms of social rather than purely biological factors. However, there is an implicit recognition in this view of gender, that what constitutes males and females is as much a product of socialisation as of biogenetic endowment. Pertinent to our discussions about the school–society relationship, cross-cultural research into gender and gender-related subjects has focused on four main aspects, namely *socialisation*, *education*, *political* and *economic* factors. Some of the research findings provide useful indicators about what the roles of the school and those of the community might be, in making gender issues, e.g. equality and female empowerment, better understood. We will examine each of the four aspects below.

Gender and Socialisation Issues

Research into behavioural differences between boys and girls often attributed them to differences in *socialisation*. The now famous study by Barry, Bacon & Child (1957) examined socialisation practices in over 100 societies, and found that boys are generally raised to achieve, to be self-reliant and independent, while girls are raised to be obedient, responsible and nurturant. However, there have been changes over the years since the work of Barry, Bacon & Child and those findings have been reanalysed by Barber, Chadwick & Oerter (1992).

Nevertheless, in many developing countries the research of Barry, Bacon & Child still holds. Overall, it seems that there are subtle differences in the way boys and girls are treated by parents. For instance, if parents treat daughters and sons on an equal basis, this may not always be seen by both genders to be the correct thing to do. Boys and girls do expect on occasions to be treated differently by their parents if even for biological reasons. Another outcome of the research on socialisation is that some societies emphasise the behaviours listed by Barry, Bacon & Child more than others; this is particularly evident in rural areas of developing countries, and in societies that follow strict Islamic religious codes, as in parts of Malaysia and in Pakistan and Saudi Arabia.

Gender and Educational Practices

Turning to cross-cultural research in *education*, it appears that in some societies it is quite common for teachers to spend more time with boys than with girls. The research of Hamilton *et al.* (1991) showed that among fifth-grade pupils in Japan and the USA boys were the targets of communication more frequently than girls. It seemed that teachers in both countries gave more negative attention to boys, and that this attention was not always directed at bad behaviour on the part of the boys. Another issue relating to gender and education, in many developing countries, is that education is considered to be more important for boys than girls.

In Zambia, fathers may be directly involved in arranging schooling for their sons, while the mother is responsible for general child care (Serpell 1993). In CHCs like Japan and China, the mother expects her sons to be better at mathematics than her daughters, while the daughters are supposed to be better at reading (Lummis & Stevenson 1990). It therefore appears that the attitudes of both teachers and parents have an impact on children's academic efforts during the early years of schooling as far as gender expectations are concerned. In view of these findings, teacher training will need to prepare teachers to be more sensitive to the different sets of gender expectations that arise from both home and school environments.

Gender and Economic Factors

Research into *economic* factors has shown that males generally receive more preferential treatment than females; in most societies, certain factors appear to influence customs that favour one gender over the other. For instance, Cronk (1993) found that in Kenya, bride price and female status are related to economic conditions. Cronk also found that high parental socio-economic status of males favours them, while the opposite is true for females.

The birth of a boy in many societies is often a much more joyful occasion than when a girl is born into the family, and this joy favours the boy throughout his life. These attitudes are common in most parts of Asia, Africa and southern Europe. Callan & Kee (1981) found that parents in Malaysia and Australia reported preferences for sons over daughters to continue the family name, for support in old age as well as the companionship of a son. Even in the USA there is a preference to have sons over daughters. However, in some developing countries these trends are beginning to change, particularly where there are close contacts with Western cultural practices. As the education of girls improves, the opportunities for highly paid work increases which eventually leads to greater access to higher-status jobs in society.

Gender and Political Empowerment

Finally, cross-cultural data on *political* factors suggest that men are more likely to be involved in political activities and to have greater power than women. The research carried out by Ross (1986) on female political participation in 90 pre-industrial societies showed that in high-conflict situations women tend to act as peacemakers, while in low-conflict situations they play no consequential part. The stereotypical dichotomy of public/male versus private/female is breaking down rapidly in most Western countries. The dichotomy features men as always in the public eye and active in industry and business, compared to women being at home and taking care of the children.

However, in most developing countries this dichotomy is still the norm. Nevertheless, as more women go out to work each day, female adolescents at school see that the roles of women are beginning to change. The female gender model, especially among professionals, is now one of both homemaker and employee. As these changing role models become the norm, there will be a greater degree of empowerment for women. These societal changes will eventually be reflected by female students having much higher levels of aspiration towards their job prospects. This in turn should have implications for career advice given by teachers to their female pupils, as they reach school-leaving age.

In this section we have examined three areas of cross-cultural research, namely I–C, cultural values and gender, which have supplied some valuable insights into the cultural dynamics of the school–society relationship. In the next section of the chapter we will focus on a key component of society, namely the family, and explore how recent research into familial influences may have a bearing on the building of cultural bridges between school and society.

FAMILY INFLUENCES AND CULTURAL BRIDGE BUILDING

In this section we will attempt to address the third question posed in the early part of this chapter, which is concerned with exploring what role parents and other caretakers have in building intercultural links between school and home. The concept of family in most Western societies usually includes the parents and their offspring, constituting what is normally labelled the nuclear family. However, in recent years the concept of the family has begun to change, so that we have single-parent families, same sex parent families, and in some cases, travelling family groups, e.g. travellers and gypsies. In collectivist societies, large extended family structures are in general still the norm. In addition to parents and their immediate offspring, extended families would include grandparents, aunts, uncles, cousins as well as in-laws.

In recent years the term "caretaker" has also been used as a substitute for parent. The term "caretaker" could cover all extended family members, as they are potential parent substitutes. In some cases where there has been family breakdown, or where children have been left orphaned due to war and epidemics, caretakers may include paid child minders, social workers and members of voluntary organisations such as Save the Children or Oxfam. Therefore, there are a myriad of interpretations of what might constitute family and particularly parents and/or child caretakers.

In the discussion that follows, we will focus on parental influences, in which principally the mother in company with the father (or extended family members) have had the main responsibility for the upbringing of the child. The main reason for this choice is that the bulk of cross-cultural research on family influences to date has been carried out on this type of family structure.

However, some reference will also be made to alternative parental models that have been mentioned above, as they are increasing in number and impact in many Western countries where traditional family structures are changing.

We will examine two key areas in our discussion of parental influences on schooling; firstly, the importance of *cultural belief systems* as they relate to children's socialisation and secondly, the role of parents and family members in the *integration of children's cultural capital* into formal schooling. Let us examine first the area of cultural belief systems.

Parental Influences and Cultural Belief Systems

To understand the nature of parental influence in different cultures, it is important to briefly examine cross-cultural research relating to parental cultural beliefs as they apply to childhood socialisation practices. The increasing interest in parents' cultural belief systems or parental ethnotheory has come about with the parallel developments in anthropology, psychology and cultural human development (Super & Harkness 1997). Historically, it was thought by most psychologists working in the field, that parents' ideas about how children should be socialised was a matter of pragmatic education. Relating specific beliefs and social attitudes to parental behaviour did not meet with much success, until they were rediscovered and became important in explaining parental influences on a child's social and emotional development.

The work of LeVine (1974) on the importance of parental goals in the socialisation of children meant that parenting was not only about getting children to do household chores, but is a process that anticipates the future of the child. This led to further observations by LeVine and others in the 1990s, to suggest that parental ambitions need to be seen as a set of hierarchical goals, ranging from basic survival to the attainment of culture-specific values. Positive parental influences would be attempts on behalf of the child to achieve as many of the goals as possible. LeVine's view of parental goals is, in reality, a set of culturally shared assumptions about being a parent. The subject of developmental expectations held by parents of their children's success relates quite naturally with viewing parenthood as meeting a set of cultural goals. For if children are brought up within a framework of goals, parents will have expectations that their children will ultimately achieve them.

However, parents' developmental expectations have been found to differ cross-culturally. Hess *et al.* (1980), comparing Japanese and American mothers, found that the latter had earlier expectations of academic achievement than their Japanese counterparts, while Japanese mothers expected earlier development of emotional control, compliance and courtesy.

Apart from cross-cultural differences, there are also intracultural differences. For instance, it has been found that educated Mexican mothers had higher developmental expectations of their children's communication skills than mothers who had not been to school. Studies by Edwards, Gandini & Giovaninni (1996), on pre-school parents' and teachers' developmental expectations (or timetables) in Italy and the USA, found that parents shared with the teachers the same expectations.

There are two frameworks that have attempted to explain the influence of cultural environment on a child's development, which are relevant to our discussions about familial and particularly parental influences. Firstly, the *ecocultural niche* framework used by Gallimore, Goldenberg & Weisner (1993), which emphasises the role of contextual influence and related activities, which structure a child's life. They identified five factors which include (a) the personnel who teach and influence children, (b) motivations of all the actors, (c) cultural scripts for conduct, (d) the nature of tasks in daily life, and (e) cultural goals and beliefs. By observing and assessing these factors, it is possible to develop child-generated learning in home circumstances which can be transferred across to school. This framework has been used by Serpell (1993) to explain school success of children whose home cultures differ from that of the school. The eco-cultural approach has been successful in identifying many cultural differences in children's learning and understanding.

The second framework has been put forward by Super & Harkness (1997) and called the *developmental niche* (see Figure 6.2). The gist of the framework puts the *child* at the centre from which he or she interacts with three outer subsystems. These subsystems include the *physical and the social setting* in which the child lives, the *culturally regulated customs* of child care and child rearing, which are deeply integrated into the larger culture, and the *psychology of the caretakers*, which includes parental influences, and the cultural belief systems they bring to the child's development. This framework is an integrative attempt to put together all four components into an interactive and reciprocal system, which provides valuable ideas for developing cultural bridges between school, the family and society.

While the eco-cultural niche framework provides the essential element of cultural context into school–family relationships,

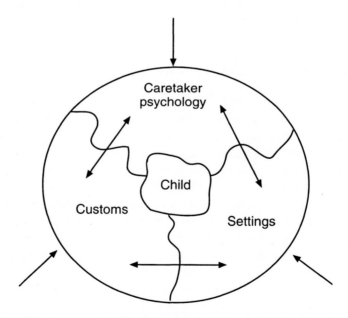

Figure 6.2: Super & Harkness's (1997) developmental niche framework

the developmental niche approach of Super & Harkness gives an insight into the cultural dynamic that exists between parents and children at home, and between children's experiences when they attend school.

The foregoing discussions covering research on parental ethnotheories, cross-cultural and intracultural differences pertaining to developmental expectations, and the conceptual frameworks of Weisner *et al.* and Super & Harkness, provide valuable guidelines and ideas for cultural bridge building between school and the family. In the next section, we will examine some case studies in which home-centred learning takes place, showing how cultural bridges can be constructed to narrow the gap between school and family life. It is hoped that by constructing such bridges, the cultural belief systems of the family will be balanced with the need for pupils to receive the essential knowledge and skills associated with schooling.

Integrating Children's Culture Capital into Formal Schooling

We have seen that children who are about to start school in developed countries, are already familiar with certain behaviours and settings they will experience when they go to school. This is because their socialisation during the first three to four years of life includes exposure to activities that will be emphasised throughout their period of schooling. These activities include developing communication skills and tackling tasks which require a child to organise and select information. The children are in effect building their cultural capital in readiness to increase its currency when they arrive at school.

This socialisation takes place mainly at home, but playgroups or pre-schools would also be possible venues. Building cultural bridges under these circumstances is less of a problem, as there is a higher level of cultural proximity between home and school. However, where the home culture is vastly different from that of the school, the cultural bridge builders (who could be teachers, parents and the children themselves) face very different sets of problems. Let us examine four case studies, the first from Hawaii, the second from Turkey, the third from Singapore and the last one from Hong Kong, where attempts have been made to build cultural bridges between the culture of the home and that of the school.

Children's Culture Capital and a Relevant Curriculum: a Hawaiian Case Study

The Kamehameha Elementary Education Project (KEEP) is a project which was based in Hawaii concerning Hawaiian and part-Hawaiian schoolchildren (Jordan & Tharp 1979; Vogt, Jordan & Tharp 1987). The KEEP team embarked upon research to find out to whom children talked and in what social settings, as this would be helpful in understanding the children's formal education. It was found that siblings figured highly in the way children communicated with each other, as their parents were often at work. In fact, older children became accustomed to acting as teachers and learners within their own peer group.

It was also found that storytelling (talk story) in Hawaiian culture plays a significant role in adult communication which filters down to children as they learn to communicate. Patterns that can be observed within the "talk story" culture extend to how people add to the story, without interrupting one another. The waiting time for each person to tell his or her bit of the story is equated with good attention span. The KEEP research team used these and many other observations to modify the school curriculum. They pinpointed four factors of importance in designing the curriculum: children need to play in groups, they defer to group set goals, they are used to playing both learner and teacher roles within their group, and they engage in "talk story" discourse.

These factors were integrated into methods for teaching reading. The Hawaiian children's culture capital was further developed by building on their collectivist cultural patterns, by introducing co-operative group learning into classroom work. The results of the KEEP programme showed that part-Hawaiian children who were exposed to more traditional-type schooling in their early years, performed less well than their Hawaiian counterparts. However, in the KEEP case, while the cultural bridge was well designed between home culture and that of the school, maintenance of the bridge fell short of what was necessary to continue this success story.

For instance, the move by many former KEEP children to schools where more traditional approaches to learning and teaching were practised meant that the momentum to make the curriculum more culture sensitive was lost. However, this does not mean that programmes like KEEP have little to offer other projects that may embark on the same task. Lessons can be learnt from having a workable "after care" plan, which all programmes of this type need in order that they can be sustained for the future.

A Turkish Case Study in Cultural Bridge Building

Kagitcibasi, Sunar & Beckman (1989) carried out an evaluation on a four-year educational programme located in Istanbul, which involved low-income families. Components of the programme included frequent parent–child interaction, encouraging feelings of competence among parents, the introduction of various cognitive skills and cognitive stimulation at home. This programme dealt explicitly with the issue of relatedness versus autonomy, relatedness being a feature which was highly prized at home, and autonomy a feature characteristic of schooling.

The issue is how can a cultural bridge be built, which will harmonise both features. Prior to the four-year educational programme, a two-year period of training was introduced, in which mothers were taught cognitive skills that could be passed on to their children. Helping and social supporting skills were also reinforced. Parents were taught the importance of their children being autonomous, in preparation for later life, and the need for children to make their own decisions, and the value of setting their own goals. Follow-up studies showed that mothers who participated in the programme learned to value their children's autonomous behaviours, but that relational and interpersonal skills, which are features of collectivist cultures, did not suffer. The effect of this programme on mothers was that they held much higher expectations of their children's education, and they also felt part of the process of schooling as they were in a better position to understand what was going when their children attended school.

Parents as Reinforcers of School Culture: the Case of High-achieving Societies

Unlike the other cases discussed above where parents and educators actively share decisions to bring the culture of school nearer to that of the community, there are some societies which would prefer the school to carry out its prime role of promoting the academic attainment of its pupils without interference from outside. Workers such as Thomas (1989), Ling *et al.* (1997) in Singapore, and King in Hong Kong (1990) have found that parental support towards their children's schooling is mainly directed towards the enhancement of levels of academic achievement.

The relationship between parent and school in these societies is of a different order from that we met in Turkey and Hawaii. It may be better described as "support without involvement". Parental support takes the form of help with homework, giving or paying for extra tuition in key subjects like English and science; attendance at non-academic classes like dancing, art and music are also seen to be part of parental support. Parents "go along" with what the school decides, and where parent support bodies and associations exist, they are not very high profile. Parents tend to be accepting of an "invitational" culture rather than a "drop-in" culture.

Unlike in Turkey and in other developing countries, where the level of parental education is generally low, in Singapore and Hong Kong the opposite is the case. As these two states are also CHCs, there is an in-built cultural zeal for formal education and learning, as it is seen as the ladder to a successful and secure life. This cultural zeal is the driving force behind the motivation for total support for the school. The research by King (1990) in Hong Kong found that although there were some changes from the past, parents still seem content to leave the school to get on with the task of educating their children, and for them to visit school when asked by the teachers.

In Singapore, the more highly achieving the pupils are, the more the parents of the children gave support to the school. Commenting on these observations from a cross-cultural perspective, it appears that strongly held values about achievement, and respect for older persons like teachers and parents, fit closely with those of the school in these societies. What is, however, rather perplexing is that from these strong collectivist cultural values, individuality through the promotion of intense competition is also being encouraged. It appears, therefore, that individualism is also part of the culture capital that filters into the cultural value system of the school with apparent ease.

In answer to the question about parental role and influences on cultural bridge building between society and the school, it is clear that parents in many parts of the world are becoming much more involved with their children's schooling, although there is some reticence in the CHCs. Parental involvement is not confined to just visiting school sporadically at the request of the head teacher, but in many instances parents are actually taking an active role in curriculum reform, bringing much needed cultural inputs into learning and teaching. In other instances, mothers act as conduits in home–school transition, in order to make the cultural changes between home and school smoother and more meaningful. In the next section we will examine another component of societal–cultural relationship with schools, namely the community.

COMMUNITY, CULTURE AND SCHOOLING

The fourth and fifth questions which appeared at the start of this chapter are concerned with the extent to which community-based educational inputs should be part of the schooling process, and how teachers can develop intercultural teaching strategies that would make these inputs effective. In this final section of the chapter we will examine these questions together as they are closely linked as far as praxis and professionalism are concerned.

A recurring argument in education development, especially in low-income countries, is that the quality of schooling would benefit if there was more input from the community. This input would be seen in human and material resources, reflecting the culture of a particular community. The argument is based on the assumption that by developing meaningful community–school relationships, schooling is made more relevant to, and therefore more effective for, its pupils. It would also have in the long term material and social benefits for the community.

Corson (1998) makes the distinction between community-based education and community education. Community-based education refers to a type of social action within a community framework, extending beyond schools as institutions. In community-based education, the members of the community are actually *involved* in the learning environment of the school. Community education is a more passive concept which questions educational structures, but leaves them in place until a radical reform comes along to change them. However, community education does have a serious role, for it sets out to educate local people about what is going on in schools, and about what changes are being contemplated as well as those that are being implemented.

For the purpose of our discussions in this section of the chapter, we accept the assumption behind the need for effective school–community relationships. The view is also taken that the community-based education model is, in the main, the best way forward for improving school–community relationships within and across cultures. In the first part of this section we will examine research from a number of cross-cultural perspectives that may have implications for community-based education. In the second and final section, we will examine some community-based education programmes that attempt to build cultural bridges between family, community and the school.

Cross-cultural Perspectives to Community-based Education

There are few, if any, cross-cultural studies relating directly to community-based education. There are, however, many cross-cultural psychological studies in fields of *social cognition, I–C, acculturation* and *values* from which it is possible to derive some interesting cross-cultural applications for community-based education and its relationship to schooling. Let us examine in brief some relevant issues from the fields mentioned above, which may have implications for effecting qualitative change in school–community relationships.

Social Cognition, I–C Dimension and Community-based Education

In view of some of the common ground that exists between social cognition and the I–C dimension, we will consider both in our discussions about community-based education and the school. The growing awareness of the psychological relevance of how a person develops culturally has recently resulted in social cognition becoming an area for cross-cultural study

(Schweder 1991). The basic idea that impacts on social cognition research is that the self is fundamentally situated within a culture or cultures. Markus & Kitayama (1991) have pointed out the essential difference between self-perceptions of independence and interdependency of the individual within a society. Cultural psychology stresses that the cultural context of social thought, is a function of the way a person can distinguish between the ego and the nature of the cultural group in which that person operates.

These distinctions translate into a person's identity and how it is culturally regulated. These views about social cognition also relate to the I–C dimension. Collectivist and interdependent conceptions of the person are found in cultural communities, in which the group has an overriding importance, and where a person's identity is reliant upon the norms of the group. Individualistic or independent conceptions of a person's identity are characterised by communities in which the individual is important, autonomy is highly prized, and where ego-centred rather than socio-centred behaviour is encouraged. This means that all cognitive processes that implicate identity will vary according to the manner in which a person's identity is shaped by the cultural context in which he or she lives.

We have seen from the cases studies on home-based schooling in Turkey and Hawaii, and in the CHCs of Singapore and Hong Kong, which were discussed in the previous section, how a child's identity changes when he or she attends school. Schooling actually encourages the development of an individual identity, promotes individuality and autonomy in most areas of the curriculum, as well as in competitive sports and games. In subjects such as creative writing, art and craft, promoting individuality can be even more intense. The requirement of a well-conceived plan for community-based education needs teachers that will supply a socio-cultural backdrop alongside the development of the individualist features discussed above. The Turkish mothers and their children in Kagitcibasi's research in Istanbul homes and schools showed it was possible to ensure that individual and socio-cognitive identity within a balance between I–C could be achieved with considerable success.

Acculturation and Community-based Education

Acculturation is one of the most complex areas of research in cross-cultural psychology, as it involves more than one culture. Acculturation is about contact between two or more cultures and because of this, the process has a strong comparative element in it. Berry (1980b) has described acculturation as cultural changes resulting from how individuals from one cultural context adapt to a new one, as a result of migration, colonialism and other intercultural encounters. Berry related processes of psychological acculturation and adaptation, as psychological changes and eventual outcomes that occur as a result of individuals experiencing acculturation. In Chapter 2 we discussed that in multicultural communities, four types of acculturation may take place; they are assimilation, integration, segregation or ethnocultural marginalisation.

This typology of acculturation may be better understood as far as schooling is concerned against a backdrop of two levels of acculturation. At one level, there is an acculturation that takes place between groups within a community, which the present author calls *community acculturation*, and is a longer-term process (measured in generations). At another level, there is the acculturation process that takes place during the time pupils attend school, which we can call *school acculturation*, which is a relatively shorter period of time (4–14 years). A community is rarely homogeneous, as one or more of the four types of acculturation process mentioned above may have contributed to its structure. The degree of heterogeneity of a community will determine the nature of the relationship between community and school. The more heterogeneous the community, the greater will be the demands on the school to deliver a culturally relevant education. This is a key issue that is being debated among educators in countries like the UK, the USA, Germany and Australia, where there are many heterogeneous communities.

However, school acculturation is also a challenge for educators, as schools in many countries must reflect the nation state regardless of its ethnocultural components. This has been the case in many newly constituted countries, after a period of colonial rule, where forging a national identity was a priority in which the school had a key role. Apart from school acculturation processes engendering a feeling of nationhood, the school has its own cultural agenda, in which pupils and teachers are closely involved, and to which they contribute. For instance, school rules, timetables, school organisation, developing certain management attitudes and traditions, the fostering of a culture of competition and individuality as well as community, are all indicators of a school culture.

Community-based education would be the richer if those responsible for the development of its curriculum, and the training of instructors responsible for its delivery, could be made aware of some of the cross-cultural perspectives on acculturation discussed above. There is an important task to be faced by teacher educators as far as the two forms of acculturation are concerned. In order that the community–school link is both meaningful and realistic, teachers will need to be trained to understand both acculturative processes and how each can be dovetailed into one another. If this can be achieved, we will be laying the foundations for the preparation of a teaching force that will be sensitive to the challenge and demands of cultural diversity within the classroom. We will return to this subject in the next chapter when we will discuss teacher education and training for multicultural contexts.

Values: Individual and Cultural

We have discussed elsewhere in this chapter and in Chapter 5 the subject of cultural values. Here we will only cover briefly the subject as it relates to school–community relation-ships, and particularly community-based education. Cross-cultural research on values takes place at two separate levels of analysis, *individual* and *cultural*. At the *individual* level, values represent motivational goals, they can also be repre-sentative of conflict and peace of mind among individuals as people go about their daily lives. They form the core of people's attitudes and behaviour and are strong determinants of children's early socialisation.

Values at the *cultural* level are less well understood, because they are even more complex than values at the individual level (Smith & Schwartz 1997). When values are used to label cul-tures, so-called shared values about what is good and what is right emerge as key concepts. Cultural values can be con-ceived in several ways; for instance, institutional values are often expressed by mission statements and institutional goals. In institutions which rate ambition and individual success highly, professionals such as lawyers, company executives and managers are expected to be very competitive, reflecting the trademark of an individualistic and capitalistic society. On the other hand, if the value system expresses group together-ness, sharing and co-operation, we have a values culture reflective of a more collectivist society.

Values at the cultural level often reflect the nature of decision making, how resources are invested, and how human and financial capital is managed. Relations between individuals in organisations often reflect values of conflict and compatibility that are reflective of goals pursued by these organisations. Group cohesion depends to a large degree upon shared values and the acceptance of authority for the well-being of the cul-tural group.

Much of community values in non-Western countries are shared values, showing a considerable degree of consensus. For instance, most CHCs share values such as filial piety, righteousness and community well-being. In African societies, well-established hierarchical relationships mean that all tribes subscribe to a deep respect for age and authority. With the advent of school as an organisational unit, which is mainly an imported idea from Western culture, with its emphasis on values such as high academic achievement, autonomy and individual freedom, shared collectivist values come under threat.

As far as the relationship between school and community is concerned, cross-cultural research on values gives us a number of useful messages. Firstly, when children grow up in a community that has a closely knit culture, they will be exposed to a whole new set of values as they embark on their formal schooling. Many of the values at the cultural level discussed above will be reflected in the organisation and management of most schools that these children will attend. In other words, there will be a *value shift* on a daily level for each child, from a cultural context with strong collectivist values, to a context in which individualist values will start to be emphasised. This daily exposure to a value shift will in the long run have marked effects on children's cultural values within their community.

The case studies from Hawaii and Turkey discussed earlier in this chapter, and those from Peru and Australia in Chapter 1, show the extent of value shift and the challenge it poses for educators and other cultural bridge builders during the daily "cross over" from community to school and vice versa. A second message from cross-cultural research on values is that much of the studies prior to the 1990s used etic (outside the culture) measures rather than emic (from within the culture), distorting the total picture of the structure of values across cultures.

As we have seen from case studies discussed in this and other chapters, there are many instances in which strong emic characteristics have been overlooked, when it comes to developing measures of assessment, promoting culture-sensitive teaching and learning styles and approaches to school and classroom management. One function, therefore, for community-based education would be to ensure that the cultural values of the community are not discarded at home or in school. Active involvement by appropriate community personnel and school authorities, in imaginative curriculum planning and useful extra-curricular activities, would go some way to providing an education that attempts to equip future citizens with a strong set of cultural values, which can exist alongside those individual values that are necessary for success in a postmodern and global world (Thomas 1997b).

Community-based Education Programmes as Part of Cultural Bridge Building

The idea behind community-based education programmes is not a new one. For centuries, and in all parts of the world, the family, village elders, religious leaders and skilled craftsmen among others have played a key role in initiating both the young, and not so young, into the knowledge, skills, beliefs, traditions and customs that are identified as part of a community. This is the essence of a community's cultural development, and in most countries this development proceeded in the absence of formal schooling over a long period of time. However, with the advent of formal schooling, much of this cultural development was either replaced or rejected, first through colonial influences, and then by education modernisers in the middle to late twentieth century. As countries became independent after WW2, the erosion of community culture as part of any educative process intensified, and the school was seen to be a panacea for successful national and economic development.

However, by the late 1970s and early 1980s it was clear that the school was not fulfilling the dreams of politicians and planners in developing countries. The school was also failing in its social, economic and educational role even in the richer industrialised countries of the West. The Jomtien conference Education for All was held in 1990, because many poor countries were not able to meet the need for basic education, and the education that was provided was not relevant for children returning to work in their community after school.

It has already been shown in this book that cross-cultural research can provide educators with valuable perspectives about the cultural context in which schooling takes place. Educators who are sensitised to some of these cross-cultural perspectives will hopefully be able to solve certain problems, such as making community-based education work within different socio-cultural constraints. Let us examine two case studies, in which attempts have been made to tap some community cultural resources, while getting community members more involved in pre-school and where basic educational provision is a starting point.

Learning Together – the *Lok Jumbish* (LJ) Programme for Basic Education in Rajasthan (India)

The word *Lok* means "people" in Hindi and *Jumbish* means "movement" in Urdu, and the rationale of the programme is founded on the belief that in reviving the educational process, it is essential to re-establish the partnership between parents, the child and the teacher. The value and respect of the teacher needed to be restored by improving his/her ability to use the knowledge and skills of the community in the schooling process. The programme is directed at the education of girls and is seen as an integral part of social development (SIDA 1993). The role of the LJ is that of developer and catalyst, influencing formal schooling from the perspective of the community. There are three overlapping components to the programme, these being community involvement, quality of learning, and management of education (see Figure 6.3).

What is pertinent to our discussion on school–society relationships is that involvement of the community in the demand

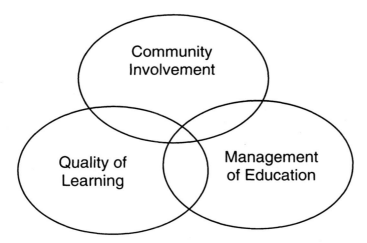

Figure 6.3: Three major components of *Lok Jumbish*

for better educational provision is seen as the starting point. However, it is expected that the community will continue the involvement, and make the programme self-sustaining. Community support is mobilised through public debate, the sharing of relevant information for informed decision making, and home surveys of children not attending school and focusing on the reasons why.

Both management and learning components are developed alongside local ideas coupled with more recent developments from other situations in India and overseas. A village education committee oversees the building and the attendance of children. A core group emerged which collaborated with teachers in both administrative and some professional matters. The core group is a change agent, getting parents to send their children to school. The core group also monitors professional standards, selecting and rejecting teachers who do not meet the standards set by the community. A key issue in the programme is to change attitudes of both women and men about enhancing the education of girls. The programme has had limited impact due to the difficulty of changing attitudes and values on the part of many of the participants. This raises a persistent cross-cultural problem, that is the need for the programme developers to carry out a thorough cultural analysis, so that individually held values and those of the cultural community can be identified. Once this has been done, there is a better opportunity for attitude and behaviour change and therefore the success of the project.

We Did It Ourselves – The Scottish Western Isles Community Education Project (CEP)

The Scottish Western Isles Community Education Project is really a community-based project as defined earlier in this chapter. In this project a group of people, mainly mothers, have been empowered to do things for themselves. It was through an awareness of the their cultural, linguistic and psychological strengths that this group was able to produce solutions to some of the challenges that faced them (Mackay 1996). The achievement of the project was the formation of a community organisation called Guth nam Parant (meaning a parent-run organisation), which is run by parents for pre-school children. The project was started in 1977 and supported by the Bernard van Leer Foundation. Although the project was completed in 1994, many of its activities and practices are still being continued by the community. Of the 30000 islanders, 80% speak Gaelic as their mother tongue, as well as English. Most live in rural villages scattered around the coasts. Crofting, weaving and fishing are the main sources of livelihood for the islanders.

The family and community are strong collectivist influences, together with the church playing a key role in maintaining a system of well-established religio-cultural values. However, by the mid 1970s, a combination of outside social and economic pressures led to a feeling among younger islanders of a lack of control over their lives and the community. This led to a slow process of migration towards urban life on the mainland, where opportunities for career prospects were seen to be much better.

Schooling was perceived to be divorced from the cultural experience of the community, and was one of the main factors in motivating young people to find work outside the islands. To counteract these problems, a Bilingual Education Project (BEP) was set up by the Island Council to encourage classroom instruction in Gaelic and English. The CEP project was set up alongside the BEP, and was aimed at getting the community to identify and tackle their own education problems. The main outcome of the CEP was the setting up of Guth nam Parant (i.e. a parent-run organisation) which got parents to take charge of the education of their pre-school children as well as providing instructor training for parents. The education and training of mothers was a key factor in sustaining the project and its ultimate success. The CEP is a truly community-based education project, in which traditional attitudes towards early childhood education have been changed.

The project has also had a spin-off for formal schooling, keeping teachers and their employers more in tune with community needs. This spin-off seems to have improved teaching and learning styles in the formal school system as well. From a cross-cultural perspective, the project has inadvertently identified the reciprocity of both collectivist and individualist attitudes to community-based educational development. On one hand, strong community togetherness meant that the project benefited from a feeling of shared ownership and co-operation, in tackling many of the organisational and peda-gogical tasks. On the other hand, parents and children were given the opportunities to develop their individual talents and interests, and make their own decisions about learning. Adap-tation in an acculturative sense also took place, as all active stakeholders in the project had to change their attitudes and behaviour for the success of improving and sustaining the empowerment of the community.

In the foregoing section, the discussion has been structured around the fourth and fifth questions posed at the start of the chapter, and it has shown how particular cross-cultural research studies have legitimate implications for developing intercultural links between school and society. We have also seen how these links can be enriched further by learning from experiences in community-based education projects that were referred to. The cross-cultural analysis which has been carried out on the various school–community projects provides educators with ample opportunities for developing ideas to improve their classroom teaching, as well as contributing to their own personal development. However, as pointed out earlier, there is little research at present being carried out by educators or cross-cultural psychologists into this very essential but challenging area of the school–society cultural dynamic. Therefore, it is hoped that some of the issues relating to bridging the cultural gap between school and community will energise educators to investigate some of the issues further, for the benefit of pupils, teachers, parents and other community members.

SUMMARY

1. Five principal questions were posed in this chapter relating to (i) the relationship between school and society and socio-cultural influences, (ii) how far can cross-cultural research throw light on the school–society relationship, (iii) the role of parents and caretakers, and intercultural links between home and school, (iv) how far should community-based education provide inputs into formal schooling and finally, (v) what strategies teachers can develop to make the school–society reciprocity more meaningful?
2. In examining the socio-cultural influences on the nature of the school–society relationship, the case for relevance is strong, not only with reference to the curriculum, but also in the ways school management relates to the community.

3. An effective reciprocity between school and society is strengthened considerably where parents, community leaders and significant others are encouraged to take an active involvement, where appropriate, in the life and work of the school; this involvement can often result in the solution of social problems inside and outside the school.

4. Cross-cultural research into areas such as *I–C*, *cultural values* and *gender* issues have important messages for understanding the cultural dynamics of school–society relationships. Some of the research on *I–C* provides a better understanding about home–school transfer as it affects pre-school children, and about how cultural bridge building can be made more effective between the community and the school.

5. Much of the cross-cultural research on *values* and on *gender* issues also has implications for school–society relationships; *values* research has provided useful profiles of community values, provided a framework to understand values differences between school and community along the I–C dimension, and supplied motivational strategies to assist students to be selective about the values they have brought with them from home.

6. Research on *gender* has covered sociology, education and political and economic aspects, providing intriguing insights into the future of female empowerment and equality that could influence the perceptions of women and girls, be they staff or students.

7. *Cultural belief systems* and the *integration of children's cultural capital into schooling* are two key areas of family influences and cultural bridge building that have been enriched by recent cross-cultural research into children's cultural development; the eco-cultural niche and developmental niche frameworks relating to child development, provide useful insights between parents and children at home, and the children's experiences when they attend school.

8. Case studies from Hawaii and Turkey show how it is possible to integrate children's culture capital into the school curriculum.

9. There are a number of cross-cultural studies in the fields of *social cognition, I–C, acculturation* and *values,* from which it is possible to derive cross-cultural applications for community-based schooling, benefiting the quality of school–society relationships.

10. Educators who are aware of certain cross-cultural research findings should be able to solve problems associated with community-based education programmes, as part of cultural bridge building.

11. Case studies from India and Scotland which emphasise the value of parental and community inputs into the school curriculum, show how cultural bridges can be built between school and community.

SUGGESTIONS FOR FURTHER READING

Barber, B.K., Chadwick, B.A. & Oerter, R. (1992). Parental behaviours and adolescent self esteem in the United States and Germany. *Journal of Abnormal and Social Psychology,* **55**, 327–332.

Corson, D. (1998). *Changing Education for Diversity.* Buckingham: Open University Press.

Kagitcibasi, C. (1990). Family and socialisation in cross cultural perspective: a model of change. In J. Berman (Ed.), *Cross Cultural Perspectives: Nebraska Symposium on Motivation.* Lincoln: University of Nebraska, pp. 135–200.

Mackay, D. (1996). We did it ourselves – Sinn Fhein a rinn e. *Early Childhood Development: Practice and Reflections,* Number 9. Berlicum, Holland: Bernard van Leer Foundation Publication.

Super, C. & Harkness, S. (1997). The cultural structuring of human development. In J.W. Berry, P.R. Dasen & T.S. Sarawathi (Eds), *Handbook of Cross Cultural Psychology,* Volume 2, *Basic Processes and Human Development.* Boston: Allyn & Bacon, pp. 1–40.

Vogt, L., Jordan, C. & Tharp, R. (1987). Explaining school failure, producing school success: two cases. *Anthropology and Education Quarterly,* **18**, 276–286.

7

TEACHER DEVELOPMENT AND TRAINING FOR CULTURAL DIVERSITY

In this, the last chapter of the book, we will focus specifically on the training and education of teachers, with particular reference to the notion of cultural diversity in the classroom. It is evident from what has been discussed about cultural influences on schooling so far, that the teacher is the ultimate key to bringing about cultural and educational change. Conversely, it could be argued that under certain circumstances, teachers may be perceived to be barriers to change, especially in countries where part of their role is seen as a guardian of cultural knowledge, traditions and religious beliefs.

Therefore, when teacher educators embark upon programmes of training they face, among other challenges, the attainment of a realistic and meaningful equilibrium between *innovation* and what may be termed *cultural retention*. To enable teachers to meet the challenge of making an equilibrium possible, teacher education programmes will need to include imaginative strategies that will on one hand promote new ideas, but on the other ensure that cultural contexts are appropriately reflected in the school curriculum and training programmes.

Furthermore, if training programmes can meet their objectives, teacher development will be given a firm foundation in addressing the issue of cultural diversity, within lifelong teacher education. However, these challenges are not easy to meet, as there are several key issues and questions that must be addressed before teacher education for cultural diversity can be a reality. Let us identify some of these issues and the key questions, before we continue our analysis of how teachers may be prepared for contexts with a high degree of cultural diversity.

ISSUES AND QUESTIONS ASSOCIATED WITH TRAINING TEACHERS FOR CULTURAL DIVERSITY

There are five issues that arise when teachers are being prepared for teaching in multicultural contexts; let us examine each of them briefly. The first issue relates to *resistance to change* on the part of communities and even teachers themselves. In certain cultural contexts the capacity for resistance may be more deep-seated than in others, e.g. indigenous societies in Peru and Cameroon, or in Islamic countries like Iran and Saudi Arabia. Therefore, for teachers to be innovative in these societies, they have to overcome cultural resistance among the school population, the community and not least the teaching profession. The effects of *cultural erosion* is the second issue, and this is especially evident in countries which have inherited a dominant colonial legacy, encapsulated within the existing system of Western-type schooling. In many instances, local and indigenous cultural influences, e.g. languages, traditions and customs, have become eroded, schooling often taking an active part in the process of cultural erosion, e.g. most Francophone and Anglophone African societies.

A third issue concerns the impact of *globalisation,* and the challenge this process poses for teacher preparation. A key aspect of the challenge of globalisation is how teachers will develop strategies to cope with the problem of selection and prioritisation of relevant information for themselves as well as their pupils. Speed of access to information will also be part of the challenge. Globalisation embraces economic, political and cultural change, all of which will have major effects on schooling as we enter the millennium. However, the relationship between global cultural change and cultural diversity will be a key issue for education and schooling.

The fourth issue is closely related to the third, as it is about the need for *innovative and special* training strategies to meet the new challenges posed by the impact of information technology (IT) on learning and teaching. Teachers will be key players in the process of curriculum planning, which tries to ensure that a balance exists between the impact of innovations like IT as well as addressing the need to prepare pupils for cultural diversity within society.

The fifth issue poses the need for a long-term strategy for the *teacher's professional development* in the context of *cultural diversity*. While education and training are different processes, they are integral to a teacher's professional development. The notion of education as a process of long-term personal development must be seen alongside training which is a process of skills learning and the acquisition of techniques required in teaching and managing classrooms. Teacher development is about the melding of both these processes, with the aim of improving the overall career prospects of the teacher. The meld will hopefully be the hallmark of a quality teaching force. It is not sufficient for teachers to be trained in new teaching methods, better management styles and innovative counselling techniques, they also need to be made aware of the fact that cultural changes inside and outside schools are as important. Much of a teacher's appeal and success stems from his or her cultural background, and a willingness to develop an empathy with colleagues and pupils, especially if there is a substantial cultural gap between all three.

Teacher development is essentially a cultural process in the broadest sense of the term, as was discussed in Chapter 3 when we examined cultures of teaching. However, teacher development is also about developing teaching and learning strategies in partnership with pupils, in order to explore, sensitise and explain cultural diversity within schools and classrooms. In Figure 7.1 an attempt is made to capture the key factors that influence teacher development for cultural diversity in the context of the multicultural classroom. The boxes depicting *knowledge of cultural contexts* and *pedagogical innovations* are reflective of the *multicultural scenario* discussed at the end of Chapter 1. These two factors contribute significantly to a cultural balance within the learning and teaching processes, as we reach the interaction phase of multiculturalism within the classroom. Cultural knowledge and its connection to innovative culture-sensitive pedagogies provide teacher development with a depth of cultural background crucial to an understanding of what cultural diversity constitutes. The two

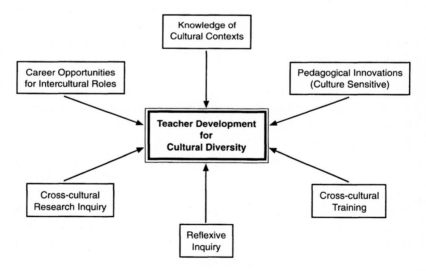

Figure 7.1: Factors influencing teacher development for cultural diversity

boxes concerned with *cross-cultural research* and *reflexion* are both *inquiry-based* factors, and are closely linked with the *cross-cultural scenario*.

It is essential that as teachers develop their experience in addressing issues related to cultural diversity, they should have the opportunity to reflect on their practice, and engage in as well as consult research studies in order to improve their expertise and personal development. The two remaining boxes, namely *cross-cultural training* and prospects for a *teacher's intercultural role*, are linked to the *intercultural scenario*. These latter factors help to introduce a sense of interculturalism into teacher development.

Through cross-cultural training, not only are teachers trained to understand existing cross-cultural patterns of behaviour in their classrooms, but they are in a unique position to observe the emergence of new cultural patterns, in the wider framework of multiculturalism. By adding interculturalism to their role as teachers, not only is their professional development enhanced, but career prospects within multicultural education are also likely to be brighter, enabling both intrinsic and extrinsic motivational goals to be set. We will discuss the factors set out in Figure 7.1 at the end of the chapter, where it is argued that they form key elements in the development of a *culture-sensitive process of teacher education and training* aimed at the preparation of teachers for cultural diversity.

In this chapter, we will examine five questions relating to teacher development and training for cultural diversity:

1. In what way do current changes in teacher education and training affect the intercultural role of teachers in promoting an appreciation of cultural diversity within society?
2. How does recent research into cross-cultural training contribute towards a greater awareness of cultural diversity during teacher training?

3. What impact would cross-cultural training for teachers have on multicultural education in schools?
4. How can teacher-training strategies be developed which focus on an appreciation of cultural diversity in the multicultural classroom?
5. What would be the prospects for the development of a *culture-sensitive teacher education*, which meets the need for preparing teachers for cultural diversity?

Let us therefore address the first of our five questions.

THE CHANGING NATURE OF TEACHER EDUCATION AND THE INTERCULTURAL ROLE OF TEACHERS

In addressing our first question about the changing nature of teacher education, it should be pointed out that since the late 1980s there have been major changes in many Western countries in the way teachers are trained, although there are differences in the nature and extent of the changes in different countries. Four areas of teacher education have been mainly affected by change; these include institutional structures, the curriculum of teacher education, teacher development, and building up research capacity among teachers and teacher educators (Thomas 1996). All areas are relevant to our discussion, but changes to the curriculum and teacher development are of particular interest to our discussions about a teacher's intercultural role in the context of cultural diversity.

A number of cultural issues transcend in particular, curriculum change and teacher development; these are *socio-cultural factors*, the current debate concerning *cultural dominance versus cultural diversity*, the nature of a *teacher's intercultural role*, and finally the need to develop an appropriate *curriculum model* for training teachers in cultural diversity. These issues are discussed below in more detail.

Socio-cultural Factors That Have Influenced Change in Teacher Education

From a socio-cultural perspective, change in teacher education has been brought about by a number of factors. Firstly, *changes due to postmodernism* that have taken place in Western educational systems and particularly in teacher education have meant that professional and social accountability on the part of teachers, and control on the part of government to ensure teacher accountability, have become inextricably linked. The teachers, as the providers, are now perceived as being accountable in delivering a service to pupils, parents and society, who are the consumers. This has meant a dilution in teachers' professional autonomy especially in the UK, Australia and New Zealand, which in turn has influenced the training and status of teachers and their professional development.

Secondly, *the changing patterns of education and training* in response to postmodernism are characterised by a greater emphasis on teacher performance in the classroom. Therefore more time is devoted to the pre-service practical work, as teacher accountability is mainly measured in terms of a teacher's ability to deliver high levels of pupil achievement, and most notably academic achievement. Therefore, much more time is spent on training teachers in mastering pedagogical and classroom management skills, and less time on studying the theoretical disciplines such as psychology and philosophy, which underpin good practice as well as contributing to a teacher's personal development. The pressures being put on teachers to concentrate on getting better pupil examination results, have also meant there is less time to prepare teachers for cultural diversity, in company with other fields of study, e.g. educational philosophy and sociology, which help to broaden a teacher's professional development.

Thirdly, the *effects of demographic changes on school populations* are not a new phenomenon; population migration has since

WW2 intensified. Among the main causes of this migration would be increased numbers of refugees as a result of local and regional conflicts, disasters due to climatic change, as well as an increase in the numbers of immigrants seeking better economic conditions, and those fleeing political and religious persecution. Countries such as the USA, the UK, Australia, Germany, Canada and France are still witnessing immigration, particularly into urban areas. Similar population movements are also being experienced in poorer countries such as India, Tanzania, Pakistan and South Africa, with even greater demands being put on already stretched financial and structural resources.

Migration has produced specific effects, where the children of migrants have been allowed access to the schools of the host country. In some instances, population profiles have become so transformed that classrooms may have as much as 60–80% non-host country schoolchildren, e.g. Latino children in Texas, Turkish children in Berlin and Bangladeshi children in London. The influx has produced major problems for the teachers who have to cope with the problems of cultural diversity. This in turn has meant that teacher education programmes have to be adapted to equip teachers to function accordingly. In countries like the USA and the UK, which have previously experienced such cultural changes to the school population, attempts have been made to produce teacher education curricula that meet the demands that classroom cultural diversity poses. However, the problems are far from being solved, as we shall discover in the course of the chapter.

A fourth factor would be *information technology and globalisation* which include recent developments in the use of personal computers (PCs), computer-assisted learning and instruction. Distance education and access to the World Wide Web with its transmission of knowledge and new ideas about teaching and learning are also having an impact on teaching and how teachers are being trained. More children in industrialised countries have access to PCs, either at home or in school, and although these developments are some way off for most children from the very poor developing countries, a growing number of children in middle-income countries like Malaysia, India, Botswana, Brazil and Ghana are already being exposed to this technology. In countries such as Australia, the UK and Singapore, teacher education programmes already include special training for the use of computers in learning. Access through the CD-ROM to educational material which informs pupils about the cultural activities of different national and ethnic groups is now widely available. A paramount task for teacher educators is to train teachers in the use of these educational materials, with the hope of promoting a better understanding of cultural diversity inside the classroom. However, there is a danger that as much of the information and innovation comes from Western sources, training approaches to cultural diversity could be heavily dominated by Western culture. Let us therefore examine this issue further below.

Cultural Dominance versus Cultural Diversity

It has been argued that countries such as the USA, the UK, France and others maintain control over the destinies of weaker countries in education, by disseminating ideas through experts, government agencies, the mass media and in the case of former colonial rulers, by the perpetuation of institutional and organisational structures (Carnoy 1974; Altbach & Kelly 1978). These influences are not confined to the non-industrialised countries and former colonial territories, but are also evident in many Western nations, where there are substantial minorities such as in the USA, the UK, France, Australia and Germany.

Although many efforts have been made to meet the educational and cultural needs of ethnic and other minorities in these countries, a cultural dominance appears to exist in both an overt and pervasive manner, leading to the alienation of cultural and ethnic minorities from their cultural main-streams. This cultural dominance has been observed by Tabachnik & Zeichner (1993) to have extended to teacher education, and which they term the "cultural imperialism" of teacher education.

In the USA, there are increasing enrolments from minority groups of over 50% in some areas of the country, while the American teaching force remains predominantly white, middle class and female, so producing a cultural gap. Unless this cultural gap can be bridged with the assistance of teacher education programmes that aim to meet the challenges of cultural diversity, the slide towards classroom cultural alienation will continue apace.

However, training teachers to meet the needs of cultural diversity has not been high on the agenda of most countries, even where there are substantive ethnic minorities. This situation is unlikely to improve as parents and employers put more value on higher academic and technical achievement, rather than on an education that prizes the development of socio-cultural skills that would assist a better understanding of cultural diversity in the classroom. Apart from Israel, the USA, Australia and the UK, where there are a number of specific programmes to teach children from different cultural backgrounds, there are many countries where there is no policy for such training, especially in the non-industrialised countries. It is clear that as the cultural profiles of school populations in many countries are becoming more multi-ethnic, teachers will be called upon to fulfil a new role, namely that of an effective intercultural communicator. It is to a discussion of this new role that we now turn.

The Teacher's Intercultural Role

The intercultural role of a teacher is, first and foremost, one of being aware of and sensitive to the cultural background of the pupils being taught. The role is also about sharing with class members the values and beliefs of all individuals. Perhaps the most difficult aspect of the intercultural role for a teacher is to put cultural sensitivity into action. This relates particularly to instruction, where cultural sensitivity may be necessary in teaching subjects like history and language. For instance, it is possible to teach history from different cultural perspectives, the colonisation by the UK of Africa had economic and political motives which from the colonisers' standpoint was to have a "civilising" effect on the indigenous peoples. But from the viewpoint of the colonised, it was seen as exploitation and the ultimate erosion of cultural values.

The same point can be made about the advent of Christian values to Africa, where again the "civilising" argument was used by the missionaries to explain their presence in the country, and to distinguish them from their less committed fellow colonisers. But these views were often countermanded by traditional religious leaders, in which they accused their "moral colonisers" of infringing their traditional values. An intercultural role also has a dynamic and formative dimension, in which the teacher makes use of the cross-cultural interfaces that exist in culturally diverse classrooms, widening pupils' perspectives to a particular issue. For instance, the teacher could explore how children who hold different cultural values could provide their own interpretations to issues such as respect for authority and preference for family values over individual values.

From such discussions, cultural-specific issues will emerge introducing relevant knowledges, and the appearance of new sets of social attitudes and behaviours. The next step would be a process of curriculum development that would reflect these experiences so that they could become embedded in the school curriculum. Let us examine what training curriculum models are on offer that would lend support to the intercultural role of teachers discussed above.

Curriculum Models for Cultural Diversity

There are a number of curriculum models which have been used by teacher educators to address the problem of cultural diversity in the classroom, so that teachers may be prepared to engage effectively in their intercultural role as a teacher. There are three models of a training curriculum which might be considered for preparing teachers for cultural diversity, all of which have been, or are being, used in different parts of the world. The first model puts an emphasis on *cultural dominance*, the second is called *minimalist multicultural* and the third model is an *issue pervasive* model.

According to Hodge (1990) the *cultural dominance* model is used in many American teacher education institutions and, in the main, downplays cultural diversity. There is a general notion that we should strive for a society which has common dominant cultural features which need to be shared by all citizens. It is a model that is based on the assumption that cultural homogeneity is the societal goal which should be worth pursuing for all. The model favours the assimilation of subordinate groups, which would give up much of their cultural capital for the benefits of accepting the dominant culture. The model does not encourage teachers to engage in cross-culturally sensitive and relevant classroom discourse.

The *minimalist multicultural* model gives token recognition that cultural diversity exists. Token recognition is manifested by introducing into an essentially monocultural teacher education curriculum, courses or study units on multi-culturism. This approach to cultural diversity concurs with the so-called "melting pot" view of society, in which all the different cultural groups are brought together into a cultural hybrid. The model could also be viewed as one that engenders the existence of different cultural identities from which we can develop a cultural mosaic. Each identity forms a part of a whole but can also be separated from it if desired.

The *issue pervasive* model stresses the need for teachers to develop an intercultural approach to cultural diversity, with a strong emphasis on infusing issues relating to cultural diversity throughout most of the teacher education curriculum. The model not only tries to address content, it goes further by melding the content of cultural diversity with the process of instruction and the general ethos of training to be a teacher. Zeichner & Tabachnik (1983) describe this model as pluralist; however, the term is rather loose to describe what is an intimate melding of three key factors, namely content, process and a teacher's cultural development.

It is clear from the above that there have been major developments in teacher education and training in the 1990s which have affected the role and status of teachers. New forms of access to information, the impact of postmodernism and changing demographic patterns to school populations are having a marked effect on the teacher's roles, leading to the need for newer training strategies to meet changing social and instructional expectations. Pertinent to the concerns of improving praxis and professionalism within changing cultural contexts, it is by tackling issues such as cultural dominance versus cultural diversity and by scrutinising the potential of a variety of curriculum models, that a truly appropriate intercultural role for teachers can be mapped out.

Recent research and development into cross-cultural training and education, which will be discussed in the next part of this chapter, will hopefully provide ideas for furthering the quality of intercultural teacher education and training, so that the outcome would be effective intercultural educators able to meet the problems concerned with cultural diversity in the classroom.

CROSS-CULTURAL TRAINING: IMPLICATIONS FOR TEACHER EDUCATION

In this part of the chapter we will address the second question posed earlier about the impact of recent research into cross-cultural training, and the implications for preparing teachers to meet the challenges of pupils from culturally diverse backgrounds. The growing interest in cross-cultural training and education in areas such as business, education, industrial organisation, international trade and tourism is testimony to the fact that more attention is being paid to improve intercultural communication between people from different cultural backgrounds, and who have constant contact with one another. Multiculturalism is rapidly becoming the norm in many societies, and therefore the incidence of cultural misunderstandings, possibly leading to some form of conflict, is likely to be greater.

There are different degrees and types of multiculturalism – in countries like the USA and the UK, multiculturalism has become firmly established within the framework of society, in which people of different cultural backgrounds have entered successfully into national life, e.g. sport, the professions, the media and all sectors of the working environment. A more transient form of multiculturalism exists with the movement of international students, businessmen and refugees, who move across cultural boundaries, but who may stay in a host country for up to four or five years.

Newly arrived and ethnically diverse immigrants will form an initial stage of multiculturalism in a society, during which they would have to adapt to their new surroundings. For the children who belong to one of these groups, the problem is often very acute, as they have to adjust to a school system which will have a different set of socio-cultural priorities from the ones which they already hold. Cross-cultural training and education are not available for all migrants who come to live in a host country that is culturally different from theirs. Where training is provided, it is likely to have different objectives and the structure of the programmes will also differ. However, in essence, the initial objective of most cross-cultural training will be preparatory and also one of sensitisation for the immigrant. Realisation of these objectives leads to further training and education, which in the long term will hopefully result in an established multicultural society.

In our discussions of research into cross-cultural training and education and its value for teacher training and development, it is important to make three points before we examine the research studies. Firstly, the amount of research into cross-cultural training for and by educators is not voluminous; there are far more studies relating to business, marketing, service industries and health than for education and teacher training. Outside the USA, there are few places where cross-cultural training has impinged on education (including teacher education). Nevertheless where cross-cultural education training programmes do exist, they tend to be focused on the practicum (teaching practice), or as a study of culture in social psychology or sociology. Secondly, in view of the above, what follows is a selection of research studies on cross-cultural training and education, together with well-documented programmes of training that have been used mainly in contexts other than education. Some of these studies and training programmes could have direct application to training school-teachers in cultural diversity and will be discussed later in the chapter.

Thirdly, it is important to make the distinction between training and education with reference to the cross-cultural research on training that is being discussed here. This is because cross-cultural training is in most cases a short-term goal, lasting anything from one week to three months, while cross-cultural education is perceived to have longer-term implications that will be intimately linked to multicultural education, the latter taking up to three years to be realised in some instances. We will now examine two main areas: firstly, the relevant research into cross-cultural training and the implications for teacher education and secondly, the transposition of some key elements from cross-cultural training to multicultural education, and its impact on the wider discussion about training teachers for cultural diversity.

Research into Cross-cultural Training Programmes and Teacher Education

Brislin & Horvath (1997) have reviewed numerous research studies and the general literature on cross-cultural training programmes. The reader is therefore referred to their work for an in-depth analysis of this subject. However, let us examine selected research on cross-cultural training that could be included in a teacher education curriculum that promotes cultural diversity. We will examine, first, research related to cross-cultural training that focuses on psychological changes, and then research that uses different methods and approaches to bring about change.

Cross-cultural Training That Attempts to Produce Psychological Change

Three main aspects of psychological change will be discussed below, namely changes in *thinking*, *affective* change and *behavioural* change.

Cross-cultural Training and Changes in Thinking Many training programmes that aim to produce change in a person's thinking have focused on how to increase that person's knowledge of culture, and the cultural differences and problems to be faced when there is cultural interaction between people. Training that changes thinking patterns provides opportunities through critical incidence techniques to increase the understanding of the other cultures, their points of view, the priorities and ways of reaching decisions. This is the essence of the role of culture assimilators or what are sometimes called culture sensitisers (Brislin *et al.* 1986; Triandis 1994). In this type of training, participants read about a case study involving persons from two or more cultures who tackle a shared task, such as negotiating a loan for aid to a developing country.

Participants learn about how decisions are taken, how time may be used as a delaying tactic and how problems are tackled without loss of face. Such training also shows how misunderstandings arise when they find that other cultures are operating along lines quite appropriate for them, but inappropriate for members of other cultures.

The value of cross-cultural training that aims to get people to see the other person's point of view has valuable lessons for teacher educators planning training programmes which aim to reinforce the notion of cultural diversity. To really understand cultural diversity, both teachers and pupils must be able to take up multiple viewpoints before some consensus can be agreed upon by all concerned.

Cross-cultural Training and Affective Change Intercultural interactions can cause various types of affective reactions (Triandis 1994). The reactions are usually one of disruption and even culture shock. Workers such as Furnham & Bochner (1986) have used the term "acculturative stress" to describe some aspects of emotional disruption caused through culture shock. Training programmes that are concerned with this aspect of behaviour have tried to emphasise the element of enjoyment in intercultural encounters (Landis, Brislin & Hulgus 1985).

Encouraging participants to actively enjoy cultural encounters rather than treat them as a formality has been found to improve the warmth and effectiveness of the interactions. Providing active enjoyment is, however, not a simple affair; any strategy that attempts to provide this approach needs to meet criteria súch as task accomplishment, reciprocity of feelings between the cultures in question, reasonable time for recovery from culture shock and the nature of the active enjoyment itself.

The time for people to overcome emotional stress and culture shock varies from one situation to another, but generally after six months most people have begun to adjust. The research on this area of training has particular application in situations where multi-ethnic immigrant children attend school in a new country for the first time. The need for teachers to receive training along the lines discussed above, would greatly help the cultural adjustment of these pupils in their new and per-plexing environment. Understanding emotional change in dif-ferent cultural contexts is particularly necessary for teachers working with refugee and street children attending school for the first time (Thomas 1998).

Cross-cultural Training and Behaviour Change Training can often lead to changes in people's behaviour, some of which can result in better interpersonal relationships, better performance in the world of work (Black & Mendenthall 1990), and in improving student acculturation when studying abroad. Westwood & Barker (1990) developed a training pro-gramme for overseas students before they embarked on a university education in Australia. The training involved developing good study skills, orientation to the academic culture of Australian universities, and interactions with Australian students who acted as cultural informants. Those students who did not have this training did not do as well as those who had. There are a number of applications to school-ing which this research into cross-cultural training might have. For instance, the setting up of co-operative learning groups which comprised host-culture peers in company with those children from minority cultures, would be a step in the right direction.

The development of group tasks that extended co-operation beyond the classroom would be another strategy that could be devised. For instance, mutual assistance with homework, shared visits linked to a school-based environmental project might also be planned. Getting to know one another's cultural traditions by visiting family homes could also help intercultural exchange considerably. Training teachers to develop these strategies for better classroom interaction would be an essential part in developing a curriculum which focuses on cultural diversity, in which the key objectives would be to change pupil attitudes followed hopefully by changes in behaviour.

Methods and Approaches Used in Cross-cultural Training

There are many methods and approaches available to cross-cultural trainers in order to improve intercultural interactions, and these have been discussed at length by Triandis, Kurowski & Gelfand (1994) and Brislin & Yoshida (1994). The main methods include *cognitive* and *attributional* training, *experiential*, *behavioural* and *self-awareness* approaches. Most of the methods and approaches have been used in training programmes that help people to adjust to life in their new surroundings. However, as we will see, some of the training methods can be applied to educational settings.

Cognitive and Attributional Training   *Cognitive training* emphasises the acquisition of facts and information concerning other cultures. The information is either culture specific or culture general. Where information focuses on aspects of the culture in which trainees will live, covering such areas as transport, climate, schooling, power relationships and male/female codes of behaviour, this would constitute information about cultural specificity. General information would include the nature of acculturative stress and culture shock, expectations by workers and managers in the workplace and threats to the trainee's cultural values. Cognitive approaches are easy to deliver, often by lecture or group seminar, which can target a large group at a time. There are, nevertheless, dangers in overuse of this approach, as too much information can be given on a single occasion, much of which will not be assimilated.

Attributional training is based on allowing trainees the opportunities to express different views about certain situations portrayed in critical incidences, involving people from different cultures. The focus is put on analysing the causes of a particular behaviour, not the behaviour itself. In an incident created by Brislin (1993) based on the I–C concept, an extremely productive American working in a software company in Japan was rated unsatisfactory by his Japanese supervisor, not because he was inefficient, but because he was perceived as being too individualistic, and failing to share his work skills with colleagues. When the attributional approach is used, an important feature of its use is that there are different interpretations of a particular incident. The American employee's attribution of the situation was that he was productive and pleasant, but the Japanese supervisor saw Peter as uncooperative and the group did not benefit from his knowledge and expertise. There are, however, no correct answers to attributional problems. But attributional training provides an awareness by all concerned in a cross-cultural situation that people behave mainly on the basis of their cultural backgrounds and the more we know about background, hopefully the less the number of intercultural misunderstandings.

In educational settings, both cognitive and attributional approaches have been used in sensitising teachers to issues in multicultural education. Cognitive inputs through the use of instructional packs containing written materials, photographs, video film, audio tapes, details of visits to anthropological museums as well as textbooks are familiar. The work of Epstein (1997) on developing a pedagogy to combat anti-racism in the UK and discussed in Chapter 1, would be an example of attempts to engage teacher trainees in using cognitive training. Case studies and role play have mainly been used alongside critical incidence in some teacher training programmes. However, critical incidences as yet are not commonly used in teacher training involving cultural diversity, but they would seem to have potential as a valuable training method for highlighting both specific and general aspects of a multicultural curriculum.

Experiential, Behavioural and Self-awareness Approaches to Cross-cultural Training Some of the above approaches to cross-cultural training have not figured very prominently in educational settings as such. However, there are some instances where these approaches have been applied to teacher training using a different label, as we shall uncover below.

Experiential approaches attempt to introduce trainees to various perspectives of other cultures as authentically as possible. In portraying the different perspectives, the use of techniques, such as role play, analysis of case studies, field-based simulation and highly structured simulation are common. Through these techniques, emotional, social and moral issues are played out to attain the maximum amount of authenticity of a situation as possible. The problem with using experiential approaches is that they can lead to disruption during the training sessions, as participants may become too involved with the issues being discussed. All the above techniques are commonly used in all forms of teacher training in many countries, but role play and field-based simulation may have particular value for sensitising teachers to the issues related to cultural diversity. By applying these methods, trainees have the opportunities to "act out" difficult situations associated with cultural interpersonal behaviours.

Behavioural approaches were widely used as intercultural training techniques during the 1960s and 1970s, but they fell into disrepute as their use became associated with an overemphasis of negative stereotypes based on Skinnerian conditioning. However, workers such as Diaz-Guerrero (1975) and Brislin & Yoshida (1994) have pointed out that it is possible to focus on certain behaviours that can lead to successful training programmes. For instance, a common behaviour pattern among CHCs is to avoid loss of face in public situations, and especially ones that involve Westerners. For Westerners to negotiate within a "loss of face" culture, it is essential that they recognise the signs and signals beyond which the Westerner should not proceed in a discussion. Both Westerner and oriental need to know the limits of what is possible in open discussion, and what eventually transpires afterwards behind closed doors. Westerners must learn to realise that decisions affecting even public events are rarely taken in a face-to-face situation; there is usually a period of private consultation before decisions are arrived at. Education settings are no different from others in this regard, as we discovered about this subject and the related topic of eye contact in Chapter 3, in which the work of Bartolome (1994) relating to visual learning cues of pupils from different cultures was discussed.

Self-awareness training deals with the trainees themselves and their perception of their own cultural background. The best-known self-awareness method is the "contrast-American simulation" which is sometimes termed "contrast culture" technique. The main feature of this technique is to put the trainee in a contrasting situation to that of the trainer, by the trainer behaving differently from that of the trainee. The sharp contrast allows the trainee to become aware of his or her attitudes, values and behaviours which are strongly influenced by their culture. The objective is to make the trainee aware that his cultural background may be very different from those of his peers and also of those he will one day teach. This is not a method that has been used very much in educational situations, but there could be potential applications in contexts where the cultural background of teachers may be so different from that of the pupils they teach, that certain contrast tactics that are features of this technique may be useful.

In answer to our second question about the value of research into cross-cultural training for teacher development and training, it is clear that the approaches discussed above have much to offer teacher trainers. The methods used to bring about changes in people's thinking, their affective responses and behavioural actions, the use of experiential and self-awareness training, all have the potential of providing trainers with valuable ideas of how to get teachers to understand cultural diversity, and help them devise a culture-sensitive pedagogy to meet the tasks associated with this diversity. Let us move on at this juncture to our third question, which addresses the impact of cross-cultural training on multicultural education programmes in schools.

Training into Education: a Transposition Challenge for Multicultural Education

Transposing training into praxis in most disciplines will always pose problems as far as effectiveness is concerned. However, in carrying out transposition to achieve a successful programme of multicultural education, the problems are particularly acute. This is due to at least four reasons: firstly, the *complex nature of multicultural education* itself, secondly, the *differing perspectives of multicultural education* held by social scientists and educators, thirdly, the problem of *extending multicultural education into the culture of schools* and fourthly, the specific problems of *transposing training into education* associated with multiculturalism. We will examine each of the reasons below.

The Complex Nature of Multicultural Education

Multicultural education and cross-cultural training have at least three common features, an emphasis on understanding differences, an acceptance of diversity, and the search for some form of common ground which lays a basis for sound intercultural discourse in society. There are many ways of conceptualising multicultural education, depending on what viewpoint is taken. Psychologists are concerned with the behavioural processes that underlie the notion of multicultural education, while sociologists, on the other hand, are more interested in how different cultures can fit into an existing host society so they have equality of opportunity and social equity. Educationists are more concerned with identifying the goals of a multicultural society and the achievement of those goals in school and society.

For instance, Banks (1989) has described multicultural education as multifaceted, in which all students should have equal opportunities to learn, that it should be at the forefront of educational reform to provide an "ongoing" process to improve all students' academic education. The phrase "ongoing" is a crucial one in the present context of teacher development and cultural diversity.

To ensure that the "ongoing" nature of multicultural education is achieved as effectively as possible in the long term, it is necessary that teachers, pupils and the community play their part. However, as teachers have such a key role in ensuring that multicultural education is meaningful and "ongoing", there is a need to concentrate on how cross-cultural training may help to sensitise teachers during their pre-service training, and their later professional development. In many countries with large numbers of diverse ethnic minorities, the focus on multicultural education has tended towards curricular addition and expansion (Cushner 1994).

Historically, this was seen as crucial in correcting the ethnocentric balance of a predominantly monocultural curriculum. However, mere knowledge infusion is not sufficient, as teachers are increasingly being called upon to teach pupils from a variety of cultural and linguistic backgrounds. Pedagogical processes have therefore become as important as content, in the drive to make multicultural education more pervasive in the school curriculum.

Differing Perspectives on Multicultural Education

There has been some confusion over the years about the label multicultural education, particularly when the term refers to the education of communities, and the interrelations between minority groups within these communities. There are two divergent views about multicultural education; one emphasises integration at the level of curriculum planning, and the other is more of a "state of mind". This dichotomy has led to different research approaches to the subject. If one poses the question why is it necessary to address the need for multicultural education and to assess its place in schooling, it might be useful to be aware of the various perspectives that are taken of the subject by educators and other professional groups.

Brislin & Horvath (1997) have identified four perspectives on multicultural education: *diversity education, non-Western education, global education* and *intercultural education*. In brief, *diversity* or *ethnic* education emphasises the development of cultural pride and aptitudes to be successful in the host community, *non-Western* education is about exposing Western peoples to other cultures, *global* education or international education aims to help students to understand and possibly participate in international relations, co-operative ventures and in education as a discipline, and finally *intercultural* education, which is a feature of pluralistic environments, focuses on cultural diversity in the school. This latter view of multicultural education is the one that is accepted by the present author as the best possible way ahead in tackling the gap between school and society, and especially where society is culturally diverse. This would apply even in societies where the need for an awareness of cultural diversity may not be perceived to be a strong feature, as in Japan or Bangladesh.

It can be argued that schoolchildren who live in such countries would benefit from being exposed to other cultures, especially nowadays as rapid forms of communication have made the world a much smaller place.

Extending Multicultural Education and Changing School Culture

From the various perspectives on multicultural education discussed above, it is clear that some of them are looser notions than others, e.g. diversity and non-Western. It is often the case that multicultural education is implemented or supplemented by training courses. However, intercultural education is the form of multicultural education which is nearest to achieving an appreciation of cultural diversity during the years of schooling. In order that intercultural education is effective in changing the culture of schools towards a greater emphasis on cultural diversity, it is important to introduce changes into the school curriculum and also changes in the way teachers are trained. It will also be necessary to monitor the changing cultural profiles of classrooms, as school populations change from year to year. In extending multicultural education to effect culture change in classrooms, three objectives need to be met: *to set realistic goals, to widen the curriculum* and *to train teachers to be innovative and adaptive.* We will explore each of these briefly.

In *setting goals* for multicultural education it is important to accept that it is a process which involves *culture learning*, which has been defined by Walsh (1979) as understanding the ways in which people from other cultures perceive reality. From this basis, the main goals of multicultural education should include getting students to predict the attitudes and behaviours of other cultural groups, and in different settings. It should increase the academic achievement of students, helping them relate to other cultural group members. To realise these goals, students need to be encouraged by their teachers to increase their mastery of events in their immediate environment, and this is often done by improving communication skills. Students should also increase their knowledge of their peers' cultural background, and to be aware of how their peers behave in different situations. To counteract feelings of alienation and lack of control, which is often the case when a student's culture does not fit easily with the culture of the school, teachers need to provide opportunities for students to take the initiative, to have books and teaching materials available which reflect key aspects of their own culture. By meeting some of these suggestions, the school will help realise the goals stated above.

Widening the curriculum should mean that students develop a greater awareness of other cultures, and culture-specific skills and customs that will provide a sure foundation for exploring the nature of cultural diversity in classrooms. The inclusion of more culturally compatible material into the curriculum would make learning for minority groups not only more meaningful but probably more enjoyable. The use of thematic approaches to learning would be another way of widening the curriculum, in this case a theme such as "Eliminating illiteracy in the world" or "Improving our neighbourhood environment" is chosen for all the class to study using group discussion, project work and field visits. Through this approach, students are encouraged to draw, where relevant, on their own cultural backgrounds to use their own initiative and ideas in the overall treatment of the theme.

Without committed *innovative and adaptive teachers*, the implementation of curriculum reform will be seriously impeded. Curriculum change has to take into account that teachers need to be adaptive to the different learning styles of their pupils and be more prepared to listen and involve their pupils in learning and teaching. In multicultural classrooms where didactic teaching is often the norm, teachers are obliged to adopt this type of teaching, because of poor classroom resources. However, with more imaginative training these difficulties can be overcome. The successful expansion of multicultural education will depend ultimately on teachers being able to fulfil their intercultural role. This means that the nature and extent of teacher training will need to address more innovative ways of sensitising teachers to preparing their pupils for a culturally diverse society.

Transposing Cross-cultural Training to Multicultural Education

We have already discussed in this and other chapters that the processes of teacher training and education can be distinguished in several ways. To reiterate the main distinction, training focuses on the acquisition of knowledge, skills and techniques which will be imparted to pupils as an essential preparation for their life prospects. However, education is a deeper process of personal development, involving enhancement of a pupil's self-actualisation and self-esteem, and a greater awareness of cultural diversity in society. The experiences of cross-cultural training have shown that, although the training is aimed at the short term and for situations that are generally not school based, they have the potential to provide a training and an education for teachers who will be at the cutting edge of making multicultural education a relevant and realistic prospect.

The translation of theory into practice is a well-known challenge for most teacher educators to meet; however, in a similar vein the transposition of cross-cultural training to improve multicultural education is an equally difficult task. This is especially so where the main focus is on developing a curriculum that puts cultural diversity high on its agenda. There is therefore under these circumstances an even greater need to examine the goals and nature of training, so that it provides a relevant and sound basis for multicultural education in the long term.

It is possible to chart a pathway from a short-term cross-cultural training programme of about three to four weeks to a longer-term course lasting several years, and in which training remains a key element in the curriculum. For instance, there are training programmes in the USA which deal with subjects such as "diversity as a challenge", "the need for cultural changes and their implementation in educational systems", and "testing the effectiveness of curriculum change" that have been expanded into longer-term courses of study. The 18-theme culture-general framework proposed by Brislin *et al.* (1986), and one of the first established programmes for cross-cultural training, has the potential to be transposed into a full course on multicultural education. Let us briefly examine the basic structure of this cross-cultural framework, and discuss the possibilities for transposing it as a component of a teacher training curriculum for cultural diversity.

The 18 themes are classified into three broad categories of concern and possible misunderstanding. The three categories are based on the assumption that people from different cultural backgrounds and who interact with one another (a) will express and receive highly charged emotions, (b) will experience conflict and misunderstanding as they operate from a different cultural base and (c) will interpret similar stimuli differently because of their cultural differences. The 18 themes are scattered among the three categories, and include issues such as anxiety, the need to belong, confronting one's own prejudices, decision making and problem solving within different cultural contexts, differences in learning styles and making judgements about others.

Each of the 18 themes can be applied to the school context, as they include issues that are day-to-day occurrences between students, and between students and teachers. Of particular relevance would be themes that relate to belonging (very important for adolescents), anxiety (in which feelings of discomfiture are common), communication problems (especially the use of the same language in different contexts and spoken differently by various minorities) and learning styles (relating to co-operative versus individual learning, and field dependence and independence). These thematic issues could form the basis for suitable content in a training curriculum that promotes an understanding of cultural diversity. In the next section we will examine different approaches to developing some teacher education programmes that focus on cultural diversity. Some of the approaches that will be discussed will include the knowledge, skills and attitudes that come from the cross-cultural training programmes discussed above, as well as using ideas that emerged from some of the research studies relating to cross-cultural training.

The third question posed at the start of the chapter raised the issue of impact. It is perhaps premature to describe with any degree of conviction the exact impact of cross-cultural training on teacher training programmes to date. This is because little has been accomplished in the field of cross-cultural teacher education, apart from some American examples to be discussed in the next section of this chapter. Nevertheless, the seminal work of Brislin, Cushner and others on cross-cultural training has laid the foundations for a more focused approach to both the training and education of teachers, as far as cultural diversity is concerned. This will hopefully lead to a cadre of teachers who will enrich the practice of multicultural education through the application of cross-cultural strategies promoting the ethos of cultural diversity.

TEACHERS FOR CULTURAL DIVERSITY: SOME STRATEGIES FOR CROSS-CULTURAL TRAINING

The need to develop cross-cultural training strategies for teachers is a message that comes over clear and persistently from much of what has been discussed so far, and constitutes the fourth question that was posed at the beginning of the chapter. It has been amply shown in countries like the UK and the USA and continental countries like the Netherlands and Germany, that the growing numbers of immigrant children in the classrooms of these countries come from a great variety of cultures (Eldering & Rothenberg 1997). This has placed teachers and teacher education in a dilemma, for it is not possible that teachers will have a knowledge of all these cultures, and it is even less likely for teachers to be able to teach about them.

This dilemma is further complicated when we examine how teachers may be trained to meet the problems that arise from it. We will examine below some teacher-training strategies that attempt to address the issue of making cultural diversity a foundation for better intercultural education in schools. We will first examine several case studies that have pioneered a pluralistic approach to training teachers in North America, followed by possible applications of ideas and practices, derived from well-established cross-cultural training programmes some of which we have discussed earlier.

Training Teachers for Diversity – Some American Case Studies

A Wisconsin Experience

A partnership between the Teacher Education Faculty of the University Wisconsin–Madison and the Madison school district aimed to prepare elementary-school teachers to use multicultural approaches to their teaching (Gomez & Tabachnik 1991). There were three objectives to the programme, to get university students (a) skilled in teaching children from low-income families and children of colour, (b) to continue to teach in the district, and (c) to contextualise theories of teaching so that teaching choices may be justified under certain classroom conditions. The programme derived strength from the close collaboration between school and faculty staff, and teacher trainees. The trainees were given opportunities to take innovative initiatives and make learning more problem centred. The programme also tried to provide a meaning to multicultural education for the trainees, teaching staff and pupils as they operated on a daily basis in multicultural classrooms.

Making multiculturalism a reality was also assisted by allowing trainees to tell "teaching stories" to each other as part of social discourse. These stories are meant to illustrate aspects of multicultural teaching (Gomez & Tabachnik 1992). The

Madison case study has meant that trainee teachers build up a considerable support network among themselves, which also means that trainees can learn about each other's culture and, in turn, pass on both the content of and approach to multicultural education to the pupils they will teach. The social discourse aspect of the programme is perhaps the most important, as far as developing teachers for cultural diversity is concerned, as it strikes at the core of what cultural diversity is about, i.e. getting to know one another's culture, and how it can be transposed to other teacher-training components such as instruction, assessment and teaching practice.

Teachers for Alaska

The Teachers for Alaska is a programme which attempts to educate teachers for diversity. It is a one-year postgraduate course which focuses on training teachers for remote Eskimo and Indian villages as well as urban multicultural schools. About 12% of the trainees are from minority groups. The programme links the training of students to the specific contexts in which trainees will work (Nordhoff & Kleinfeld 1991). The underlying philosophy of the course, is that experience with pupils from different cultural backgrounds is necessary for teachers to make sense of the training they receive at a college or university. The course makes extensive use of case material or themes written by practising teachers.

These case materials help embed specific teaching of social and cultural issues familiar to the pupils in schools. For instance, "Malaise of the spirit" (Finley 1988) is one such case used in training and deals with racial tension in the classroom, and also school–community relationships. There is an intense exposure to ethnic minority communities, and also to problems of classroom teaching. While prospective teachers are given extensive information on the culture of the region beforehand, the main emphasis is on helping trainees learn how to learn from the culturally diverse pupils and communities in which the school exists. The Alaska programme is essentially about preparing teachers for culturally diverse settings, and to learn to match their instruction and rapport to the students' cultural backgrounds.

Preparing Teachers for Their Intercultural Roles – a Cross-cultural Modular Approach

The 18-theme general culture framework for intercultural training devised by Brislin *et al.* (1986), which has already been discussed earlier in this chapter, has been used by Cushner (1994) as the basis for a module on "Preparing teachers for an intercultural context". The module provides the trainee teacher with information, numerical data and a set of study materials on cultural situations that the teacher will know about when he or she is faced with teaching a group of heterogeneous students. The module also provides strategies and incidences which help the trainee to understand and solve problems relating to cultural differences. In keeping with the 18-theme framework, the module written by Cushner has the following contents:

1. *A self-assessment test*, which contains a list of questions relating to teacher education in a multicultural society. The trainee grades his/her response on a six-point scale A–F; A is an excellent answer and F would mean the trainee would not know where to start. There are 12 questions in the test containing examples such as:
   Q1: What percentage of children in schools in your country in the 1990s are children of colour?
   Q2: Identify three to five aspects of your cultural upbringing that may present obstacles as you interact in a culturally diverse classroom setting.
2. *Case studies containing critical incidences*, which contain accounts of typical incidents which a teacher may meet at school. This is followed by a series of questions for discussion among a group of trainees.
3. *Skill concepts*, which address in some detail key issues that arise when training teachers for diversity in education. This section forms the content of the training module dealing

with concepts such as anxiety, communication and learning styles.

4. *Skill applications*, which use a series of statements which amplify in detail issues such as value orientations, communication differences and family-related roles. Trainees will use these statements to explore the issues further.

5. *Field exercises*, which will include visits to schools and observations of classrooms where intercultural teaching is taking place.

Implications of Experiences in Cross-cultural Training for Teacher Preparation

Cushner's training module identifies a number of competencies that all teachers need to develop. These include applying *prognostic* and *diagnostic* competencies, so that the teacher can find out as much as possible about the background of the cultural contexts that may make up the pupil classroom profile. The self-assessment and case study critical incidence components of the module train teachers to develop the competencies of prognosis and diagnosis. The modular components of skill concepts and skill applications, emphasise the importance of being competent in the *theoretical knowledge* and practical *application* of that knowledge to culturally diverse situations in the classroom. The modular component of field exercises may develop competencies such as *observational diagnosis*, opportunities to apply *culture-sensitive instruction* including use of an indigenous language, construction and use of teaching materials that reflect traditional customs.

From the analyses of the case studies and the modular approaches to training teachers for cultural diversity, it is clear that exciting new approaches are in the making for preparing teachers to take up their intercultural roles. However, there appears to be a gap between the existing training strategies for teachers who work in multicultural classrooms, and the increasing amount of knowledge and skills that cross-cultural researchers and practitioners have developed in the context of cross-cultural training.

It is possible to detect in the case studies from Wisconsin and Alaska on teacher training that the use of cognitive, experiential, behavioural methodologies are implicit in the training regimen, rather than being explicit. Similar gaps appear in the more recent work of Liston & Zeichner (1996) in their excellent case studies concerning "School and home", "Curriculum and culture" and "Teachers and cultural identities". An analysis of these case studies from a cross-cultural perspective shows how important it is to have a sound understanding of cultural context. These forward-looking programmes and case studies could be enriched further, if they were able to adapt some of the ideas from the modular approach which Richard Brislin and others have pioneered. It would seem that both praxis and professionalism, as far as teachers for cultural diversity are concerned, stand to benefit substantively if the more pertinent aspects of theory, practice and research on cross-cultural training find their way into all teacher education programmes that aim to produce teachers for cultural diversity.

If this were to happen, we might be approaching the exciting prospect of a *culture-sensitive teacher education*, a subject that was raised earlier in the chapter, as the last of our five questions. In concluding this chapter, we will attempt to sketch out what a *culture-sensitive teacher education* might entail.

TOWARDS A CULTURE-SENSITIVE TEACHER EDUCATION

In the course of this chapter it will not have escaped the reader that there has been a constant theme running throughout, the theme being a need for teachers to be trained as key agents in promoting an understanding of cultural diversity among their pupils in multicultural schools and colleges (see Figure 7.1).

In Chapter 3 we discussed the development of a culture-sensitive pedagogy, in making such a teaching approach available to teachers. Employing a culture-sensitive approach in classroom teaching enables teachers to provide a more in-depth understanding of the cultural contexts that are familiar to their pupils, as well as for them as professionals. At a more comprehensive level, it is equally necessary that the whole process of teacher education and training is also made more culture sensitive, so that it can meet the challenge of cultural diversity in the process of schooling.

In order to make teacher education and training more culture sensitive for future generations of teachers, it is clear from the research discussed relating to the cultural dynamics of learning in Chapter 2, that teachers will need to improve their knowledge about the cultures which are represented in many multicultural classrooms. Teachers who are trained to apply a variety of pedagogical models, be they folk or integrative, to teaching and learning processes, should make their teaching not only effective, but relevant as well.

A culture-sensitive teacher education is also one that requires teachers to be trained in innovative cross-cultural methods of instruction. It is clear from our discussion in the present chapter that the pioneering work of Cushner and Brislin provides useful signposts for the future development of more in-depth and school-centred teacher training, which will hopefully meet the demands of cultural diversity in the classroom.

In recent years reflective inquiry has become a very important part of teacher preparation in many countries, for it enables teachers to re-examine praxis and theory at all stages of their teaching. When teachers are faced with the extra challenges of coping with culturally diverse situations in class, the ability to be reflective becomes even more important and should be part of any up-to-date teacher-training curriculum. In many cases, reflective inquiry should not stop short at reflection; it should lead to useful classroom-based research that might shed valuable light on improving successful praxis in the multicultural school.

Finally, any changes aimed at making teacher education more responsive to training teachers for cultural diversity need to take account of the professional development of teachers. It is essential that teachers who have been specifically trained to take on intercultural roles in order to promote a better understanding of the dynamics of cultural diversity among pupils should be given the opportunity to study disciplines related to cross-cultural issues and problems. These teachers should also have the opportunity to embark on career pathways that would provide them with the motivation needed to enable them to become effective in cultural bridge building as well as other intercultural roles. In answer to the fifth and final question posed at the start of this chapter, the case for a *culture-sensitive teacher education* is not only a viable prospect and is clearly desirable, it is also long overdue.

SUMMARY

1. When teacher educators embark on teacher-training programmes for cultural diversity, they face the challenge of maintaining an equilibrium between innovation and cultural retention.
2. Five main questions were addressed in this chapter relating to (i) the changing nature of teacher education and the intercultural roles of teachers, (ii) the contribution of recent cross-cultural training research on teacher training, (iii) the impact of cross-cultural training on multicultural education, (iv) how teacher-training strategies can focus on cultural diversity as part of multicultural education, and (v) the prospects for a culture-sensitive teacher education?
3. Five key issues are linked to training teachers for multicultural education: *resistance to change* on the part of teach-

ers, *cultural erosion*, the impact of *the information revolution*, the need for *special training strategies*, and for long-term *teacher professional development*.

4. Among the major areas of teacher education that have been affected by change, the curriculum and teacher development and training are the two most pertinent as far as the cultural influences on schooling are concerned. Transcending these two areas are a number of factors which have influenced the nature of change, these include *socio-cultural factors, cultural dominance versus cultural diversity, the teacher's intercultural role* and *the development of an appropriate curriculum model* for teacher training.

5. The number of research studies on cross-cultural training that have been carried out by and for educators is not large; however, what research on cross-cultural educational training exists has focused on the practicum (teaching practice).

6. Research into cross-cultural training falls into two areas, research which focuses on *psychological aspects*, targeting thinking, affectivity and behavioural change, and research which focuses on *methodologies* such as the use of cognitive, attributional, behavioural and self-awareness techniques.

7. Multicultural education and cross-cultural training have three common features: an emphasis on understanding differences, acceptance of diversity, and the search for a common discourse.

8. Effective teacher education must aim at meeting the challenges posed by the common features (mentioned in 7 above), in order to provide teachers who will be sensitive to the demands of cultural diversity in schools.

9. To apply cross-cultural training methods to the problems of teacher training in multicultural contexts, it is important to realise that (a) multicultural education has different perspectives, (b) to be effective it needs to become part of the school culture and (c) the transposition of training into education in the context of cultural diversity is as smooth as possible.

10. In order to develop training strategies to meet the inter-
    cultural roles which teachers are required to perform
    in culturally diverse school contexts, there have been
    several examples from the USA which usefully employ
    "on the job" training, curricula which emphasise cultural
    diversity.
11. The use of modular strategies in cross-cultural training for
    classroom instruction promoting better training for cul-
    tural diversity, may improve the prospects for a more cul-
    turally sensitive teaching profession.
12. The development of *culture-sensitive teacher education and
    training* programmes would, in the long run, provide a
    teaching force which would be better prepared for
    meeting the challenges of cultural diversity in multicul-
    tural classrooms.

SUGGESTIONS FOR FURTHER READING

Brislin, R.W. & Horvath, A.M. (1997). Cross-cultural training and
multicultural education. In J.W. Berry, M.S. Segall & C. Kagitcibasi
(Eds), *Handbook of Cross Cultural Psychology*, Volume 3, *Social
Behaviour and Applications*. Boston: Allyn & Bacon, pp. 327–369.

Cushner, K. (1994). Preparing teachers for an intercultural context.
In R.W. Brislin & T. Yoshida (Eds). *Improving Intercultural Interac-
tion: Modules for Cross Cultural Training Programs*. Thousand Oaks,
Calif.: Sage, pp. 109–128.

Epstein, D. (1997). *Changing Classroom Cultures: Anti-racism, Politics
and Schools*. Stoke on Trent: Trentham Books.

Tabachnik, B.R. & Zeichner, K.M. (1993). Preparing teachers for
cultural diversity. In P. Gilroy & M. Smith (Eds), *International
Analyses of Teacher Education*. Abingdon: Carfax Publications, pp.
113–124.

Thomas, E. (1996). Teacher education in South East Asia: prospects
for a North–South dialogue with a difference. In C. Brock (Ed.),
Global Perspectives on Teacher Education. Wallingford, Berks:
Triangle Press, pp. 123–151.

REFERENCES

Adler, N. & Bartholomew, S. (1992). Academic and professional communities of discourse: generating knowledge on transactional human resource management. *Journal of International Business Studies*, **23**(3), 551–570.

Aikman, S. (1994). School curriculum as a forum for articulating intercultural relations with particular reference to the Peruvian Amazon. In E. Thomas (Ed.), *International Perspectives on Culture and Schooling: A Symposium Proceedings*. London: University of London, Institute of Education Publication, pp. 197–218.

Aikman, S. (1999). *Intercultural Education and Literacy*. Studies in Written Language and Literacy, 7. Amsterdam: John Benjamins Publishing Company, pp. 167–171.

Alderfer, C.P. (1972). *Existence, Relatedness, and Growth*. New York: Free Press.

Altbach, P. & Kelly, G. (1978). *Education and Colonialism*. New York: Longman.

Anastasi, A. (1988). *Psychological Testing* (6th edn). New York: Macmillan.

APEID/UNESCO (1988). *Multiple Class Teaching in Primary Schools: A Methodological Guide*. Bangkok: UNESCO Publication.

Apple, M. (1982). *Education and Power*. London: Routledge.

Bagby, J.W. (1957). A cross cultural study of perceptual dominance in binocular rivalry. *Journal of Abnormal and Social Psychology*, **54**, 331–334.

Bajunid, I.A. (1996). Preliminary explorations of indigenous perspectives of educational management: the evolving Malaysian experience. Paper presented at the Eighth International Conference of the CCEA, Indigenous Perspectives of Educational Management, IAB, Genting Highlands, Malaysia.

Baker, C. (1993). *Foundations of Bilingual Education*. Clevedon: Multilingual Matters.

Ballenger, C. (1992). Because you like us: the language of control. *Harvard Educational Review*, **6**(2), 199–208.

Banks, J.A. (1989). Multicultural education: characteristics and goals. In J.A. Banks & C.A. McGee Banks (Eds), *Multicultural Education: Issues and Perspectives*. Boston: Allyn & Bacon, pp. 2–26.

Barber, B.K., Chadwick, B.A. & Oerter, R. (1992). Parental behaviours and adolescent self esteem in the United States and Germany. *Journal of Management and the Family*, **54**, 128–141.

Barry, H., Bacon, M.K. & Child, I.L. (1957). A cross cultural survey of some sex differences in socialisation. *Journal of Abnormal and Social Psychology*, **55**, 327–332.

Bartolome, L.I. (1994). Beyond the methods fetish: towards a humanising pedagogy. *Harvard Educational Review*, **64**(2), 173–194.

Bass, B.M. (1985). *Leadership and Performance beyond Expectations*. New York: Free Press.

Baumgart, N. & Elliot, A. (1996). *Promoting the Study of Asia across the Curriculum: An Evaluation of the First Three Years of the Asia Education Foundation*. Sydney: University of Sydney, Nepean.

Bennett, N. (1993). Knowledge bases for learning to teach. In N. Bennett & C. Carre (Eds), *Learning to Teach*. London: Routledge, pp. 1–17.

Ben-Peretz, M. (1998). Classroom management in Israel: issues and concerns. In N.K. Shimahara (Ed.), *Politics of Classroom Life*. New York: Garland Inc., pp. 265–277.

Ben-Peretz, M. & Steinhardt, M. (1996). Student perceptions of classroom situation in multicultural contexts. Paper presented at the ECER, the Second International Conference of the European Educational Research Association, Seville, September.

Berry, J.W. (1980a). Ecological analysis for cross cultural psychology. In N. Warren (Ed.), *Studies in Cross Cultural Psychology*, Volume 2. London: Academic Press.

Berry, J.W. (1980b). Social and cultural change. In H.C. Triandis & R. Brislin (Eds), *Handbook of Cross Cultural Psychology*, Volume 5, Boston: Allyn & Bacon, pp. 211–279.

Berry, J.W. (1984). Cultural relations in plural societies: alternatives to segregation and their sociopsychological implications. In N. Miller & M. Brewer (Eds), *Groups in Contact*. New York: Academic Press, pp. 11–27.

Berry, J.W. (1990). The psychology of acculturation. In J. Berman (Ed.), *Cross Cultural Perspectives: Nebraska Symposium on Motivation*. Lincoln: University of Nebraska Press, pp. 201–234.

Berry, J.W. (1991). Cultural variation in field dependence–independence. In S. Wagner & J. Demick (Eds), *Field Dependence–Independence: Cognitive Styles across Cultures*. Hillsdale, NJ: Erlbaum, pp. 289–308.

Berry, J.W. & Sam, D.L. (1997). Acculturation and adaptation. In J.W. Berry, M.S. Segall & C. Kagitcibasi (Eds), *Handbook of Cross Cultural Psychology*, Volume 3, *Social Behaviour and Applications*. Boston: Allyn & Bacon, pp. 291–326.

Best, D. & Williams, J. (1997). Sex, gender and culture. In J.W. Berry, M.S. Segall & C. Kagitcibasi (Eds), *Handbook of Cross Cultural Psychology*, Volume 3, *Social Behaviour and Applications*. Boston: Allyn & Bacon, pp. 163–212.

Bhawuk, D. & Brislin, R. (1992). The measurement of intercultural sensitivity using the individualism and collectivism concepts. *International Journal of Intercultural Relations*, **16**, 413–436.

Bickersteth, P. & Das, J.P. (1987). Syllogistic reasoning among school children from Canada and Sierra Leone. *International Journal of Psychology*, **16**, 1–11.

Biggs, J.B. (1979). Individual differences in study processes and the quality of learning outcomes. *Higher Education*, **8**, 381–394.

Biggs, J.B. (1988). The role of metacognition in enhancing learning. *Australian Journal of Education*, **32**, 127–138.

Biggs, J.B. (1993). What do inventories of students' learning processes really measure? A theoretical review and clarification. *British Journal of Educational Psychology*, **63**, 3–19.

Biggs, J.B. (1996). Western misconceptions of the Confucian-heritage learning culture. In D.A. Watkins & J.B. Biggs (Eds), *The Chinese Learner: Cultural, Psychological and Contextual Influences*. Victoria: CERC & ACER, pp. 45–68.

Biggs, J.B. & Watkins, D.A. (1996). The Chinese learner in retrospect. In D.A. Watkins & J.B. Biggs (Eds), *The Chinese Learner: Cultural, Psychological and Contextual Influences*. Victoria: CERC & ACER, pp. 269–285.

Black, J. & Mendenthall, M. (1990). Cross cultural training effectiveness: a review and a theoretical framework for future research. *Academy of Management Review*, **15**, 113–136.

Blanchard, K., Zigarmi, P. & Zugarmi, D. (1985). *Leadership and the One Minute Manager*. London: Fontana/Collins.

Bloom, B.S. (Ed.) (1956). *Taxonomy of Educational Objectives*, Book 1, *Cognitive Domain*. London: Longmans.

Blumenfeld, P.C. (1992). Classroom learning and motivation: clarifying and expanding goal theory. *Journal of Educational Psychology*, **84**, 272–281.

Bordieu, P. (1971). Systems of education and systems of thought. In M. Young (Ed.), *Knowledge and Control*. London: Collier Macmillan, pp. 189–207.

Bottger, P.C., Hallein, I.H. & Yetton, P.W. (1985). A cross national study of leadership: participation as a function of problem structure and leader power. *Journal of Management Studies*, **22**, 358–368.

Bradley, D. & Bradley, M. (1984). *Problems of Asian Students in Australia: Language, Culture and Education*. Canberra: Australian Government Printing Service.

Brislin, R.W. (1986). The wording and translation of research instruments. In W.J. Lonner & J.W. Berry (Eds), *Field Methods in Cross Cultural Research*. Newbury Park, Calif.: Sage, pp. 137–164.

Brislin, R.W. (Ed.) (1990). *Applied Cross Cultural Psychology*. Newbury Park, Calif.: Sage.

Brislin, R.W. (1993). *Understanding Culture's Influence on Behaviour*. Fort Worth: Harcourt.

Brislin, R.W. (1994). Individualism and collectivism as the source of many specific cultural differences. In R.W. Brislin & T. Yoshida (Eds), *Improving Intercultural Interactions: Modules for Cross Cultural Training Programs*. Thousand Oaks: Sage, pp. 71–88.

Brislin, R.W., Cushner, Cherrie C. & Yong, M. (Eds) (1986). *Intercultural Interactions: A Practical Guide*. Newbury Park, Calif.: Sage.

Brislin, R.W. & Horvath, A.M. (1997). Cross cultural training and multicultural education. In J.W. Berry, M.S. Segall & C. Kagitcibasi (Eds), *Handbook of Cross Cultural Psychology*, Volume 3, *Social Behaviour and Applications*. Boston: Allyn & Bacon, pp. 327–369.

Brislin, R.W. & Yoshida, T. (Eds) (1994). *Improving Intercultural Interaction: Modules for Cross Cultural Training Programs*. Thousand Oaks, Calif.: Sage.

Bronfenbrenner, U. (1979). *The Ecology of Human Development*. Cambridge, Mass.: Harvard University Press.

Bruner, J.S. (1966). *Toward a Theory of Instruction*. Cambridge, Mass.: Harvard University Press.

Burg, B. & Belmont, I. (1990). Mental abilities of children from different cultural backgrounds in Israel. *Journal of Cross Cultural Psychology*, **21**, 90–108.

Burns, J.M. (1978). *Leadership*. New York: Harper Row.

Callan, V.J. & Kee, P.-K. (1981). Sons or daughters? Cross cultural comparisons of sex preferences of Australian, Greek, Italian, Malay, Chinese and Indian parents in Australia and Malaysia. *Population and Environment*, **4**, 97–108.

Cara, F. & Politzer, G. (1993). A comparison of conditional reasoning in English and Chinese. In J. Altarriba (Ed.), *Cognition and Culture: A Cross Cultural Approach to Cognitive Psychology*. Amsterdam: Elsevier, pp. 283–298.

Carnoy, M. (1974). *Education as Cultural Imperialism*. New York: Longman.

Carraher, T.N., Carraher, D.W. & Schliemann, A.D. (1987). Written and oral mathematics. *Journal for Research in Mathematics Education*, **18**, 83–97.

Carroll, J.B. (1983). Studying individual differences in cognitive abilities: implications for cross cultural studies. In S.H. Irvine & J.W. Berry (Eds), *Human Assessment and Cultural Factors*. New York: Plenum, pp. 213–235.

CCC (1987). Chinese values and the search for culture free dimensions of culture. *Journal of Cross Cultural Psychology*, **18**, 143–164.

Ceci, S.J. (1994). Schooling. In R.J. Sternberg (Ed.), *Encyclopedia of Human Intelligence*, Volume 2. New York: Macmillan, pp. 960–964.

Clement, R. (1980). Ethnicity, contact and communicative competence in a second language. In H. Giles, W.P. Robinson & P. Smith (Eds), *Language: Social Psychological Perspectives*. Oxford: Pergamon Press, pp. 147–154.

Cole, M. & Griffin, P. (1983). A socio-historical approach to remediation. *Quarterly Newsletter of the Laboratory of Comparative Cognition*, **5**, 69–74.

Cole, M. & Scribner, S. (1977). Developmental theories applied to cross cultural cognitive research. *Annals of the New York Academy of Sciences*, **285**, 366–373.

Cole, N.S. (1990). Conceptions of educational achievement. *Educational Researcher*, **19**(3), 2–7.

Commonwealth Secretariat and Donors to African Education Working Group on the Teaching Profession (1994). *Training and Support Programme for School Heads in African: An Evaluation Report on Working Papers*. London: Commonwealth Secretariat.

Corson, D. (1998). *Changing Education for Diversity*. Buckingham: Open University Press.

Court, E. (1994). How culture influences children's drawing performance in rural Kenya. In E. Thomas (Ed.), *International Perspectives on Culture and Schooling: A Symposium Proceedings*. London: University of London, Institute of Education Publication, pp. 219–260.

Cronk, L. (1993). Parental favoritism toward daughters. *American Scientist*, **81**, 272–279.

Crooks, T.J. (1988). The impact of classroom evaluation practices on students. *Review of Educational Research*, **58**, 438–481.

Cummings, J. (1987). L'éducation bilingue: théorie et mise en œuvre. In Centre pour la recherche et l'immigration dans l'ensignement (Ed.), *L'éducation multiculturelle*. Paris: OECD, pp. 323–353.

Cushner, K. (1994). Preparing teachers for an intercultural context. In R.W. Brislin & T. Yoshida (Eds), *Improving Intercultural Interaction: Modules for Cross Cultural Training Programs*. Thousand Oaks, Calif.: Sage, pp. 109–128.

Dasen, P.R. (1982). Cross cultural aspects of Piaget's theory: the competence/performance model. In L.L. Adler (Ed.), *Cross Cultural Research at Issue*. New York: Academic Press, pp. 163–170.

Dasen, P.R. & Heron, A. (1981). Cross cultural tests of Piaget's theory. In H.C. Triandis & A. Heron (Eds), *Handbook of Cross Cultural Psychology*, Volume 4. Boston: Allyn & Bacon, pp. 295–342.

De Boer, C. (1978). The polls: attitudes towards work. *Public Opinion Quarterly*, **42**, 414–423.

Delpit, L.D. (1988). The silenced dialogue: power and pedagogy in educating other people's children. *Harvard Educational Review*, **58**(3), 280–298.

Deregowski, J. (1980a). Perception. In H.C. Triandis & W.J. Lonner (Eds), *Handbook of Cross Cultural Psychology*, Volume 3. Boston: Allyn & Bacon, pp. 21–115.

DES (Department of Education and Science) (1990). *Developing School Management: The Way Forward. A Report by the School Management Task Force*. London: HMSO.

DFE (Department for Education) (1992). *Effective Management in Schools*. London: HMSO.

Diaz-Guerrero, R. (1975). *Psychology of the Mexican: Culture and Personality*. Austin: University of Texas Press.

Edwards, C.P., Gandini, L. & Giovaninni, D. (1996). The contrasting developmental timetables of parents and preschool teachers in two cultural communities. In S. Harkness & C.M. Super (Eds), *Parents' Cultural Belief Systems: Their Origins, Expressions and Consequences*. New York: Guilford Press, pp. 270–288.

Eldering, L. & Rothenberg, J.J. (1997). Multicultural education: approaches and practice. In K. Watson, C. Modgil & S. Modgil (Eds), *Educational Dilemmas: Debate and Diversity*, Volume 1, *Teachers, Teacher Education and Training*. London: Cassell, pp. 306–316.

Entwistle, A. & Entwistle, N. (1992). Experiences in understanding in revising for degree examinations. *Learning and Instruction*, **2**, 1–22.

Entwistle, N. & Waterson, S. (1988). Approaches to studying and levels of processing in university students. *British Journal of Educational Psychology*, **58**, 258–265.

Epstein, D. (1997). *Changing Classroom Cultures: Anti-racism, Politics and Schools*. Stoke on Trent: Trentham Books.

Eysenck, H.J. (1988). The biological basis of intelligence. In H.S. Irvine & J.W. Berry (Eds), *Human Abilities in Cultural Context*. New York: Cambridge University Press, pp. 70–104.

Fan, F. (1993). How examinations affect students' approaches to writing. In J.B. Biggs & D.A. Watkins (Eds), *Teaching and Learning in Hong Kong: What Is and What Might Be*. University of Hong Kong, Education Papers No. 17.

Feather, N.T. (1975). *Values in Education and Society*. New York: Free Press.

Feiman-Nemser, S. & Floden, R.E. (1986). The cultures of teaching. In M.C. Wittrock (Ed.), *Handbook of Research on Teaching* (3rd edn). New York: Macmillan.

Fiedler, F. (1967). *A Theory of Leadership*. New York: McGraw-Hill.

Fijneman, Y.A., Willemsen, M.E. & Poortinga, Y.H. *et al*. (1995). Individualism–collectivism: an empirical study of a conceptual issue. *Journal of Cross Cultural Psychology*, **27**, 381–402.

Finley, P. (1988). *Malaise of the Spirit: A Case Study*. Fairbanks, Alaska: Center for Cross Cultural Studies, College of Rural Alaska, University of Alaska-Fairbanks.

Furnham, A. & Bochner, S. (1986). *Culture Shock: Psychological Reactions to Unfamiliar Environments*. London: Methuen.

Gagné, R.M. & Driscoll, M.P. (1988). *Essentials of Learning for Instruction* (2nd edn). Englewood Cliffs, NJ: Prentice-Hall.

Gallimore, R., Goldenberg, C.N. & Weisner, T.S. (1993). The social construction and subjective reality of activity settings: implications for community psychology. *American Journal of Community Psychology*, **21**, 537–559.

Gardner, H. (1989). *To Open Minds*. New York: Basic Books.

Gardner, H. (1991). *The Unschooled Mind: How Children Think and How Schools Should Teach*. New York: Basic Books.

Gearing, F. (1979). A reference model for a cultural theory of education and schooling. In F. Gearing & L. Sangree (Eds), *Toward a Cultural Theory of Education and Schooling*. The Hague: Mouton Press, pp. 169–230.

Gibbons, J.L., Stiles, D.A. & Shkodriani, G.M. (1991). Adolescents' attitudes toward family and gender roles: an international comparison. *Sex Roles*, **25**, 625–643.

Gibson, E.J. & Levin, H. (1975). *The Psychology of Reading*. Cambridge, Mass.: MIT Press.

Giles, H., Bourhis, R.Y. & Taylor, D.M. (1977). Towards a theory of language in ethnic group relations. In H. Giles (Ed.), *Language, Ethnicity and Intergroup Relations*. London: pp. 307–348.

Gomez, M. & Tabachnik, B.R. (1991). Preparing preservice teachers to teach diverse learners. Paper presented at the Annual Meeting of the American Educational Research Association, Chicago, Ill.

Gomez, M. & Tabachnik, B.R. (1992). Telling teaching stories. *Teaching Education*, **4**, 129–138.

Grauwe, A. & Bernard, D. (Eds) (1995). *Developments after Jomtien: EFA in the South-East Asia and Pacific Region*. Paris: IIEP Publication.

Grossman, H. (1995). *Classroom Behavior Management in a Diverse Society*. Mountain View, Calif.: Mayfield Publishing Co.

Gumperz, J.J. (1982). *Discourse Strategies*. Cambridge: Cambridge University Press.

Hamilton, V.L., Blumenfeld, P.C., Akoh, H. & Miura, K. (1991). Group and gender in Japan and American elementary classrooms. *Journal of Cross Cultural Psychology*, **22**, 317–346.

Hargreaves, A. (1992). Cultures of teaching: a focus for change. In A. Hargreaves & M.G. Fullan (Eds), *Understanding Teacher Development*. London: Cassell, pp. 216–240.

Hargreaves, D. (1983). The occupational culture of teachers. In P. Woods (Ed.), *Teacher Strategies: Explorations in the Sociology of the school*. London: Croom Helm, pp. 125–148.

Hatano, G. (1990). The nature of everyday science: a brief introduction. *British Journal of Developmental Psychology*, **8**, 245–250.

Hess, R.D. & Azuma, M. (1991). Cultural support for schooling: contrasts between Japan and the United States. *Educational Researcher*, **20**(9), 2–8.

Hess, R.D., Kashiwagi, K., Azuma, H., Price, G. & Dickinson, W.P. (1980). Maternal expectations for mastery of developmental tasks in Japan and the United States. *International Journal of Psychology*, **15**, 259–271.

Hill, M.J.D. (1991). *The Harambee Movement in Kenya: Self Help, Development and Education among the Kamba of Kitui District*. London: Athlone Press, pp. 216–254.

Ho, D.Y.F. (1981). Traditional patterns of socialisation in Chinese society. *Acta Psychologica Taiwanica*, **23**, 81–95.

Ho, D.Y.F. (1991). Cognitive socialisation in Confucian Heritage Cultures. Paper presented to Workshop on continuities and discontinuities in the cognitive socialisation of minority children. US Dept. of Health and Human Services. Washington, DC, 29 June–2 July.

Hodge, C. (1990). Educators for a truly democratic system of schooling. In J. Goodlad & P. Keating (Eds), *Access to Knowledge: An Agenda for Our Nation's Schools*. New York: College Entrance Examination Board.

Hofstede, G. (1980). *Culture's Consequences: International Differences in Work Related Values*. Beverley Hills: Sage.

Hofstede, G. (1991). *Culture and Organisations: Software of the Mind*. London: McGraw-Hill.

Hofstede, G. & Bond, M.H. (1984). Hofstede's cultural dimensions: an independent validation using Rokeach's value survey. *Journal of Cross Cultural Psychology*, **15**, 417–433.

Hollos, M. & Richards, F.A. (1993). Gender associative development of formal operations in Nigerian adolescents. *Ethos*, **21**, 24–52.

Hui, C.H. (1988). Measurement of individualism–collectivism. *Journal of Research in Personality*, **22**, 17–36.

Hui, C.H. (1990). Work attitudes, leadership styles, and managerial behaviours in different cultures. In R.W. Brislin (Ed.), *Applied Cross Cultural Psychology*. Newbury Park, Calif.: Sage, pp. 186–208.

Hui, C.H. & Chung Leuk Luk (1997). Industrial/organisational psychology. In J.W. Berry, M.S. Segall & C. Kagitcibasi (Eds), *Handbook of Cross Cultural Psychology*, Volume 3, *Social Behaviour and Applications*. Boston: Allyn & Bacon, pp. 371–414.

Hutchins, E. (1991). The social organisation of distributed cognition. In L.B. Resnick, J.M. LeVine & S.D. Teasley (Eds), *Perspectives on Socially Shared Cognition*. Washington, DC: American Psychological Association, pp. 283–307.

Illich, I. (1991). A plea for research on lay literacy. In D.R. Olson & N. Torrance (Eds), *Literacy and Orality*. Cambridge: Cambridge University Press, pp. 28–46.

Inagaki, T. (1986). School education: its history and contemporary status. In H.W. Stevenson, H. Azuma & K. Hakuta (Eds), *Child Development and Education in Japan*. New York: Freeman, pp. 75–92.

Jackson, P.W. (1968). *Life in Classrooms*. New York: Holt, Rinehart & Winston.

Johnson, D. (1995). Developing an approach to educational management in South Africa. *Comparative Education*, **31**, 223–242.

Jordan, C. & Tharp, R. (1979). Culture and education. In A. Marsella, R. Tharp & T. Cirobowski (Eds), *Perspectives on Cross Cultural Psychology*. New York: Academic Press, pp. 265–285.

Kagitcibasi, C. (1987). Individual and group loyalities: are they compatible? In C. Kagitcibasi (Ed.), *Growth and Progress in Cross Cultural Psychology*. Lisse: Svets & Zeitlinger, pp. 94–104.

Kagitcibasi, C. (1990). Family and socialisation in cross cultural perspective: a model of change. In J. Berman (Ed.), *Cross Cultural Perspectives: Nebraska Symposium on Motivation*. Lincoln: University of Nebraska, pp. 135–200.

Kagitcibasi, C. (1997). Individualism and collectivism. In J.W. Berry, M.S. Segall & C. Kagitcibasi (Eds), *Handbook of Cross Cultural Psychology*, Volume 3, *Social Behaviour and Applications*. Boston: Allyn & Bacon, pp. 1–49.

Kagitcibasi, C. & Berry, J.W. (1989). Cross cultural psychology: current research and trends. *Annual Review of Psychology*, **40**, 493–531.

Kagitcibasi, C., Sunar, D. & Beckman, S. (1989). *Preschool Education Project*. Ottawa: IDRC Final Report.

Kalleberg, A.L. & Reve, T. (1992). Contracts and commitment: economic and sociological perspectives on employment relations. *Human Relations*, **45**, 1103–1132.

Keats, D.M. (1985). Strategies in formal operational thinking: Malaysia and Australia. In I. Reyes Lagunes & Y.H. Poortinga (Eds), *From a Different Perspective: Studies of Behaviour across Cultures*. Lisse: Svets & Zeitlinger, pp. 306–318.

Kellaghan, T. & Greaney, V. (1992). Using examinations to improve education: a study in fourteen African countries. *World Bank Technical Paper No. 165*, Washington: World Bank Publications.

King, C. (1990). Linking school and home: liaison between teachers and parents in aided secondary schools. In M. Bray (Ed.), *Educational Administration in Hong Kong: Personnel and Schools*. Education Papers 5, Hong Kong: University of Hong Kong, pp. 89–99.

Kirkbride, P. & Tang, S. (1992). Management development in the Nanyang Chinese societies of South East Asia. *Journal of Management Development*, **11**, 94–106.

Kolb, D. (1984). *Experiential Learning*. Englewood Cliffs: Prentice-Hall.

Kornadt, H.J. (1987). The aggression motive and personality development: Japan and Germany. In F. Haslich & J. Kuhl (Eds), *Motivation, Intention and Volition*. Berlin: Springer-Verlag, pp. 115–140.

Kruger, A.C. & Tomasello, M. (1996). Cultural learning and learning culture. In D.R. Olson & N. Torrance (Eds), *Handbook of Education and Human Development: New Models of Learning, Teaching and Schooling*. Oxford: Blackwell, pp. 369–387.

Kulasena, K.G. (1992). Preparing headmasters for increased responsibility at the institutional level. *Report*, Colombo, Sri Lanka: NIE.

Kulkarni, S.S. & Puhan, B.N. (1988). Psychological assessment: its present and future trends. In J. Pandey (Ed.), *Psychology in India: Personality and Mental Processes*, Volume 1. New Delhi: Sage.

Kwan-Terry, A. (1994). Culture and learning: a Singapore case study. In E. Thomas (Ed.), *International Perspectives on Culture and Schooling: A Symposium Proceedings*. London: University of London, Institute of Education Publication, pp. 261–277.

Lambert, W.E. (1977). The effect of bilingualism and the individual: cognitive and sociocultural consequences. In P.A. Hornby (Ed.), *Bilingualism: Psychological and Educational Implications*. New York: Academic Press, pp. 15–27.

Landis, D., Brislin, R. & Hulgus, J. (1985). Attributional training versus contact acculturative learning: a laboratory study. *Journal of Applied Social Psychology*, **15**, 466–482.

Lave, J. (1977). Cognitive consequences of traditional apprenticeship training in Africa. *Anthropology and Educational Quarterly*, **7**, 177–180.

Lave, J. & Wenger, E. (1991). *Participation in Practices*. Cambridge: Cambridge University Press.

Lee, W.O. (1996). The cultural context for Chinese learners: conceptions of learning in the Confucian tradition. In D.A. Watkins & J.B. Biggs (Eds), *The Chinese Learner: Cultural, Psychological and Contextual Influences*. Victoria: CERC & ACER, pp. 45–68.

LeVine, R.A. (1974). Parental goals: a cross cultural review. *Teachers College Record*, **76**, 226–239.

Lin, Y.N. (1988). Family socio-economic background, parental involvement and students' academic performance by elementary school children. *Journal of Counselling*, **11**, 95–141.

Ling, Q.M., Sharpe, P., Lim, A. & Heng, M.A. (1997). Home and parental influences on the achievement of lower primary school children in Singapore. In J. Tan, S. Gopinathan & H.W. Kam (Eds), *Education in Singapore*. Singapore: Prentice-Hall, pp. 315–337.

Liston, D.P. & Zeichner, K.M. (1996). *Culture and Teaching*. Mahwah, NJ: Lawrence Erlbaum Associates, Publishers.

Little, A. (1994). Learning for all: bridging cultures. In E. Thomas (Ed.), *International Perspectives on Culture and Schooling: A Symposium Proceedings*. London: University of London, Institute of Education Publication, pp. 65–75.

Little, P.W. (1982). Norms of collegiality and experimentation: workshop conditions of school success. *American Education Research Journal*, **19**, 325–340.

Lonner, W.J. (1990). An overview of cross cultural testing and assessment. In R.W. Brislin (Ed.), *Applied Cross Cultural Psychology*. Newbury Park, Calif.: Sage, pp. 56–76.

Lonner, W.J. & Berry, J.W. (Eds) (1986). *Field Methods in Cross Cultural Research*. Newbury Park, Calif.: Sage.

Lonner, W.J. & Ibrahim, F. (1989). Assessment in cross cultural counselling. In P. Pedersen, J.G. Draguns, W.J. Lonner & J.E. Trimble (Eds), *Cross Cultural Counselling* (3rd edn). Honolulu: University of Hawaii Press.

Lortie, D. (1975). *The Schoolteacher*. Chicago: University of Chicago Press.

Lummis, M. & Stevenson, H.W. (1990). Gender differences in beliefs and achievement: a cross cultural study. *Developmental Psychology*, **26**, 254–263.

Luria, A.R. (1976). *Cognitive Development: Its Cultural and Social Foundations*. Cambridge, Mass.: Harvard University Press.

Mackay, D. (1996). We did it ourselves – Sinn Fhein a rinn e. *Early Childhood Development: Practice and Reflections*, No. 9.

McInerney, D. (1994). Psychometric perspectives on school motivation and culture. In E. Thomas (Ed.), *International Perspectives on Culture and Schooling: A Symposium Proceedings*. London: University of London, Institute of Education Publication, pp. 327–353.

McShane, D. & Berry, J.W. (1988). Native North Americans: Indian and Innuit abilities. In H.S. Irvine & J.W. Berry (Eds), *Human Abil-*

ities in Cultural Context. New York: Cambridge University Press, pp. 385–426. Berlicum, the Netherlands: Bernard van Leer Foundation Publication.

Mak, G.C. (1998). Classroom management in China: personalising groupism. In N.K. Shimahara (Ed.), *Politics of Classroom Life.* New York: Garland Inc., pp. 239–260.

Mandler, J.M., Scribner, S., Cole, M. & de Forest, M. (1980). Cross cultural invariance in story recall. *Child Development,* **51,** 19–26.

Mao Zedong (1953). Talk with the commission members of the 2nd National Conference of Chinese Youth League, June.

Markus, H.R. & Kitayama, S. (1991). Culture and the self: implications for cognition, emotion and motivation. *Psychological Review,* **98,** 224–253.

Marso, R.N. & Pigge, F.L. (1991). An analysis of teacher made tests: item types, cognitive demands and item construction errors. *Contemporary Educational Psychology,* **16,** 279–286.

Marton, F. & Saljo, R. (1976). On qualitative differences in learning. 1: Outcome and process. *British Journal of Educational Psychology,* **46,** 4–11.

Maslow, A.H. (1954). *Motivation and Personality.* New York: Harper.

Metz, M.H. (1978). *Classrooms and Corridors: The Crisis of Authority in Desegregated Secondary School Classrooms.* Berkeley: University of California.

Mishra, R.C. (1997). Cognition and cognitive development. In J.W. Berry, P.R. Dasen & T.S. Sarawathi (Eds), *Handbook of Cross Cultural Psychology,* Volume 2, *Basic Processes and Human Development.* Boston: Allyn & Bacon, pp. 143–175.

Misumi, J. (1985). *The Behavioral Science of Leadership: An Interdisciplinary Japanese Research Program.* Ann Arbor: University of Michigan Press.

Mohanty, A.K. & Perregaux, C. (1997). Language acquisition and bilingualism. In J.W. Berry, P.R. Dasen & T.S. Sarawathi (Eds), *Handbook of Cross Cultural Psychology,* Volume 2, *Basic Processes and Human Development.* Boston: Allyn & Bacon, pp. 217–254.

MOW International Research Team (1987). *The Meaning of Work.* New York: Academic Press.

Murphy, D. (1987). Offshore education: a Hong Kong perspective. *Australian University Review,* **30,** 43–44.

Negandhi, A.R. (1984). Management in the third world. *Advances in International Comparative Management,* **1,** 123–154.

Nevis, E.C. (1983). Cultural assumptions and productivity: the United States and China. *Sloan Management Review*, **24**, 17–29.

Nik Hishun, I. (1998). Perceptions of leadership among ethnic Malay residential secondary school pupils in Peninsula Malaysia, in the context of national development. Unpublished Ph.D. thesis, University of London.

Noblit, G.W. (1993). Power and caring. *American Educational Research Journal*, **30**(1), 23–38.

Nordhoff, K. & Kleinfeld, J. (1991). Preparing teachers for multiculticultural classrooms: A case study in rural Alaska. Paper presented at the Annual Meeting of the American Educational Research Association, Chicago, Ill.

Nunes, T. (1994). Cultural diversity in learning mathematics: a perspective from Brazil. In E. Thomas (Ed.), *International Perspectives on Culture and Schooling: A Symposium Proceedings*. London: University of London, Institute of Education Publication, pp. 357–370.

Nunes, T., Schliemann, A.D. & Carraher, D.W. (1993). *Street Mathematics and School Mathematics*. New York: Cambridge University Press.

Ogundare, S. (1988). Curriculum development: a description of the development of the national curriculum for primary social studies in Nigeria. *Educational Studies*, **14**, 43–50.

Olson, D.R. (1991). Literacy as a metalinguistic activity. In D.R. Olson & N. Torrance (Eds), *Literacy and Orality*. Cambridge: Cambridge University Press, pp. 251–270.

Olson, D.R. & Bruner, J.S. (1996). Folk psychology and folk pedagogy. In D.R. Olson & N. Torrance (Eds), *Handbook of Education and Human Development: New Models of Learning, Teaching and Schooling*. Oxford: Blackwell, pp. 9–27.

Parsons, O.A. & Schneider, J.M. (1974). Locus of control in university students from Eastern and Western societies. *Journal of Consulting and Clinical Psychology*, **42**, 456–461.

Peterson, M.F. (1988). PM theory in Japan and China: what's in it for the United States? *Organisational Dynamics*, **16**, 22–38.

Piaget, J. (1971). *Science of Education and the Psychology of the Child*. London: Longman.

Price-Williams, D. (Ed.) (1969). *Cross Cultural Studies*. Penguin Modern Psychology Readings. Harmondsworth: Penguin, pp. 11–15.

Purdie, N. & Hattie, J. (1996). Cultural differences in the use of strategies for self regulated learning. *American Educational Research Journal*, **33**, 845–871.

Reder, S.M. (1987). Comparative aspects of functional literacy: three ethnic American communities. In D.A. Wagner (Ed.), *The Future of Literacy in a Changing World*. New York: Pergamon, pp. 250–270.

Reed, H.J. & Lave, J. (1979). Arithmetic as a tool for investigating relations between culture and cognition. *American Anthropologist*, **6**, 568–582.

Reid, W.A. (1987). Institutions and practices: professional education reports and the language of reform. *Educational Researcher*, **168**, 10–15.

Revans, R. (1982). *The Origins and Growth of Action Learning*. Bromley: Chartwell-Bratt.

Rodwell, S. (1998). Internationalisation or indigenisation of educational management development? Some issues of cross cultural transfer. *Comparative Education*, **34**(1), 41–54.

Rogoff, B. (1990). *Apprenticeship in Thinking: Cognitive Development in Social Context*. New York: Oxford University Press.

Rohner, R.F. (1984). Towards a conception of culture for cross cultural psychology. *Journal of Cross Cultural Psychology*, **15**, 111–138.

Ronen, S. (1986). *Comparative and Multinational Management*. New York: John Wiley.

Ronen, S. (1994). An underlying structure of motivational need taxonomies: a cross cultural confirmation. In H.C. Triandis, M.D. Dunette & L.M. Hough (Eds), *Handbook of Industrial and Organisational Psychology* (2nd edn), Volume 4. Palo Alto: Consulting Psychologists Press.

Ross, M.H. (1986). Female political participation: a cross cultural explanation. *American Anthropologist*, **88**, 843–858.

Roulet, E. (1980). *Langue maternelle et langue secondes, vers une pédagogie intégrée*. Paris: Hautier-CEDRIF.

Roulet, E. (1995). Peut-on intégrer l'enseignement-apprentissage décale de plusieurs langues? *Babylonia*, **2**, 22–26.

Rushton, J.P. (1995). *Race, Evolution, and Behaviour: A Life History Perspective*. New Brunswick, NJ: Transaction.

Safavi, N. (1992). The world of management development in the 1990s: challenges beyond our imaginings. *Journal of Management Development*, **11**, 62–72.

Salili, F., Hwang, C.E. & Choi, N.F. (1989). Teachers' evaluative behaviour: the relationship between teachers' comments and perceived ability in Hong Kong. *Journal of Cross Cultural Psychology,* **20**, 115–132.

Samuelowicz, K. (1987). Learning problems of overseas students: two sides of a story. *Higher Education Research and Development,* **6**, 121–134.

Santerre, R. (1971). Aspects conflictuels de deux systèmes d'enseignment au Nord-Cameroun. *Revue Canadienne des Etudes Africaines,* **2**, 157–169.

Santerre, R. (1975). La Pédagogique coranique. *Recherche, Pédagogique et Culture,* **20**, 12–17.

Saunders, G. (1988). *Bilingual Children: from Birth to Teens.* Clevedon: Multilingual Matters.

Schliemann, A.D. (1995). Some concerns about bringing everyday mathematics to mathematics education. In L. Meira & D. Carraher (Eds), *Proceedings of the XIX International Conference for Psychology of Mathematics Education,* Volume 1, Recife, Brazil: pp. 45–60.

Schliemann, A.D. & Acioly, N.M. (1989). Mathematical knowledge developed at work: the contribution of practice versus the contribution of schooling. *Cognition and Instruction,* **6**, 185–221.

Schliemann, A.D. & Carraher, D.W. (1992). Proportional reasoning in and out of school. In P. Light & G. Butterworth (Eds), *Context and Cognition: Ways of Learning and Knowing.* New York: Harvester Wheatsheaf, pp. 47–73.

Schliemann, A.D., Carraher, D. & Ceci, S.J. (1997). Everyday cognition. In J.W. Berry, P.R. Dasen & T.S. Sarawathi (Eds), *Handbook of Cross Cultural Psychology,* Volume 2, *Basic Processes and Human Development.* Boston: Allyn & Bacon, pp. 177–216.

Schmeck, R.R. (Ed.) (1988). *Learning Strategies and Learning Styles.* New York: Plenum.

Schon, D. (1983). *The Reflective Practitioner.* New York: Basic Books.

Schwartz, S.H. (1992). Universals in the content and structure of values: theoretical advances and empirical tests in 20 countries. In M. Zanna (Ed.), *Advances in Experimental Social Psychology,* 25. Orlando, Fla: Academic, pp. 1–65.

Schwartz, S.H. (1994). Beyond individualism/collectivism: new cultural dimensions of values. In U. Kim, H.C. Triandis, C. Kagitcibasi, S.-C. Choi & G. Hoon (Eds), *Individualism and Collectivism: Theory, Method and Applications.* Thousand Oaks, Calif.: Sage, pp. 85–119.

Schweder, R.A. (1990). Cultural psychology, what is it? In J.W. Stigler, R.A. Schweder & G. Herdt (Eds), *Cultural Psychology Essays on Comparative Human Development*. Cambridge: Cambridge University Press, pp. 1–43.

Schweder, R.A. (1991). Cultural psychology, what is it? In R.A. Schweder (Ed.), *Thinking through Cultures*. Cambridge, Mass.: Harvard University Press, pp. 73–110.

Scribner, S. & Cole, M. (1981). *The Psychology of Literacy*. Cambridge, Mass.: Harvard University Press.

Serpell, R. (1993). *The Significance of Schooling: Life-long Journeys in an African Society*. Cambridge: Cambridge University Press.

Serpell, R. & Hatano, G. (1997). Education, schooling and literacy. In J.W. Berry, P.R. Dasen & T.S. Sarawathi (Eds), *Handbook of Cross Cultural Psychology*, Volume 2, *Basic Processes and Human Development*. Boston: Allyn & Bacon, pp. 340–376.

Shaw, M. & Welton, J. (1996). The application of education management models and theories to the processes of education policy making and management: the case of compound cross cultural confusion. Paper presented at the Eighth International Conference of the CCEA, Indigenous Perspective of Educational Management, IAB, Genting Highlands, Malaysia.

Shea, J.D. (1985). Studies of cognitive development in Papua New Guinea. *International Journal of Psychology*, **20**, 33–61.

Shenkar, O. & Ronen, S. (1987). The cultural context of negotiations: the implications of Chinese interpersonal norms. *The Journal of Applied Behavioural Science*, **23**, 263–275.

Shimahara, N.K. (1998). Classroom management in Japan: building a classroom community. In N.K. Shimahara (Ed.), *Politics of Classroom Life*. New York: Garland Inc., pp. 215–238.

Shulman, J. (1986). Paradigms and research programmes in the study of teaching: a contemporary perspective. In M.C. Wittrock (Ed.), *Handbook of Research in Teaching* (3rd edn). New York: Macmillan.

Shulman, J. (1987). Knowledge and teaching: foundations of the new reforms. *Harvard Educational Review*, **57**, 1–22.

SIDA (1993). *Lok Jumbish – Learning Together*. Jaipur: Kumar Press.

Sims, D. & McCaulay, I. (1995). Management learning as a learning process: an invitation. *Management Learning*, **26**, 15.

Singhal, S. & Mohanty, N. (1994). Psychological differentiation and school performance of tribal and non-tribal children in their cultural context. In E. Thomas (Ed.), *International Perspectives on*

Culture and Schooling: A Symposium Proceedings. London: University of London, Institute of Education Publication, pp. 392–406.

Sinha, D. (1983). Human assessment in the Indian context. In S.H. Irvine & J.W. Berry (Eds), *Human Assessment and Cultural Factors*. New York: Plenum, pp. 17–34.

Sinha, J.B.P. (1973). *Some Problems of Public Sector Organisations*. Delhi: Concept.

Sinha, J.B.P. (1994). Cultural embeddedness and the developmental role of industrial organisations in India. In H.C. Triandis, M.D. Dunette & L.M. Hough (Eds), *Handbook of Industrial and Organisational Psychology* (2nd edn), Volume 4. Palo Alto: Consulting Psychologists Press, pp. 727–764.

Smith, P.B. & Schwartz, S.H. (1997). Values. In J.W. Berry, M.S. Segall & C. Kagitcibasi (Eds), *Handbook of Cross Cultural Psychology*, Volume 3, *Social Behaviour and Applications*. Boston: Allyn & Bacon, pp. 77–118.

Steffensen, M.S. & Calker, L. (1982). Intercultural misunderstandings about health care: recall of descriptions of illness and treatments. *Social Science and Medicine*, **16**, 1949–1954.

Sternberg, R.J. (1985). *Beyond IQ: A Triarchic Theory of Human Intelligence*. New York: Cambridge University Press.

Stewart, E. (1966). The simulation of cultural differences. *Journal of Communication*, **16**, 291–304.

Street, B. (1984). *Literacy in Theory and Practice*. Cambridge: Cambridge University Press.

Super, C. & Harkness, S. (1997). The cultural structuring of human development. In J.W. Berry, P.R. Dasen & T.S. Sarawathi (Eds), *Handbook of Cross Cultural Psychology*, Volume 2, *Basic Processes and Human Development*. Boston: Allyn & Bacon, pp. 1–40.

Tabachnik, B.R. & Zeichner, K.M. (1993). Preparing teachers for cultural diversity. In P. Gilroy & M. Smith (Eds), *International Analyses of Teacher Education*. Abingdon: Carfax Publications, pp. 113–124.

Tang, C. & Biggs, J. (1996). How Hong Kong students cope with assessment. In D.A. Watkins & J.B. Biggs (Eds), *The Chinese Learner: Cultural, Psychological and Contextual Influences*. Victoria: CERC & ACER, pp. 159–182.

Tannenbaum, A.S. (1980). Organisational psychology. In H.C. Triandis & R.W. Brislin (Eds), *Handbook of Cross Cultural Psychology*, Volume 5. Boston: Allyn & Bacon, pp. 281–334.

Tanon, F. (1994). A cultural view on planning: the case of weaving in Ivory Coast. *Cross Cultural Psychology Monographs*, 4. Tilburg: Tilburg University Press.

Tape, G. (1994). *L'intelligence en Afrique: Une étude du raisonnement experimental*. Paris: L'Harmattan.

Teasdale, R. & Teasdale, J. (1994). Culture and schooling in Aboriginal Australia. In E. Thomas (Ed.), *International Perspectives on Culture and Schooling: A Symposium Proceedings*. London: University of London, Institute of Education Publication, pp. 174–196.

The Economist (1997). World Education League: Who's top? 29 March.

Thomas, E. (1989). *Pupils' Perceptions of Parental Influences on Schooling*. A Research Report. London: University of London, Institute of Education Publication.

Thomas, E. (1990). Filial piety, social change and Singapore youth. *Journal of Moral Education*, 19(3), 192–205.

Thomas, E. (1992). Schooling and the school as a cross cultural context for study. In S. Iwawaki, Y. Kashima & K. Leung (Eds), *Innovations in Cross Cultural Psychology*. Amsterdam: Swets & Zeitlinger, pp. 425–441.

Thomas, E. (1993). The professional development and training of teacher educators. In E. Thomas, E. Sharma, M. Khanna & H. Jatoi (Eds), *Policy and Practice in Initial Teacher Training*. London: Commonwealth Secretariat Publications, pp. 1–19.

Thomas, E. (1994). Overview. In E. Thomas (Ed.), *International Perspectives on Schooling and Culture: A Symposium Proceedings*. London: Institute of Education, University of London Publication, pp. 4–30.

Thomas, E. (1996). Teacher education in South East Asia: prospects for a North–South dialogue with a difference. In C. Brock (Ed.), *Global Perspectives on Teacher Education*. Wallingford, Berks: Triangle Press, pp. 123–151.

Thomas, E. (1997a). Teacher education and values transmission: cultural dilemmas with difficult choices. In K. Watson, C. Modgil & S. Modgil (Eds), *Educational Dilemmas: Debate and Diversity*. London: Cassell, pp. 246–259.

Thomas, E. (1997b). Developing a culture sensitive pedagogy: tackling a problem of melding "global culture" within existing cultural contexts. *International Journal of Educational Development*, 17, 13–26.

Thomas, E. (1997c). Models of teacher education and their role in educational planning. In J. Lynch, C. Modgil & S. Modgil (Eds), *Education and Development: Tradition and Innovation*, Volume 3. London: Cassell, pp. 106–121.

Thomas, E. (1998). Education and the rights of the child: understanding some cross cultural contexts with reference to policy and practice. Paper presented to World Dialogue Conference on Children's Rights and Wrongs. Nicosia, Cyprus, 5–6 November.

Thomas, E. (1999). Cross cultural challenges of a culture sensitive pedagogy within an emerging "global culture". In J.G. Lasry, J. Adair & K.L. Dion (Eds), *Latest Contributions to Cross Cultural Psychology*. Amsterdam: Swets & Zeitlinger, pp. 304–317.

Tjosvold, D. (1984). Effects of leader warmth and directiveness on subordinate performance on a subsequent task. *Journal of Applied Psychology*, **69**, 422–427.

Tobin, J.J., Wu, D.Y.H. & Davidson, D.H. (1989). *Preschool in Three Cultures: Japan, China and the United States*. New Haven, Conn.: Yale University Press.

Tomasello, M., Kruger, A.C. & Ratner, H. (1993). Cultural learning. *Behavioural and Brain Sciences*, **16**(3), 495–511.

Triandis, H.C. (1980). Values, attitudes and interpersonal behaviour. In M.M. Page (Ed.), *Nebraska Symposium on Motivation: Beliefs, Attitudes and Values*, Volume 27. Lincoln: University of Nebraska.

Triandis, H.C. (1988). Collectivism and individualism: a reconceptualisation of a basic concept in cross cultural psychology. In G.K. Verma & C. Bagley (Eds), *Personality, Attitudes and Cognitions*. London: Macmillan.

Triandis, H.C. (1994). *Culture and Social Behaviour*. New York: McGraw-Hill.

Triandis, H.C., Kurowski, L. & Gelfand, L. (1994). Workplace diversity. In H.C. Triandis, M. Dunnette & L. Hough (Eds), *Handbook of Industrial and Organisational Psychology* (2nd edn), Volume 4. Palo Alto: Consulting Psychologists, pp. 769–827.

Triandis, H.C., McCusker, C. & Hui, C.H. (1990). Multimethod probes of individualism and collectivism. *Journal of Personality and Social Psychology*, **59**, 1006–1020.

Trimble, J.E., Lonner, W.J. & Boucher, I. (1983). Stalking the wily emic: alternatives to cross cultural measurement. In S.H. Irvine & J.W. Berry (Eds), *Human Assessment and Cultural Factors*. New York: Plenum, pp. 259–273.

Trompenaars, F. (1993). *Riding the Waves of Culture*. London: Brealey.

UNESCO–EPP (1986). *Development and Evaluation of Standard Training Materials (in the Field of Educational Planning, Administration and Facilities)*. Paris: UNESCO.

Van Rensburg, P. (1978). *The Serowe Brigades: Alternative Education in Botswana*. London: Macmillan Education Ltd.

Vernon, P.A. (1969). *Intelligence and Cultural Environment*. London: Methuen.

Vernon, P.A. (1990). The use of biological measures to estimate behavioural intelligence. *Educational Psychologist*, **25**, 293–304.

Vogt, L., Jordan, C. & Tharp, R. (1987). Explaining school failure, producing school success: two cases. *Anthropology and Education Quarterly*, **18**, 276–286.

Wagner, D.A. (1985). Islamic education: traditional pedagogy and contemporary aspects. In T. Husen & T.N. Postlethwaite (Eds), *International Encyclopedia of Education: Research and Studies*. New York: Pergamon, pp. 2714–2716.

Wagner, D.A. (1993). *Literacy, Culture and Development: Becoming Literate in Morocco*. Cambridge: Cambridge University Press.

Waller, W. (1932). *The Sociology of Teaching*. New York: Russell & Russell.

Walsh, J.E. (1979). *Humanistic Cultural Psychology*. Honolulu: The University Press of Hawaii.

Wang Gang (1996). Educational assessment in China. *Assessment in Education*, **3**(1), 75–88.

Ward, C. & Kennedy, A. (1996). Crossing cultures: the relationship between psychological amd sociocultural dimensions of cross cultural adjustment. In J. Pandey, D. Sinha & D.P.S. Bhawuk (Eds), *Asian Contributions to Cross Cultural Psychology*. New Delhi: Sage, pp. 289–306.

Ward, C. & Rzoska, K. (1994). Cross cultural perspectives on cooperation and competition: educational applications in plural societies. In E. Thomas (Ed.), *International Perspectives on Culture and Schooling: A Symposium Proceedings*. London: University of London, Institute of Education Publication, pp. 455–482.

Watkins, D.A. (1996). Learning theories and approaches to research: a cross cultural perspective. In D.A. Watkins & J.B. Biggs (Eds), *The Chinese Learner: Cultural, Psychological and Contextual Influences*. Victoria: CERC & ACER, pp. 1–24.

Watkins, D.A. & Biggs, J.B. (Eds) (1996). *The Chinese Learner: Cultural, Psychological and Contextual Influences*. Victoria: CERC & ACER.

Weinstein, C.S. (1998). Classroom management in the United States: a shifting paradigm. In N.K. Shimahara (Ed.), *Politics of Classroom Life*. New York: Garland Inc., pp. 49–83.

Westwood, M. & Barker, M. (1990). Academic achievement and social adaptation among international students: a comparison groups study of the peer pairing program. *International Journal of Intercultural Relations*, **14**, 251–263.

Whyte, W.F. (1983). Worker participation: international and historical perspectives. *The Journal of Applied Behavioral Science*, **19**, 395–407.

Wittrock, M.C. (Ed.) (1986). *Handbook of Research on Teaching* (3rd edn). New York: Macmillan.

Zavalloni, M. (1980). Values. In H.C. Triandis & R.W. Brislin (Eds), *Handbook of Cross Cultural Psychology*, Volume 5. Boston: Allyn & Bacon, pp. 73–120.

Zeichner, K.M. (1983a). Alternative paradigms of teacher education. *Journal of Teacher Education*, **34**(3), 3–9.

Zeichner, K.M. (1983b). Individual and institutional factors related to the socialisation of teaching. In G.A. Griffin & H. Hukill (Eds), *First Years of Teaching: What are the Pertinent Issues?* R&DCTE Report No. 9051, pp. 1–59.

Zeichner, K.M. (1992). Conceptions of reflective practice and teacher education. In G. Harvard & R. Dunne (Eds), *Westminster Studies in Education*, 15.

Zeichner, K.M. & Tabachnik, B.R. (1983). Teacher perspectives in the face of institutional press. Paper presented at the American Educational Research Association, Montreal.

Zhang, H. (1988). Psychological testing and China's modernisation. *Bulletin of the International Test Commission*, No. 27.

AUTHOR INDEX

SUBJECT INDEX

Lightning Source UK Ltd.
Milton Keynes UK
11 November 2009

146103UK00001B/97/A